ESSAYS ON JOHN COWPER POWYS

PLATE 1

Portrait by Raymond Jonson, 1917.

ESSAYS
ON
JOHN COWPER POWYS

Edited by
BELINDA HUMFREY

CARDIFF
UNIVERSITY OF WALES PRESS
1972

First published 1972

I.S.B.N. 0 7083 0456 7

Printed in Wales by CSP Ltd., Fairwater, Cardiff.

The ending forever of the Guilt-sense and God-sense,
The ending forever of the Sin-sense and Shame-sense,
The beginning forever of the Peace paradisic,
The 'I feel' without question, the 'I am' without purpose,
The 'It is' that leads nowhere, the life with no climax,
The 'Enough' that leads forward to no consummation,
The answer to all things, that yet answers nothing,
The centre of all things, yet all on the surface,
The secret of Nature, yet Nature goes blabbing it
With all of her voices from earth, fire, air, water!
Whence comes it? Whither goes it: It is nameless; it is shameless;
Time haunted no more by a Phantom Eternal:
It is Godless; but its gods are as sea-hands in number;
It's the Square with four sides that encloses all circles;
Four horizons hath this Tetrad that swallows all Triads;
It includes every creature that Nature can summon.
It excludes from Annwfyn nor man, beast, nor woman!

CONTENTS

APPENDICES

Appendix I

Some hitherto unpublished letters and poems by J. C. Powys

Continued overleaf

Appendix II

Appendix III

ILLUSTRATIONS

1. Painting of J.C.P. by Raymond Jonson, 1917 (by kind permission of Phyllis Playter and Peter Powys Grey who owns the portrait and has written that "at one childhood point when (his) relationship with Jack was particularly ambivalent (he) shot three arrows through it!")

2. Photograph of J.C.P. as a young man (by kind permission of E. E. Bissell).

3. J.C.P. on the steps of the house at Phudd Bottom (so named by him), otherwise Hillsdale, New York, where he lived and wrote, 1930–1934. See the extracts from letters of these years in Appendix I(b). Photograph by kind permission of Phyllis Playter.

4. Photograph of J.C.P. in 1940 (by kind permission of C. Benson Roberts). Phyllis Playter explained that having been given a Hallowe'en mask she took some snapshots of J.C.P. as an exorciser and the ghost. He is wearing a paper party-cracker hat. J.C.P.'s inscription on the back of the photograph reads: "From the old Welsh Cagliostro in his hud a lledrith a gwisg y Bardd ac Ofydd." (A Druid's power is described as "hud and lledrith" in *Porius* (1951), p. 151. Here a translation appears to be, "magic and fantasy and Poet's and Ovate's dress": Ovate being one of the orders of the Gorsedd. J.C.P. was installed as a bard at a Corwen Eisteddfod in 1936.)

5. Painting of J.C.P. by Gertrude Powys (in the National Museum of Wales). See J.C.P.'s letter to C. Benson Roberts of October 16th 1944.

6. Portrait bust of J.C.P. by Jonah Jones, 1957. Photograph from the plaster cast for bronze in possession of Anthony Bland. See *Athene Provides*.

7. Letters from J.C.P.
   (a) First and last sides of the letter to Theodore F. Powys, March 10th [1901].
   (b) Inside pages of the letter to Theodore F. Powys, March 15th 1902.
   (c) First side of the letter to C. Benson Roberts, November 14th, 1951.

Acknowledgements

I am very grateful for the goodwill and helpfulness of E. E. Bissell (from whose collection of Powys manuscripts have come the extracts from J. C. Powys's letters to his brothers and the poems published in Appendix I), Malcolm Elwin, G. Wilson Knight, Phyllis Playter and Francis Powys.

June, 1972   Belinda Humfrey

INTRODUCTION

Belinda Humfrey

In 1963, in the January number of *A Review of English Literature* devoted to John Cowper Powys, Angus Wilson conjectured that the work of Powys had been neglected because of highly enthusiastic reviewing suggesting "amazement rather than comprehension" and "insufficient" analytic criticism. Yet, since then, although there have been scattered essays and chapters, there have been only two complete books on J. C. Powys's work, G. Wilson Knight's "map" of his subjects, plots and themes, *The Saturnian Quest* (1964), and H. P. Collins's critical survey, *John Cowper Powys, Old Earth Man* (1966). The present volume of essays should at least clear further ground and begin or provoke more of the close critical study which this generous writer merits.

It seems to me that the titles of the essays in this collection sufficiently explain their main concerns for readers who seek first a specific approach to Powys's works, such as the man, the metaphysic or philosophy, symbols, themes, individual novels. The essays by M. Greenwald and T. Hyman are perhaps the most widespread in range.

I have placed J. Hooker's essay on the *Autobiography* (a "middle" work, 1934) at the beginning of the collection because it indicates a sound, central approach to Powys's whole work, especially as it points his identification with the Proteus poet Taliesin and as it reveals how the fictional J. C. Powys of the *Autobiography* embodies the creative J. C. Powys. But thereafter, the critical essays, mainly devoted to Powys's novels, follow the chronological order of his writings, as far as possible. First M. Greenwald analyses Powys's early philosophical work, *The Complex Vision* of 1920, which anticipates the subjects and nature of the novels to come because "philosophy for him is essentially fictive." There follow two essays on the early group of novels (1915–1925) by G. Cavaliero and D. Fernandez (who includes discussion of the Poems (1896–1922) and links the early novels with the later *Wolf Solent*). Then there is an approach to Powys's personality by F. Davies which, incidentally, describes his lecturing (1894–1928). The central essays are mainly devoted to various aspects of the middle group of novels, all set in Dorset, *Wolf Solent*, *A Glastonbury Romance*, *Weymouth Sands* and *Maiden Castle* (1929–1936). G. F. Miles's essay links these with studies of the two large Wales novels, *Owen Glendower* (1942) by R. Mathias and *Porius* (1951) by J. A. Brebner who also discusses the late fantasies (1952–1960). Thus, although one such collection of essays cannot be comprehensive, J. C. Powys's long and variously experimental writing career is examined. Also, the critical essays begin and end, as Powys would wish, with discussions of his principal concern: imagination, man's fictive power.

The extracts from John Cowper Powys's letters in the Appendix supplement the critical approach to his work. They show something of his attitude to himself and his writings in years which include the astonishingly creative 1928 to 1934 spent in New York State but yet are very thinly documented by published letters (most of which are in Louis Wilkinson's *Welsh Ambassadors*, 1936), whereas for the later years, 1935 to 1956, we have the rich *Letters to Louis Wilkinson*.

* * *

There are various, complementary, and conflicting interpretations and assessments of J. C. Powys's characteristics and methods as a novelist, and criticisms of both his faults and virtues as a creative writer, throughout this collection of essays. However it seems to fall to me as introducing editor to offer an opinion as to the "place" of J. C. Powys among novelists. I shall work to this, first, through his mythological images (using two of the poems in Appendix I(d)) and, second, through his own critical views of the developments within the novel since the nineteenth century. From this, it seems to me we can discover that, although he emerged from Cambridge a year after the publication of *The Celtic Twilight*, Powys can be strongly identified with the major novelists between the World Wars, and that he is also an outstanding writer of what have become recognised from a recent perspective as "anti-novels". (The best work on the anti-novel is G. Josipovici's *The World and the Book*, 1971.) I shall first outline the nature of these two categories: they overlap in part, and, although the anti-novel, especially, has European ancestors of very much earlier centuries, both are heavily indebted to the advent of Proust.

The general interior characteristics of some important inter-war novelists, Proust, Woolf and Joyce, are distinguished by E. Auerbach in the penultimate chapter of *Mimesis* of 1946. These include the author's declining authoritative knowledge of his characters, multipersonal representations of consciousness, exterior events releasing and interpreting inner events (in place of the opposite process), the disintegration of the continuity of exterior events, the shifting of narrative viewpoint, the stratification of time resulting from representation of interior time, and a tendency to represent a very limited portion of time and to hold to minor, random, everyday events, even for an encyclopedic work such as *Ulysses*. These characteristics Auerbach sees as a reflection of the disintegration into multiple ways of life and endeavour in the Europe of this era and of its hopelessness. The consequently fragmented reality of the novel and its "exploratory type of representation" he sees as having two benefits, the realisation of the wealth and depth of life in every moment to which we surrender ourselves without prejudice, and, a levelling process, the unification and simplification of men's lives.

It is very obvious that Powys exploits all the characteristic methods of the inter-war novel described by Auerbach, but sprawlingly, unsystematically, some will say. Yet, he also stays half outside the group because of his attitude to the two benefits of Europe's disintegrating consciousness which Auerbach sees posited by the new novel. The deep surrender to moments Powys would have more positive by willed imagining: the surrender is for him not compensatory but primary and creative. Secondly he is against levelling, against unity, which might destroy individuality, so he preaches multiple consciousness as man's hope and glory. Hence his novels can only have the shape of trees, and, although they attain interior coherence through repeated imagery, they cannot have even an illusory picture-framed shape, such as is suggested in *To the Lighthouse* by Lily Briscoe's picture.

Fundamentally the anti-novel is not concerned with the representation of reality but with itself, the artefact. It has the same origin as the inter-war novel, the realisation that linear narrative is a falsification of experience. But, in English literature, we can see its kinship with the work of a central line of twentieth century poets, with Hardy as master, who replace the romantic concept of the Bard with convictions by the concept of the Maker with impressions[1] ("For poetry makes nothing happen", says Auden in his elegy on Yeats), so that the reader's concentration falls upon the artefact and his participation in its making. Hence the writer does not communicate (except in provoking our afterthoughts) but brings the reader into the writer's artistic self-consciousness and so into an exploration of the nature of experience by exploration of how it is being captured and represented.

It seems probable that Powys came to be an anti-novelist not from any consideration of structure, or artistic form, but from his personal metaphysic, namely his faith in man's fictive power, as revolution, the perpetual creation of new life. In the *Autobiography's* part-parody of *The Prelude* (and the schoolboy Powys's self-dedication to poetry between urinal and stars (104–5[2]) is in the same vein as Auden's comic rewriting, in *Letters from Iceland* (1936), of Wordsworth's "vows Were then made for me") Powys's discovery that he, self-created, self-analysed, self-mocked, was to be his poetry (155) indicates his primary inspiration. (His amusing discovery here, and its accidental nature, contrasts with the young Yeats's earnest decision, revealed in his *Autobiographies*, to make his life into poetry, himself his own artefact.) His novels invite our conscious cooperation in making, because his concern is how we each make ourselves and our lives, and so what we all make of life.

Yet, before he first went to America, Powys began the ambition, still held at sixty, as he wrote the *Autobiography*, to write "a sort of mystic-humorous, Pantagruelian, Shandean,

Quixotic Romance" (314). Here his proposed masters are great eccentrics concerned with structural process that ridicules customary structure, and concerned to break down fossilised attitudes and to put their readers at unease. The prototypes of the anti-novel are to be found in literature long before "the rise of the novel" and Powys is a modern because of his sympathy with its grander ancestors. Although and because he writes as a prophet against the tyrannies and conformities of mechanised man of the twentieth century, he has masters like Homer (admiring Homer for the same reasons as Addison did, namely his representation of the permanent and natural in man) and Rabelais (whose exploration of the overlap in man of the excremental and the sacramental is imitated in *A Glastonbury Romance*). His novels are akin to earlier English works, of such different kinds as *The Faerie Queene* and *King Lear*, which move outside traditional literary forms, away from symmetry and exterior form in search of "unaccommodated man" and so push nature and experience to "the very verge of her confine".

An essential characteristic of Powys as creator is that he is bookish, "a bookworm turned novelist", as he says in the 1953 Preface to *A Glastonbury Romance*. He puts it more extremely in a letter to Louis Wilkinson on December 5th, 1949: "I can't sit and think—books think for me." This is sometimes placed whole into his novels. In *Porius*, Brochvael's reading puts current domestic and large social events in the perspective of the permanent. His clash with his daughter about her wish not to marry Porius is juxtaposed with a moth crossing a page of Ovid's *Metamorphoses* (431[3]), and his night-thoughts about personal and national problems against passages from Aristophanes' "eleven rhapsodies on the enthralling follies of human life" (440–43). Men are the same in the time of the Athenian dramatist, in Brochvael's fifth century, and in the twentieth century, for evidently the comprehensive forest of *Porius*, with its complex of races and creeds, is Powys's mirror of fluid, multiple, present-day Europe.[4]

Powys incorporates myth and mythical allusion in the same way as bookishness, not for contrast, like Eliot and Joyce, but for a more hopeful stress on continuity in human nature. The contemporary writer most like him in this is Golding, although his reapplication of myth is in slenderer novel-forms. Powys and Golding similarly work through a multiple interpretation of a few images; but in this, in form, Golding is writing a *Tempest* to Powys's *King Lear*. The assertion of the material continuance of mythical concepts is at its most daring in *Porius*, Powys's last romance and his declared "masterpiece" of eight years writing. *Porius* is centrally, sympathetically described and analysed by J. A. Brebner in this collection, but, as it has mainly received neglect and adverse criticism previously, I shall concentrate on it as an example of Powys's creative skill, to give an impression of his place in the world of literature.

> The ending forever of the Guilt-sense and God-sense,
> The ending forever of the Sin-sense and Shame-sense,
> The beginning forever of the Peace paradisic,
> The 'I feel' without question, the 'I am' without purpose,
> The 'It is' that leads nowhere, the life with no climax,
> The 'Enough' that leads forward to no consummation,
> The answer to all things, that yet answers nothing,
> The centre of all things, yet all on the surface,
> The secret of Nature, yet Nature goes blabbing it
> With all of her voices from earth, fire, air, water!
> Whence comes it? Whither goes it: It is nameless; it is
>   shameless;
> Time haunted no more by a Phantom Eternal;
> It is Godless; but its gods are as sea-sands in number;
> It's the Square with four sides that encloses all circles;
> Four horizons hath this Tetrad that swallows all Triads;
> It includes every creature that Nature can summon.
> It excludes from Annwfyn nor man, beast, nor woman!

This ending to the "windy gust of oracular obsession" by Taliessin in the middle of *Porius* is the poem form of the visionary hope which pervades all Powys's writings and which is finally most perfectly realised into an artefact, through our collaboration with the story, characters and images, of this *Romance of the Dark Ages*. In accord with the ideal described in the poem, not only is the poem incomplete, for Taliessin is chanting it to himself as he works upon it, but it describes the awareness conjured by the entire novel 250 pages before we, the novelist and the readers, have worked to it. The poem is Powys's blue-print as a creator of fiction. No-one who reads the *Autobiography* can miss the deliberately outrageous repetition of "I am", Powys's assertion "without purpose", for the book ends in a beginning. Similarly for Powys, a "great modern novel" (such as he attempts at least in *A Glastonbury Romance* and *Porius*) which "ought to include just *everything*"[5], "every creature that Nature can summon" and gods "as sea-sands in number" is identical with "the Peace paradisic", and so will convey "life with no climax". (See T. Hyman's approach to this.)

From the very beginning of his novel-writing, Powys saw his virtue as leaving "large tolerant after-thoughts" in the reader when the book had finally been put away, but through the large novels he wrote himself into a fuller magnanimity so that in *Porius* he achieves something like the awareness of King Lear's "Come let's to prison" speech. In action this is realised when Porius, having come from hearing his master, the Pelagian Brother John, declare in his dying speech that "No one is to be punished . . . we are all angels and we are all devils. The good is always stronger than the bad" (549), in sympathy allows the destroyer, Medrawd, to go free (572). Significantly, Taliessin identifies himself with Pelagius in the first half of his poem.

However, though, like Shakespeare and Blake, Powys moves in his final works to his most emphatic stress on giving all for nothing, on forgiveness, he thinks and feels consistently throughout his writing, and everything we examine of his relates to the guiding concept proclaimed in the Taliessin poem.

Perhaps Powys's best poems are those given to Jason Otter in *Wolf Solent* and Taliessin in *Porius*. The three poems in the Appendix to this collection of essays are interesting as examples of some of the verse written after Powys's last published volume, *Samphire* of 1922, and during the period of the middle group of novels.

Teiresias, the person of one poem, haunts Powys's work, often mentioned, seldom congruously. In the poem, Teiresias is imagined as sensitive to the consciousness of inanimate things, which makes him like the similarly fate-driven, pre-ternatural and yet most natural magician-prophet Myrddin Wyllt (Merlin the Wild) of *Porius*. Porius thinks of Myrddin as "the only true prophet . . . since Tiresias" (597) and Myrddin himself conjectures that Taliessin's "obscure modern poetry" is "the sort of writing the old Greek prophet Tiresias might have dictated to his disciples" (410).

Teiresias embodies Powys both in his three main mythological characteristics and in the metamorphosis to wind (an extension of the prophet's mythical properties) conjured in the poem. The obvious shared characteristic is an interior knowledge of the feelings of women. This, Powys declares in the *Autobiography*, he enjoys with Shakespeare and Wordsworth. He proves it in the novels: H. P. Collins in his essay quotes one example, Perdita in *Weymouth Sands*, and the last and best entry into a woman's feelings and thoughts in love and in love-making is Morfydd in *Porius*. Understandably, Powys's critics tend to rejoice in the unusual in his work, including the descriptions of "abnormal" sexual relationships. Perhaps here is the place to remark that he probably provides the fullest and most emotionally entrancing descriptions of "normal" hetero-sexual relationships in twentieth century literature. One of Powys's few attacks on contemporary novelists is on Joyce and Lawrence for losing a sense of the uniqueness and separateness of persons in their too "representative" characters:

> They do not *stand out*, these dissected perambulatory pathoids. . . . they reveal to a wonder their "streams of

24

consciousness"; but their loves and hates are like the loves and hates in fish-ponds and aquariums. The psychology of sex has dehumanised them.[6]

Then we come to the less easily defined characteristics of Teiresias, all associated with the dark, elusive, possibly evasive, side of Powys which baffles readers while it strengthens his fictions. One of the identifications is with Euripides' "soothsayer" Teiresias of *The Bacchanals* who danced before Dionysius. This Powys makes in the *Autobiography* in answer to two charges made by his brother Llewelyn, first, that he is "spiritually insincere", second, that he is undignified, "a Prize Ninny". The first Powys interprets:

> The truth is that what he finds most difficult to tolerate in me is my trick of *living up* to my poetical mythology.
> By this I mean my way of behaving as if the imaginations of the ancient poets concealed more than mere subjective fancies.

To the second charge he replies:

> what is the deepest, secretest purpose of my life? I can answer categorically: 'To enjoy the sensations that I like enjoying, when I am most entirely and shamelessly myself.' (536–8)

This shameless enjoyment of his own sensations (which he recommends to us all in his metaphysical works like *In Defence of Sensuality* (1930) and through its practice by some of his fictional characters) for him includes the cult of his natural ninny-ism. Ninny-ism he declares is "the profoundest of all religious gestures and far the oldest" and "in my ninny-ism the madness of the mystics of all ages rises up." There is in this jugglery the defence of "the 'I feel' without question" of Taliessin's poem, which Powys develops into the assertion of our free will to be wild, unorthodox, disorderly, disunified, inartistic, to be multitudes or whatever we will. It is part of his championing of the misfits and mad, an exaggeration of Wordsworth's half-humorous, half-serious cult of tramps, leechgatherers and idiots ("worshipped in the east"[7]), for the sake of his defence of men's redeeming power to imagine, "to tell themselves stories".

The third, shared mythical characteristic appropriated by Powys is Teiresias's retention of prophetic power underground, among the dead (*Odyssey, XI*). In this Teiresias is a shadowy duplication of the primary mythological figure of his work, Saturn. Saturn, invoked throughout the philosophical and critical works as well as fiction, as an image of Millennial hope, must be brought up from the abyss, pictured in *Morwyn* (1937), in accordance with Greek myth, as not only below Earth but below Hell. There seem to be several possible interpretations of what Powys's imagination was sinking to here.

In *The Saturnian Quest*, G. Wilson Knight suggests it is a search for the golden age "through evil" (associating evil here with Powys's claim to cerebral sadism) and what Shakespeare called "the dark backward and abysm of time". Perhaps "through evil" is too strong in the context of the novels: they describe cruelties, but as wholes they speak against evil, showing it as self-defeating. This is made absolute in *Porius*, *the* Saturn book. There is, of course, a wealth of imaginative literature, known to Powys, on the process of attaining deity or paradise, ranging from St. Paul's concept of the crucified Christ becoming sin, to Keats's sketch, at the end of *Hyperion*, of Apollo becoming a god through a dying agony. (Powys wrote an admiring essay on St. Paul and spent many early years writing a book on Keats—which remains unpublished.)

There also appears to be some personal basis for the inclusion of an abyss of horror, about which one can only conjecture, and which is not artistically relevant. It is suggested by Powys's often saying that we should *force* ourselves to be happy, and by the *Autobiography*'s revelations of his "self-tormenting incarnations of Fear . . . from Hell" (188), and of his forty years' torment by a Demon (248–9). (There may be some play with his inheritance from Cowper here.) It is represented less

starkly by his admission of basic pessimism (375) and by
Llewelyn's identification of him with their mother who "loved
the side of the moon away from the earth."[8]

An abyss is suggested in some novels, distinct from the
existentialists' abyss, but posited by the novels' acceptance of
every man's loneliness, which may be the basis of his strength.
At the end of *Porius* comes an abyss of time of waiting (or
story-telling?) in hope or unhope, for the Millennium. Here
we are not given entry into the consciousness of Myrddin,
"the Being in the Pit". Instead we have Porius's

> "This," he thought, "is what I've often feared as pure
> madness. And yet it doesn't seem madness now; or is it
> that . . . a person *can* enjoy being alone in absolute dark-
> ness? . . . alone among millions of universes and yet
> enjoying himself, as small and weak and helpless in the
> abysses of existence as a worm or a fly, and yet able to
> rescue a God?" (679)

In a very long, detailed, interesting letter to Powys, of
December 20th–23rd, 1941, recording his response to the
"epic tragedy" *Owen Glendower* (which, he decided, gave him
the same experience as reading the *Paradiso* and the Second
Part of *Faust*), the poet J. Redwood Anderson struggled success-
fully to explain his realisation that this was not "a historical
novel" but that the characters, with varying degrees of awareness (Meredith, Owen's son, he thought, "the axis of the work"
and "a man who has no self") are beyond life and death,
concerned with the Abyss, the "Hinterland of existence, that
Annwn, 'the world which is not—and yet was and shall be'
(890)":

> suddenly I saw them all
> ". . . like workings of one mind, (not yours)
> *Of the same face*, blossoms upon one tree,
> Characters of the great Apocalypse . . ."
> and the final significance of your *Owen Glendower* came
> upon me. This is not a tissue of events woven by the

27

various characters, but an *Event*, itself symbolical, which for its expression takes to itself these various characters . . . all . . . are but the limbs of the *Ineffable*.[9]

It is not "through evil" but through knowledge of the Abyss, some inarticulate darkness, that Powys attempts to represent, if not in the person (or "*Event*") of his most melancholy and straggling novel *Owen Glendower*, in the person of Glendower himself, prince both of Wales and *Annwn* (925) and the human image of the past as the eternal (415). *Owen Glendower* is an ambitiously experimental novel,[10] and Owen himself reads like "a try-out" in a historical figure for the composite metaphorical-mythical being, wisely put off-centre, in *Porius*, Myrddin-Cronos. The representation of the possibility of our reaching the Millennium via the Abyss, Powys achieves in *Porius* by working to it essentially through images instead of characters, and by violating historical probability by boldly blending it with myth. In the last Powys was supported by his agreement with Paracelsus that thoughts when visualised and long brooded upon become entities:[11] thus story-telling is actually objective, history is the product of creative imagination.

As Porius is the accomplice of Saturn in his Cronos aspects so Man's creative power should work with time: this is Powys's central concern as a creative artist. Taliessin, earlier in his poem, part-quoted above, declares:

> I was the first word on the lips of Tiresias
> When he lapped at the blood between Ocean and Hades.

In view of the images of Teiresias, articulate of life among the dead, and Saturn, a corpse god explicitly associated with creative power in *Porius*, it seems to me that Powys's feeling for the Dark of the earth is primarily for something like Boehme's *ungrund*, the abyss of unarticulate deity. In fact, this is made very clear in the "Pair Dadeni" (Cauldron of Rebirth) essay of *Obstinate Cymric* (1947) (see pages 99–100), the essay itself an explanation of much of the thought-content in *Porius*.

The wind, subject of the poem "Teiresias", has many and varied significances for Powys. "I am a worshipper of the wind", he says on the last page of the *Autobiography*. In this there is self-mockery at his verbosity and "windy art of dithyrambic analysis" (533). (Here, in "dithyrambic", is an association with the Bacchanalian Teiresias again.) But his serious association of wind with prophecy is seen when he declares:

> I regard myself as a voice crying in the wilderness, an individual with a devilish shrewd inkling as to the hidden tricks of the creative and destructive forces of the cosmos, and with something more than an inkling as to the craftiest, foxiest and wisest way of seeking happiness for myself and of giving happiness to the entities I encounter.

This "claim" he admits is regarded by his enemies as megalomaniacal folly and by "enemy-friends as a lovable weakness in a windy oracle". (225–6) In the novels winds often figure large and have malefic or restorative powers according to their quarters. (See *Rodmoor* (1916), pages 349–350, for an early example.) They participate in the novels' dramas by inspiration and influence. In *Porius*, which is wind-filled, the Prince and Taliessin each has his favourite, activating wind, and Myrddin receives messages by wind and puts "the burden of his prophecy on the air". Winds for Powys, throughout his prose and poetry, carry memories of previous incarnations, race-memories and race-inspirations.

Most obviously, the wind represents freedom. One freedom is from possessing and being possessed. This is for Powys a personal need:

> I have never liked being held, not even by the wisest and most affectionate of human hands. I am like the wind. I have to blow *where I list*.[12]

It is also a general ideal, linked to his wish to rewrite the most important two of the Ten Commandments.[13] In *Porius*, Taliessin, anticipating the enchantress Nineue's attempt to bury Merlin in the ground for her own use throughout a thousand years, explains his contrasting use of his poetry:

> I like freeing people from love. Instead of keeping them
> shut up for thousands and thousands of years, I tell them
> to rush out when the winds blow free . . . and to fill all they
> meet with the magic of liberation! (422–3)

Such freedom allows construction of the future. Powys's
Mandragora and *Samphire* volumes contain many poems
showing worship of the wind. One of the earliest, "Wayfarers",
celebrates the Proteus power of immersing oneself into every
form of experience, always passing on to the next, which is
our experience in reading (explicitly described in *The Pleasures
of Literature* (1938), page 75). In this dialogue poem, the
poet's shivering heart is led on by the cold wind, at his soul's
bidding, to the city of Dis, to the city of God, to the City of
Dreams, and yet onward:

> And still they follow and follow,
> Beyond each ultimate shore;
> And Aldebaran shines before them
> And Arcturus shines before.
> And when my poor heart murmurs,
> "When we left those gates we sinned!"
> My soul thro' the darkness answers her—
> "Follow the wind!"

The wind represents an ideal of endless becoming, endless
possibility. It may not image "spiritual insincerity", but it does
image a life of spiritual or cerebral promiscuity, the life of the
creative writer.

The "Saturn" poem of 1928 is interesting as a counterpart
to the "Saturn" published in *Mandragora* in 1917. In the
longer, early poem, despite the hope of "every fragile, quivering
thing" at dawn, not the old buried god but the tyrannous sun
is resurrected. The later poem is a successful invocation of the
god, just after sunset. These poems' cold, forest and vegetation
god or idea, "Saturn", served by Powys, has fully risen in all
his riches of moss, lichen and fungus in *Porius*.

Powys's bookishness served him well here: Saturn/Cronos
of *Porius* has every characteristic to be collected from ancient

literature. The collection of the characteristics of Saturn by R. Klibansky, E. Panofsky and F. Saxl in *Saturn and Melancholy* (1964)[14] reveals that the Greek god Cronos who merged with the originally good Roman Saturn is distinguished by *a dual nature*. For Homer (and the most detailed source of information is Powys's loved *Iliad*) this father of gods and men was both "great" and "of crooked counsel". He was a benevolent god of agriculture, enjoyed by freemen and slaves alike, ruler of a Golden Age of abundance and natural innocence, lord of the Islands of the Blessed. But he was also the gloomy, dethroned and solitary god "dwelling at the uttermost end of land and sea", "exiled beneath the earth", ruler of nether gods; he was even a prisoner (Hesiod) in or beneath Tartarus, and, later, he was even the god of death and the dead. He obtained attributes of cold, wind, and old age when linked in idea with the star Saturn. It was later that the Neoplatonists identified Cronos with Chronos, Time.

All these ambivalent characteristics of the ancient god, possessed by Myrddin, "crooked counseller" to Emperor Arthur, are arranged to supply the *story* of *Porius*. However, though Powys's capturing of the traditional Saturn is complete (and Myrddin even has the main visual characteristics of ancient murals and medieval portraiture), it is cunningly slanted to his own imaginings and artistic purposes. The early "Saturn" poem includes the medieval psychological association of Saturn with madness. Powys relates it to older tradition by a story: Saturn was exiled because he was thought "mad". Here Saturn becomes one with Powys in his identifying championship (often too strident, as in Chapter X of *Auto-biography*) of outsiders, social exiles and misfits, lyrically explained in his "Moon madrigal", "The Epiphany of the Mad" which begins:

> I am the voice of the outcast things,
> The refuse and the drift.

The poems' Saturn is the same whom Porius, himself instinctive protector of the imaginatively eccentric, the emotionally disturbed, the nervously deranged (536), at the end of his story forsees will redeem "innumerable weak and terrified and unbeautiful and unconsidered and unprotected creatures" (681).

Powys, however, could only have achieved this end-vision of the novel by blending the classical Saturn with this island's war-maddened, green or savage man of the woods and master of animals, Merlin.[15] And, from this blending, Myrddin in the Cave of Mithras can reveal a slow-worm coiled about his wrist which identifies him with the statue of Cronos entwined by a tail-eating serpent, conveniently but, unlike the authentic Mithraic torches, astonishingly found there.[16] Given this association, it is no imaginative shock to us when, afterwards, Myrddin, drifting in a boat on the forest's stream, in reverie, relives his own history as Cronos, defeater of tyrranic Zeus, but himself overthrown. One outstanding achievement of this superimposed series of idea-images is that we have seen Time in a Cave, which is one important, repeated, actual and mental image of *Porius*. Here we come nearer to an appreciation of the artistic form of *Porius*, and to an assessment of Powys as a novelist.

Powys is happy to describe himself in the *Autobiography* as "a terrifyingly formidable genius" (225), but when an account of himself as a novelist is drawn from him, he writes simply, as in the letter to Louis Wilkinson of July 31st, 1956, rejoicing in his complicated stories, host of characters and exciting situations, big crowded scenes, describing himself as "an Inventor of Fairy Tales". Moreover, repeatedly, he declares that though he is "poetical" and imaginative" he is "not an artist". "To the devil with 'art' " he cries in the *Autobiography*, but mentioning there that he can convey "the cubic solidity" of his vision in fiction (641–2). We can see something of what his non-artistry does not exclude by finding which other novelists he considers non-artists.

In *The Pleasures of Literature* (1938), which provides much detail of Powys's values as a novelist, Dostoievsky is described as "a great artist" because his writing has such close veri-similitude to "the startling, corrosive, explosive stuff of our universal experience" (87) and for parallel Powys has to move outside prose to Shakespeare. Powys in some ways emulated Dostoievsky, and here cannot have used "artist" to signify alienation from his own aims. It is not surprising to have Dickens described as a non-artist, taken over by his creative energy (136). It is astonishing and significant to find Proust and Joyce put into the same category:

> I am old enough now to have lived through three great literary dictatorships. When I was at college, Dostoievsky and Nietzsche were the rulers of our spirit. When I first visited America Anatole France and Thomas Hardy were our masters. But all the way through the decade that is now closing, the more serious booklovers among us, I mean those who are concerned with real original genius and not with mere skilful craftmanship, have turned, perforce, . . . to Proust and Joyce. (650)

In this essay on Proust, Powys appears to use "artist" per-joratively to signify the writer concerned primarily with technique, whose composition is rigidly selective:

> Proust permits himself to do to the limit the very thing that is anathema to the artist type of author, that is, to interpose his fiction with what is not so much a "stream of consciousness" as a stream of Proustian commentaries upon consciousness! (642)

Powys has strong sympathy with the Proust of "madeleine moments", and he is deft in his essay's explication of *A la Recherche* which, imposing his own ideal, he finds "like the masterpieces of all great novelists . . . a whole world in itself . . . in which you can dwell." But two observations seem especially relevant to his own art as a novelist. One, on Proust's "*method of writing*" or "*aesthetic science*", is his discovery of:

> the imaginative bringing together of ideas or essences, or images that in objective reality are scattered through many various levels and dimensions, but can be fused together

> by our power of feeling things, not in their isolation, like
> instruments of torture in a museum, or like nectarines in
> cotton wool, but in their living, breathing, fluctuating
> environment, permeated by the airs and sounds and
> smells about them, and by our complicated feelings with
> regard to them. (640)

This seems to describe the method of Powys's novels from
Wolf Solent onwards. The second is the rather inaccurate
observation about *A la Recherche:*

> Time is the Antagonist of this book; and the Timeless—
> revealed in Art and revealed in these rare outbursts of the
> Self that is eternal—is the Protagonist. (631)

This notion, which suggests giving "vision" or awareness
"cubic solidity", forms a basis for Powys's novel construction.
At its simplest he makes the atmosphere of a place or landscape
the protagonist of a novel, or an archetypal image, like the
Grail Cup and the Life poured into it, as he explains in the
1953 Preface to *A Glastonbury Romance*. More bold, in *Porius*,
he incarnates awareness, which is here Time itself. Thus
Powys blends Proust's two methods, assembling and fusing
idea-images "that in objective reality are scattered through
many various levels and dimensions" by his presentation of
them in their living, fluctuating environment.

Wolf Solent, on the surface a very lucid, easily readable
novel, composed of a linear series of events, is a simple version
of Powys's method of composition which grew more complex
and comprehensive. *Wolf Solent* is the struggle of a solitary
soul with "symbolic" events, which Powys says in explaining
the art of his *Autobiography* (46) is all we want in a story. But
the mental climax of the novel (there is no climax of action),
Wolf's acceptance of life through full realisation of his solitude,
splendid and in accord with Powys's philosophy and also with
"real life" verisimilitude as it is, after the body of the novel,
is almost as inadequate as Wordsworth's explanation of his

benefits after his confrontation of *The Leech Gatherer*, or Coleridge's moral that we should be kind to animals at the end of *The Ancient Mariner*.

In the body of the novel there are sustained images, equally actual and mental, such as the grinning skull and the pond (which never left Powys), but places and characters rather than objects are used mainly as images for a mythology of life. Wolf's "mythology" (and the word "mythology" is important here, as when Powys uses it of himself in the *Autobiography* (64), for it indicates fictive action fit for universal use), his "subterranean vice" of imagining a dualistic conflict in the universe, corresponds with exterior events in his own little world (and also comically simplifies and exaggerates it).

But the events of the novel are arranged so that we brood upon certain figurations and interpret them. Thus (to take up just one strand, the meditation on alternative kinds of male-female love relationship), on the first day of Wolf's arrival into the novel he is forced to speculate on the two different forms of relationship his dead father must have had with two very different women, his wife and Selina Gault. On the following day (as he is becoming aware of a different duplication, himself and the former employee of Urquhart) he meets two similarly different girls. Such cerebral patterning, even in events, makes it clear that we are not, afterwards, to reflect on one particular man's experience in particular circumstances, as we may, perhaps, after *Jude the Obscure* (nor, probably, are we to see the two women as externalisations of components of the hero's self, a sort of body—soul dialogue: and we *could* interpret Wolf as Jude has been interpreted, especially as Wolf also marries the sensually attractive of two women). *Wolf Solent* has more kinship with *Robinson Crusoe* and makes even less social comment than that novel: it studies not Wolf *Obscure* but Wolf *Solent* and has more kinship with Proust's "commentaries on consciousness" than anything in Hardy's narratives.

That we are to dwell upon figurations and images is indicated too by Powys's use in the novel of an interior commentary on the art of writing. This, having a history book or chronicle written within the novel, he was to use several times again. (This has become almost a cliché of modern writing.) Early in *Wolf Solent*, when we are settling into a linear narrative, we encounter Urquhart's theory, attractive to Wolf, of a book with "organic" not "logical" development.[17] Urquhart's explanations of it come just before and just after the first chapter's "straight" narrative of Wolf's thoughts and feelings at objects and events ends with a vision of a selection of these being jumbled and fused or imposed upon one another arbitrarily in reverie as he falls asleep.

After *Wolf Solent* Powys abandoned "that Henry James rule of 'straining' the whole thing through one . . . consciousness"[18] and crammed his books with many varieties of consciousness, even inanimate. *Porius*, which rests mainly on object images, is outstanding for its whole entry into a series of consciousnesses, as the titles of the central group of chapters indicate. Throughout this romance, the chronicler and "tale-teller" Henog sits writing. He asks a writer's questions, such as "Have you noticed . . . how the mind works when real events occur?" (85) He also joins the novel's commentary on Time (97). More importantly, in Myrddin's tent, he forms a comic comment on those who might accuse Powys of historical inaccuracies for he takes down distorted facts from Merlin's mischievous page, Neb. But Henog's vital appearance is later in the book at a central scene and image, the cell in which Brother John is dying and the Jewish doctor's wife gives birth.

Porius enters the cell and overhears Henog reciting a story appropriate to his own predicament. Henog's tale ends midway and Porius discovers:

> He had in fact been reading from *what he was in the midst of composing*. And in doing this he was absolutely self-centred and self-sufficient. . . . "He's alone in space," Porius thought, "and only space has the power of reflecting his stories in such a manner that all their faults are lost and all their virtues remain. . . . Perhaps everybody who

listens to the Henog . . . is resolved into this paradigm, or perfect pattern, of an ideal myth; and by becoming a part of it himself, is transformed into the . . . perfection . . . Thus, while the Henog's hearers . . . may actually be tearing to pieces the tale he is telling them, they are . . . irresistibly compelled to assume the role of small and unimportant portions of the perfect pattern of his vision." (543–4)

Space, like Time, is only one object of the pattern of Powys's tale. Throughout *Porius* Time is identified with Earth, Space with Sky (562). Morfydd, meeting a time-vacuum where myth and her human world blend (personified in the owl-maiden), is aware of the two cosmic motions, the stream of events in time and the growth of events in space (633). Of course a novel works with time and space, the time of events narrated, the time of reading, the space of the universe caught therein, the space occupied by words. But these events and this universe are independent of time and space outside the writer and reader; they are alone in space. In the above passage, Powys upturns the old lie about the mimetic novel. He says that the story-teller is a magician, that there is a correlation between the artefact and the "real" world, because the real, in the persons of readers, is "transformed" into the verisimilitude of fiction. His gain here, as a novelist, is that by his hero's self-conscious realisation of himself as a fiction, we readers become conscious of our part with the writer's composing.

Porius ends on a mist-covered mountain peak, the Prince physically "alone in a world without a sky . . . space gone" (673). Having come from his ideal relationship with Morfydd, he does not succumb to the enchantress Nineue and is left to remove Myrddin (creative Time) from the cavernous gateway to the World of the Dead. As Nineue rides away Porius has the sense of holding Space in his hands (676). (For Powys, the storyteller, he is, at its end, holding the entire novel in his hands.) As he swings Zeus's thunderbolt to drop onto Myrddin to release him from his trance, Porius feels that he, the child of Time, is "alone with this necessary illusion . . . called Space."

The story has ended for him: we see that he has moved from the power "to create or to destroy", to the power "simply to enjoy" (678); thus he steps outside the novel.

These two scenes hold other thematic images which the readers accumulate throughout the book. One is death. The book, or forest, contains an astonishing variety of deaths with many "unnecessary" peripheral ones, such as of the Saxon soldier who staggers to Arthur (365), of the ancient princess in an ecstacy of long-frustrated embrace (471) ("Death is life's high meed"), of the "little ghost" servant girl Teleri who has slept with Medrawd in place of her lady (613–16). In addition to these studies of death, there are various forms of death worship, healthy as by the ancient, noble Cadawg who venerates the Cauldron of Rebirth (322) and by Brother John for its ending pain (549), and unhealthy as by Medrawd (570). There are death longings by Porius (571) who eventually decides that life and death must be kept separate (642) and by Myrddin, who is rescued by a water rat sitting on his knuckle (286). Hence we are involved in a long meditation on death.

But the book also traces and ends in a love story, though we learn quite early not to think of "love" as ideal, but Golden Age common-sense, kindness, indulgence, and leaving people alone (276). The novel's eight days show the development to ideal understanding by Porius and Morfydd, which begins by their deciding to marry for political purposes, though Porius is detached and Morfydd wants Rhun, the third of a triangle built from childhood. We realise the development not only by experience of the impact of events and observation of other relationships on the two characters' consciousnesses, but by a play on accumulated images of union for our and the characters' comparison. There is Morfydd's leap at Rhun, to bite his neck, in parting before her marriage (295) (blood itself is a strong image throughout the novel), her flinging Rhun from her bed at his approach on her wedding morning, the consummation of the marriage ("If it suited *his* method of existence to take possession of her with no more than a tenth part of his personality, it suited *hers* to be so taken.") (491–3), Porius's union with the compliant and passionate giantess (517), and, after Morfydd's realisation that she likes Porius more than Rhun (625), there is Porius's carrying her to "their childhood's Home-Rock" to ecstatic union and sympathy (contrasted with the marriage union) and a parting kiss which draws blood (634–40). The central pair are surrounded by a wide variety of others, including not only major characters but the young servants Gwythyr and Nesta, the ancients Cadawg and Princess Tonwen, the children Neb and Gunta, so that the space of the novel is heavy with love and liking.

In his marriage bed, Morfydd asleep, Porius imagines his "long, slow, tranquilly rolling ripples of sex-satisfaction" resemble the contented feelings of every child "in its first independent falling asleep after its navel string is cut." (493) Such linkages are central to Powys's exploration in the novel, its groping to comprehend the primeval and permanent in human life, through scenic juxtapositions of marriage bed and death bed and birth, which would appear crude were they not surrounded in the novel by swirling multitudes of thoughts and details and by an awareness of an extra dimension, the enveloping inanimate forest and elements.

The image uniting death and love with birth is the cave. Caves are numerous, of Mithras, of the Aunties, of the Druid (underground), of Brother John's cell. The cave links the "historical", Porius world with the mythical, Saturn world of Myrddin. Porius yearns for his aboriginal, cave-dwelling ancestors. Myrddin, who as Time ends by imprisonment in and escape from a "cosmogonic cavern", has a body reeking of "thousands . . . of earth-chasms full of the black leaf mould of the original planetary forests" (99). Porius's inner life he calls "cavoseniargising", which G. Wilson Knight has con-jectured involves enlargement and energising with his cave-wish.[19] Porius's opportunity to materialise his cave-wish comes when two giants, father and daughter, appear with the corpse mist to feed on the slain. His union with the giant girl swiftly results in her death and both giants' drowning in a cavernous lake. Later, exhausted in Brother John's cell, Porius reimagines the sight in "that clear green water":

> suddenly, clean through the blood and the hair and the staring eyes a chasm opened into something deeper yet, an ecstasy of life-worship, indescribable in words . . . (538)

The Jewish doctor's wife crawls in, and Porius, leaning over the unconscious body of Brother John, and fighting against the "feeling that he was moving from the past into the future like a shadow upon a dial" looks as

> once before that day, through a mist of water and wet hair and torn flesh at a human head smeared with blood. (546)

At the book's end, having caught the murmur of a second Golden Age, he again has the vision of floating blood, strewn hair and green water. (681) By this time we may have the sensation that the novel has been a "cosmogonic cavern". But, after this process, after this working through accumulated and superimposed images, exploring their pattern, we emerge. What then?

Porius at the embodiment of Birth and Death was left only, as Morfydd was elsewhere (619), with the astonished realisation that he could not predict his own emotions, and with a sense of being in a boat on an unknown sea (550). Despite his complicity with materialised Time and a glimpse of future hope, he ends deciding to "just accept this crazy loneliness in this unbounded chaos" (681). The bounded space, the syntheses of images, the illusion of the novel, is at an end, and we, the readers, become aware of our complicity in its creation. We are left with an unfinished object for contemplation, a story which is incomplete in many strands, and with a baffling hoard of primary images. This Porius seems to consider enough. He remains content with uncertainties and doubts. It is significant that this Prince, who displays Powys's admired virtues of courage, magnanimity and an open mind, who is articulate and capable of choice, yearns for a primeval language, of wise sounds which, when discovered, he cannot communicate even to his sensitive and wedded Morfydd (641–2). Thus he yearns for the inarticulate, meaningful to him alone, not for communication. The giants' incommunicable gibberish about endurance lies at the heart of the romance with Taliessin's poem about the structure of "peace paradisic".

It has been, we realise, an amazing book. Powys has used the word "grotesque" throughout, too often but appropriately. Though the year of its placing, 499 A.D., could justify its collection of manifold creeds and races in one forest, though the men and women are more normal than usual for Powys, though human relationships, especially family ones, father-daughter, son-father, nephew-aunt, are conveyed and analysed with detailed verisimilitude, this is more than a realistic novel, more than a Romance of the Dark Ages. It seems an extravaganza and critical burlesque of the traditional historical novel, like Scott's, and of the twentieth century novel of the type of Proust or Virginia Woolf. As a historical document the work sets off its "modern novel's" assertion of men's omnitemporal interior lives as flamboyantly rebellious. But there are also mythical ingredients which juxtapose another view, Man's interior life. Places, objects, the rich inanimate world, and animals are important participants, and, mixing with the ordinary mortals there are a magician, an enchantress and aboriginal giants. A strong obsession of some novelists since Proust has been time and its various workings. Powys goes further and makes thought into material entity by creating Time as a complex person in his fiction. For example, in one simple aspect Myrddin resembles the modern novelist's mental time when he keeps his head to the earth, negligent of battle raging round him.

In all this Powys writes in the manner of the English epic poets who each exploited, criticised and made something new of traditional ingredients. An explicit example is *Paradise Lost* in which the reader must recognise that Satan out-heroes all previous epic heroes and so bears in person Milton's exaggeration (and distortion) of the traditional form and concept which he, the new epic poet, is discarding for his own new conception of hero and literary form alike. Powys's personified Time, Myrddin, is feeble and vulnerable, too easily captured. To be the Future, Time needs man's fictive, free imagination.

The forest of *Porius*, comprehensive of crowds and solitary quests, alive with people and events, historical, mythical and allegorical, resembles the forest of Spenser's *The Faerie Queene* which Coleridge rightly says is "composed of a wondrous series of images as in our dreams." The work, he explains, lacks particular time and space:

> it is truly the land of Faery, that is, of mental space. The poet has placed you in a dream . . . and you neither wish, nor have the power to enquire how you got there.[20]

H. P. Collins finds Glastonbury of the *Romance* "an island outside space and time."[21] Coleridge exaggerates in his account of *The Faerie Queene* (like Collins on the *Romance* he records a relevant critical impression, not facts) and we would exaggerate to apply it entirely to *Porius* as an escape "world to dwell in" of the "Inventor of Fairy Tales". *Porius* has emphatic relationship with the actual world of birth, passion and death. H. P. Collins declares, however, that in *Porius* "drama is merged in dream".[21]

In some ways, dream vision is a discovery of the inter-war novelists, and indeed Auerbach notes their capturing of "the dream like wealth of a process of consciousness which transverses a whole subjective universe" in "a brief span of time". But Powys's ancestors are obviously earlier. It was the English Romantic writers who first consciously explored the relationship of the processes of dream-experience and of creative imagination, particularly Wordsworth, Keats and Coleridge, whose thoughts and imagery are frequently glimpsed throughout Powys's work, and De Quincey, with whom Powys often identifies himself. Wordsworth, who Powys says in *Obstinate Cymric* (1947) had nourished him for sixty years,[22] did not furnish Powys's attitude to the inanimate natural world (Powys's is his own and equally defies simple description), but from Wordsworth come not only his outsiders and idiots,

"the self-sufficing power of solitude", a brooding on imaginative
and spiritual "power", a concern with the "individual Mind
that keeps her own Inviolate retirement", but very possibly a
veneration for the "Forests of Romance" (*The Prelude* (1805),
V,477) and a sympathy with romancers, "Forgers of lawless
tales" "Who make our wish our power, our thought a deed"
(*The Prelude* (1850), V,524,528). Certainly Coleridge's scattered
prose discussions of the phenomena of dreams and reverie
(such as the relationship of sensations to images, the suspension
of belief, of surprise, of judgement and moral sense, the
combination and association of images, the "transmutation of
the succession of Time into the juxtaposition of Space") and
the relation of these to the "self-power of the imagination"
and the composition of fairy-tales, are relevant commentary
both on the contents of Powys's works as wholes, compounded
of scenic images, and on the experience of some of his characters. Porius alone, and it is he who has insight into Neneue,
conjunction with Myrddin and a giant, moves without surprise,
in a semi-dream state in that novel. He seems, in some ways,
heir to the experience of Coleridge's Ancient Mariner and
Christabel.

It has been said that Powys's characters are unaware of social
pressures. (In this volume this is asserted by H. P. Collins, of
Weymouth Sands, but rejected by J. A. Brebner, of *Porius*.)
Such an impression also relates the novels to dream process.
Certainly most of Powys's major characters have strong
interior lives to which to retire from everyday life. It is not
surprising that the two Wales novels, accentuating this, should
have, at their centres, princes who should play public roles
distinct from their interior lives. Shakespeare thoroughly
explored the special similiarity of kings and actors. Powys, "a
born actor", as he so often tells us, in accord with the concern
with masks and personae of some important poets of this
century, contemplated acting to various interpretations, mainly
as escape from others, and as a means of self-endurance.[23]
In the *Autobiography* he describes his enjoyment of acting "the
sceptical" Shakespeare's tragic heroes at school, early suspecting

"the solidity of the objective world" and regarding "the whole astronomical universe" with detachment as "the mere *material stage* for playing whatever romantic, picturesque, or fantastical role a person's life-illusion might arbitrarily select." He discovered that Homer's "primeval" and "elementary heroes were just as addicted to this vision of themselves as acting a spectacular part before gods and men." Thus Powys learned early the consolation of enduring and enjoying things as an actor, "as though . . . you could play out your part before your own awareness, and be to the end both performer and audience!" (121–2) Later, remarking his own combination of metaphysical system-making and scepticism, Powys describes himself as "always . . . an actor in ideas". (135–6) In this awareness, transferred to many of his creations, not only to *Porius*, Powys again captures a dream experience, of which one of the best descriptions is by Addison. It is unlikely that the schoolboy, comically searching for erotic stimulation through the volumes of the *Spectator* in his father's library,[24] came across Addison on dreams on September 18th, 1712, but the essayist was partly embellishing the view of Sir Thomas Browne who Powys did enjoy.

> (The soul) converses with numberless beings of her own creation, and she is transported into ten thousand scenes of her own raising. She is herself the theatre, the actors and the beholder. This puts me in mind of a saying . . . which Plutarch ascribes to Heraclitus, "That all men whilst they wake are in one common world; but that each of them, when he is asleep, is in a world of his own.

This, or such a concept, probably contributed to the *Reverie* experience of Coleridge's isolated Ancient Mariner. It describes the predicament represented in Powys's lone heroes. It explains the feebleness of Time in *Porius* (although the artefact, the novel, is in control of its eight days). It explains even the sensation that Space, in which a storyteller (like Henog) is alone, is an illusion. The objective world lacks solidity. The book is a private world, a created illusion of Time and Space, outside unsolid Time and Space, in which "the individual soul" of writer or reader can "disport itself in sweet security".[25]

Therefore the more copious and jagged and inclusive the novel is, the better. By the overflow of imagery and by withdrawals from dramatic finishes, Powys reveals his fictions as triumphs of imaginative will and power. A "Magician-wish", like his own, lends itself to enjoyment of this bewildering universe.[26] In Powys's books the writer, and so the reader, is acting "Lord of Hosts", inventing complicating, destroying, making and keeping "all doors open".[27]

Obviously, Powys does not wish to be placed, tied down, labelled, in the multiverse of literature. He overcrowds his large novels with experience, almost as if he is in rivalry with, or must absorb, all the great, romantic, universal writers of the past. He tends to be an over-emphatic imagist, too extravagantly articulate. He strains towards the inarticulate, to include "dimensions" outside the novel's grasp. Amazement at his magician powers, or attempted magician powers, and "our becoming a part" of his patterns of "ideal myth", should not preclude our attempts at analytic comprehension, with the recognition that Powys's explorations within "the art of the novel" need magical powers, because of his determination that it is the "most comprehensive of all arts".[28]

NOTES

1. F. E. Hardy, *The Life of Thomas Hardy* 1840–1928, 1962, pp. 377–378.
2. My textual page references in parentheses throughout are to the 1967 edition of the *Autobiography* (1934).
3. My textual page references in parentheses throughout are to the only edition of *Porius*, 1951.
4. Powys explains this similarity at length in the "Pair Dadeni" essay of *Obstinate Cymric*, 1947.
5. *Dostoievsky*, 1946, p. 184.
6. *The Pleasures of Literature*, 1938, "Dickens", p. 132.
7. W. and D. Wordsworth, *Early Letters*, ed. E. de Selincourt, 1935, (To J. Wilson, June, 1802), p. 297.
8. *Skin for Skin*, 1926, p. 73.
9. This letter was generously loaned to me by Mrs. Redwood Anderson. It was abbreviated, at considerable loss, in *The Dublin Magazine*, June, 1942.

[10] *Owen Glendower*, astonishingly, for, though it is rich and interesting, it is, I think, Powys's least manageable, worst-constructed work, seems to have had more critical analysis lavished on it than any of his other works. (One essay, J. A. Brebner's, sees the Fourth Dimension it reaches for as different from *Annwn*.) R. Mathias's essay in this collection tackles, at last, the *first* problem, hitherto unnoticed by critics (including J. Redwood Anderson), its historical inaccuracies and incredibilities.

[11] *Autobiography*, p. 11.

[12] *Ibid*., p. 529.

[13] *Ibid*., pp. 375–376.

[14] See especially pp. 133–136; 154.

[15] For secondary works which discuss these characteristics of Merlin, see, for example, J. D. Bruce, *The Evolution of Arthurian Romance*, Gottingen and Baltimore, 1923, pp. 136–143 (an account of Geoffrey of Monmouth's *Vita Merlini* and its sources), or, better, A. O. H. Jarman, *The Legend of Merlin* (an Inaugural Lecture), University of Wales Press, 1960, pp. 12–25.

[16] Did Powys know about and interpret a Mithraic Aion? (See Plate 9 of R. Klibansky et al., *Saturn and Melancholy*, 1964.) Or did he impose a medieval image upon an ancient cult unlikely to include it? (See F. Saxl, *Lectures*, 1957, "Mithras I and II".) Some Mithras reliefs showed the history of the world from Chaos, including Cronos's overthrow of Zeus (which Powys did not need in the Cave). The reliefs usually had serpents, representing earth catching the slain bull's blood for renewal. Powys's Myrddin is guided by the earth, and has an earthy slow-worm, but obviously Powys preferred to forget the traditional Mithraic earth-serpent.

[17] *Wolf Solent*, 1929, pp. 42 and 58; 1961, pp. 34 and 50.

[18] *Autobiography*, p. 544.

[19] *The Saturnian Quest*, 1964, p. 80.

[20] S. T. Coleridge, *Miscellaneous Criticism*, ed. T. M. Raysor, 1936, p. 35.

[21] *John Cowper Powys, Old Earth Man*, 1966, p. 199. On *Porius*, pp. 144–145.

[22] "My Philosophy", p. 164.

[23] *The Pleasures of Literature*, "Shakespeare", pp. 297–298.

[24] *Autobiography*, p.118.

[25] *Ibid*., p. 123.

[26] *Ibid*., p. 7.

[27] *The Pleasures of Literature*, "Rabelais", p. 114.

[28] *Ibid*., "Dostoievsky", p. 95.

II

"A TOUCH OF CARICATURE":
THE AUTOBIOGRAPHY OF
JOHN COWPER POWYS

Jeremy Hooker

To a considerable extent, this book of mine, the "Autobiography" of a tatterdemalion Taliessin from his third to
his sixtieth year, is the history of the "de-classing" of a
bourgeois-born personality, and its fluctuating and wavering approach to the Communistic system of social justice:
not however to the Communistic philosophy: for I feel
that the deepest thing in life is the soul's individual struggle
to reach an exultant peace in relation to more cosmic
forces than *any* social system, just or unjust, can cope with
or compass.

What is wrong with so many clever people today is the
fatal distrust lodged in their minds—and lodged there by
a superstitious awe in the presence of transitory scientific
theories—of the power in their own souls. What we need—
and the key to it lies in ourselves—is a bold return to the
magical view of life. I don't mean to the magic of Madame
Blavatsky, but to that kind of faith in the potentialities of
the ego, with which all great poetry and all great philosophy
has been concerned. That feeling of exultant liberation
from the immediate pressure of practical life, which any
"logos" from the arena of Goethe, or Spinoza or Leonardo,
or Plato, or Heraclitus, or Epictetus, or the old Chinese
Taoists conveys, is what we need.

Science has not changed the human soul. Science has
not changed the basic relations between the human soul
and the mystery surrounding it. We are still potential
magicians as long as we have faith in the power within
us to create and to destroy. (626)[1]

The tone of this passage is not uncommon in the *Autobiography*
and especially in the final chapters, although it is one among
many belonging to a voice with a wide range of expressiveness.
For the time being the "tatterdemalion Taliessin" is once more
upon the rostrum, his solitary reader transformed into a large
audience. Such passages should prevent us from forgetting
that the habit of self-depreciation, which is often a refreshing
feature of the *Autobiography* and all the writings, including his

letters, where Powys "caricatures" himself, serves the aims of a propagandist for a philosophy of life. There is every reason for taking Powys very seriously indeed when a few pages later he writes,

> My writings—novels and all—are simply so much propaganda, as effective as I can make it, for my philosophy of life. It is the prophecy and poetry of an organism that feels itself in possession of certain magical secrets that it enjoys communicating. And, by the way, I certainly feel conscious of conveying much more of the cubic solidity of my vision of things in fiction than it is possible to do in any sort of non-fiction.

> It is for this reason that my instinct has led me in this "Autobiography" to treat myself as if I were one of my own fictional characters, even at the risk of making myself out more of a rascal and more of a fool than my friends have supposed me to be. *Caricaturing* is the master trick! And that is why the discreet, dignified, plausible autobiographies are so insipid and unconvincing. A touch of caricature is what we *must* have, if we are to compete, even in this analytic job, with the beautiful madness of Nature. (641–642)

It should be clear from Powys's remarks in letters, and in the *Autobiography* itself, that he had given a great deal of thought to the task of writing about his own life, including what to say and what to leave unsaid, and the manner of approach to adopt. This is generally accepted to be true, especially in certain respects such as the virtual absence of women from the book, an absence which is a shaping factor in its construction. In fact, however, the *Autobiography* does examine in depth Powys's apprehension of the feminine principle, and especially as it constitutes a vital element in his own psyche, so that the paucity of references to actual women is not felt to impoverish the fulness of the work: the importance of Powys's particular attitude to woman for his understanding of life balances the weight given to the father. Apart from his

49

theme, and the recognition that Powys is an artist of some kind—though an idiosyncratic one it is often maintained, as if most great artists were anything else in times of spiritual upheaval—he is not thought by many people to have a maker's cunning. Certainly, one's initial image of the creation of the *Autobiography* tends to be of a book that was talked into existence, its coherence of a kind that is organic to the personality of the talker rather than of a deliberately willed and cleverly wrought form. This is an attractive image, but I believe that it cannot survive a clearer understanding of the nature of Powys's self-presentation.

When Powys tells us that he is writing propaganda it would be wrong to think in any simple-minded way about the nature of the propaganda or of its expression, since the act of writing propaganda is related by the propagandist himself to the process of creating fiction. And besides, "prophecy and poetry" are strange bedfellows for what the word propaganda is usually taken to mean. The *Autobiography* discloses sensitively, sometimes painfully, often exuberantly, the tissue of a remarkable man's inner life, and it is what emerges from the life itself that constitutes the propaganda. In my experience, when Powys writes about the major ideologies of the day and sets them against each other, in the novels, he is almost totally unconvincing, a manipulator of large ideas which solidify his fluid, very acute intelligence into a number of static poses. Fortunately, the novels contain a lot more than discussions of communism, fascism, and capitalism. And in the *Autobiography* he is almost invariably true to one of the strongest impulses in his work: to reestablish the primacy of the imagination for a time desperately in need of it. His understanding of the nature of the imagination is such that its isolation in any one passage reveals the stuff out of which the whole is made. Given certain basic impulses and influences, Powys's life is, literally, his own creation.

Powys's reference to himself as a "tatterdemalion Taliessin" in the first passage quoted above combines his use of caricature with the serious claim to embody a power of the imagination alien to most categories of modern thought about this creative faculty. But before outlining my view of the importance of Taliessin for Powys, it would be useful to include a brief sketch of the myth associated with this figure together with a contemporary idea of its significance.

In the Welsh Story of Taliesin, the witch Ceridwen prepares in her cauldron a magic brew which, after a year's boiling, will yield three blessed drops. Whoever swallows these drops will know all the secrets of the past, the present, and the future . . . The drops fly out of the cauldron and fall on the finger of Gwion Bach, the boy who has helped to tend the fire underneath the cauldron. He puts his finger in his mouth, and then, realizing his danger, flees. Ceridwen sets out in pursuit. Gwion transforms himself successively into a hare, a fish, a bird, and a grain of wheat; she gives chase in appropriate forms— a greyhound, an otter-bitch, a hawk, and a hen. In this last form, she swallows the grain of wheat, and in the fulness of time, Gwion Bach is reborn of her as the wizard-poet Taliesin. . . . The child Taliesin, in a poem replying to the king's question as to who he is and whence he has come, envisages himself as a ubiquitous presence which has witnessed the history of the world and will endure to the end . . . In a poem in the Book of Taliesin he claims to have witnessed the fall of Lucifer, the Flood, and the birth and the Crucifixion of Christ . . . Some of the poems in this Book are replete with utterances beginning 'I have been', and the things he has been include inanimate objects—stock, axe, chisel, coracle, sword, shield, harp-string, raindrop, foam; animals such as bull, stallion, stag, dog, cock, salmon, snake, eagle—and a grain which grew on a hill . . . Taliesin is everything, and it is a fair inference that among the Celts, as in India and other lands, there existed alongside the belief in individual reincarnation, a doctrine that there is essentially only One Transmigrant. As Ovid expresses it: 'The spirit wanders, comes now here, now there, and occupies whatever frame

51

it pleases. From beasts it passes into human bodies, and from our bodies into beasts, but never perishes."[2]

The myth and the poems associated with Taliessin (or Taliesin) have been fertile for a number of modern writers seeking access to something beyond the socially-conditioned points of view that characterise the retreat from religion and nature—to an apprehension of cosmic forces, to an immediate sense of other times, and to an awareness that transcends the limits of merely personal experience; but for no-one have they been more fertile than for John Cowper Powys. Moreover, it is clear from the *Autobiography* that he associates the power of Taliessin with the imagination, and thus with his own life-illusion as a "magician". Furthermore, whatever antic disposition he may put on in speaking of these matters, Powys is never joking. The figure of Taliessin is at the root of his belief in the "magical view of life", and so of the kind of man and writer he is, but he does not claim an exclusive right to "magical secrets" so that this aspect of the *Autobiography* is what makes Powys such a great liberator for those trapped within a narrow conception of their human potentiality.

> But the more I soak myself in the work of Shakespeare and Dostoievsky the more I recognise that both these men have the magic power of *becoming women*. *That* is the point. That is where the intelligencies of our modern critics are so dull. They do not understand what the meaning of the word "Imagination" is.

> But it was not only into women I could transform myself when the old Druidic spirit, the spirit of Taliessin of the many incarnations, took possession of me! I could feel myself into the lonely identity of a pier-post, of a tree-stump, of a monolith in a stone-circle; and when I did this I *looked* like this post, this stump, this stone. (528)

The principal theme, and it is one to which everything in the book is organic, of the *Autobiography* follows the desire of a small boy in a Victorian vicarage "to play the part of a magician" until, through experience of the growing power of his imagination, the man can assert with total conviction the primacy of the "magical view of life". And if the story reads like a tall one, Powys would be right, I think, to infer that this is because we "do not understand what the meaning of the word "Imagination" is" whereas, for all his "charlatanism", he does. This is Powys's propaganda, and it is expressed as a justification for his way of life with an assertiveness that no conventional memoir could outdo, if only because Powys is bound to show the utter futility of conventional notions of "success" when set against the spirit he is possessed by. For this reason, too, "a touch of caricature" is essential to his aim.

Without his absurdities Powys would be ridiculous; with them he is both very human and a great liberator. After all, consider how ludicrous his task might have been made to appear: to write about the upper-middle class upbringing, in Victorian times, of an English gentleman, of a man respectful enough of the traditional continuities to send his son to his old Public School, who was destined for a Curacy but became instead a bookish itinerant lecturer, while the dominant life-illusion of this same man was the belief that he possessed magical powers derived from the strain of wizard-poets in his remote Welsh ancestry. It is the very disparagements of his self-portrayal—the references to himself as a "Loch Ness Monster", the self-depreciating epithets that accompany most of the assimilations to his own personality of the power of Taliessin, Owen Glendower, Merlin and the Druids—that establish his humanity while showing that the power of the imagination is no less human and real. The "touch of caricature" is both Powys's means for conveying the truth and an example of his artistic tact. The "fictional" John Cowper Powys embodies the great creative spirit of the actual man very effectively indeed.

The portrait of the father, which is recognised as one of the book's principal triumphs, also helps to achieve the success of Powys's propaganda for his own life-illusion. This may seem a heartless way of putting it, but it is intended to indicate that the magnificent portrait of the father, as well as being a tribute

53

of love to the man, presents him as fundamental to Powys's own creativity, and is thus a double tribute. Obviously, in Powys's feeling for "the romance of race" Wales occupies a very special position as the source of his idea of the imagination. True to the nature of this power, as it is derived from the identification with Taliessin, is the Protean quality of Powys's imagination, its fluidity, its capacity to become the object of his contemplation, and its embodiment in the art of "dithyrambic analysis". In the act of self-creation which the *Autobiography* describes Powys reveals himself to be a great shape-shifter, and he conceives this faculty of his creative will as akin to the elements of water and air: he flows into and becomes what he wills to become. But he also has an earth-rooted, massive solidity, so that "old earth-man", the subtitle of Mr. Collins's book about him, is singularly appropriate; and this solidity, containing volcanic but withheld emotion, also characterises the father. But it is from the father, too, that Powys derives his initial romantic attachment to Wales, despite the fact that C. F. Powys is more readily identifiable with Wessex as a man hewn from the very earth he loves. In John Cowper, on the other hand, the feminine principle is a determining factor in his apprehension of the imagination, so that what emerges from the conjunction of the two great portraits, of the father and of John Cowper himself, is a sense of differences based on a deep-rooted affinity. Sometimes, it seems as if what John Cowper is articulating *is* the father.

What I am trying to show by bringing together Powys's portrait of his father and the depiction of his own dominant life-illusion can be illustrated from a curious passage near the end of the book.

> But as for my father, every morning as I stop to stare at the foaming torrent of our spring-and-autumn stream, as it swirls round the rocks within a bow-shot of this little garden, I cry aloud, to the astonishment of my friend "Sis," the unruly hornless cow, upon whose milk I live and between whom and me there is such a singular understanding, "*It's not so cold, John, my boy!*" For I envisage

> at these times the majestic form of my progenitor standing
> stark naked in this swirling stream, encouraging me to
> face all the Preston Brooks of the world, and finally the
> deep West Bay of death itself. (643)

Rising from the waters, the father is at the source of life itself—
one thinks of the waters of baptism and the waters of birth—
and yet he is also associated with one of the elements analogous
to the Protean nature of imagination. But the father is no
shape-shifter. He is like a rock in the water, thus partaking of
the element and rising above it with a massive, earth-rooted
solidity. Still, it is his spirit, the spirit that has strengthened
Powys in the determination to dance his own dance and sing
his own song, that this image evokes as a challenge to death.
Later on, on the final page, the differences between father and
son are clearly stated: "My father was an inarticulate man.
I am an only too voluble one. My father was a man of rock.
I am a worshipper of the wind." The father is a presence
throughout the book, and the process of Powys's self-realization
as a man of imagination is, in a sense, his discovery of how to
use for his own creative purposes, in life and in literature, the
powers that his father possessed as a man of nature and of
faith. Not surprisingly, then, this final evocation of the father
leads Powys to exclaim:

> But now when from this resting-place, this ledge, this
> slab of stone, in the wavering Indian trail of my migrations
> and reversions, I look back at the path behind me and
> the path before me it seems as if it had taken me half a
> century merely to learn with what weapons, and with what
> surrender of weapons, *I am to begin to live my life*. (652)

The slab of stone is also the rock, "my father".

The *Autobiography* was written toward the end of Powys's
exile, albeit a happy and creative exile, in America, but it is a
feature of the book's inner coherence, that is an artistic coherence cunningly wrought in terms of the inner coherence of
the life itself, that it should point forward in a direction of
which Powys himself, at that time, may or may not have been

aware: the whole movement of the book is towards his identification, partly through the spirit of his father, with his idea of
Wales as one of the last places on earth where his kind of
imagination could be at home. It is not easy to think of the
spirit of Taliessin as associated in any way with the figure of
C. F. Powys, and yet it is by showing the twin sources of
John Cowper's imagination in all their stark differences but
also as a confluence of two powerful streams that the *Autobiography* achieves a form that no other kind of maker could
have given it. And the "touch of caricature" is organic to this
form; for without it the gigantic task of disclosing coherence
where most people would see only absurdly disparate elements,
and enormous pretentions in the attempt to bring them together, would have defeated even Powys himself. In the event,
however, the *Autobiography* is able to encompass so much
(both urinal and stars between which the boy Powys vowed to
be a poet) and yet, as a great work of art, remain the source of
a zest for life and a faculty of self-creation that is more badly
needed today than when the book was written. If Powys's
retreat to Wales constitutes a rejection of the modern world,
more and more readers will feel compelled to find him in his
work, by the very pressures he sought to avoid there. And
what they will discover, in his propaganda, is that the world
we have created and called "modern" is, as a constricting
area of consciousness in which it is impossible to live fully,
one that the creative will can refashion in the image of a
larger, more generous human spirit.

NOTES
[1] Numerals in parentheses refer to pages of the *Autobiography* (1934), 1967.
[2] Alwyn Rees and Brinley Rees, *Celtic Heritage*, 1961, pp. 229–231.

III

POWYS'S COMPLEX VISION

Michael Greenwald

Near the beginning of *The Meaning of Culture* (1929) John Cowper Powys declares that "to be a cultured person is to be a person with some kind of original philosophy."[1] At the same time he insists that this philosophy is not fundamentally an intellectual system nor even a discipline to be mastered and consciously articulated, but something corresponding to a person's "life-illusion". Hence culture, in contrast to mere education, is essentially the process whereby each person appropriates to himself that which fortifies his own unique way of viewing the world and integrates his opinions with his personality. Ultimately "to philosophise is not to *read* philosophy; it is to *feel* philosophy"[1].

Lest this attitude be too readily dismissed as merely amateurish or naive, it should be pointed out that important philosophers of the late nineteenth or early twentieth century such as Nietzsche, James and Bergson, all of whom influenced Powys, had also come to recognise and even emphasise this subjective aspect of philosophy. In 1909 William James, in the Hibbert Lectures on the Current Situation in Philosophy later published as *A Pluralistic Universe*, had told an Oxford audience that "every one is . . . prone to claim that his conclusions are the only logical ones, that they are necessities of universal reason, they being all the while, at bottom, accidents more or less of personal vision which had far better be avowed as such; for one man's vision may be much more valuable than another's, and our visions are usually not only our most interesting but our most respectable contributions to the world in which we play our part."[2] It was this sort of awareness that made Russell, Whitehead, Wittgenstein, and their successors dissatisfied with metaphysics and led them to seek out a more valid, if also more abstract, objectivity in their studies of mathematical logic and the epistemology of language. But in *A Pluralistic Universe* James remained attracted to metaphysics and he praised at length the obscure German philosopher Fechner for creating a metaphysical system thick with an "intense concreteness" and "fertility of detail" in contrast to the abstract thinness of transcendental idealism. Indeed, Fechner's passionate animism,

58

as described by James, with its cosmos made up of planetary souls vitalising what appears to be unconscious matter, in many respects strongly anticipates that of Powys. It seems probable that Powys was influenced by the example of Fechner, if only through James's description which he had certainly read.[3]

In any case, Powys regards philosophy as primarily subjective in viewpoint and evocative in detail rather than objective and systematically exact. In *Wolf Solent*—published in the same year as *The Meaning of Culture*—one of the things that draws Wolf to the bookish Christie, despite his more conventional attachment to Gerda, is the similarity of their attitudes toward philosophy. When he asks her if she is fond of it, she hesitates before replying:

> 'I don't understand half of what I read' Christie began, speaking with extreme precision. 'All I know is that every one of those old books has its own atmosphere for me.'

> 'Atmosphere?' questioned Wolf.

> 'I suppose it's funny to talk in such a way,' she went on, 'but all those queer non-human abstractions, like Spinoza's "substance" and Leibnitz's "monads" and Hegel's "idea" don't stay hard and logical to me. They seem to melt.'

Wolf pretends not to understand so that he can enjoy in her self-consciously "awkward way of putting things" both the transparent originality of her point of view and its delightful similarity to his own:

> 'What I mean to say *is*,' she went on, with a little gasp, flinging out the words almost fiercely, 'I regard each philosophy, not as the "truth", but just as a particular country, in which I can go about—countries with their own peculiar light, their Gothic buildings, their pointed roofs, their avenues of trees—But I'm afraid I'm tiring you with all this!'

> 'Go on, for heaven's sake!' he pleaded. 'It's just what I want to hear.'

'I mean that it's like the way you feel about things,' she explained, 'when you hear the rain outside, while you're reading a book. You know what I mean? Oh, I can't put it into words! When you get a sudden feeling of life going on outside . . . far away from where you sit . . . over wide tracts of country . . . as if you were driving in a carriage and all the things you passed were . . . life itself . . . parapets of bridges, with dead leaves blowing over them . . . trees at crossroads . . . park-railings . . . lamplights on ponds . . . I don't mean, of course,' she went on, 'that philosophy is the same as life . . . but—Oh! Can't you *see* what I mean?' She broke off with an angry gesture of impatience.

Wolf bit his lip to suppress a smile. At that moment he could have hugged the nervous little figure before him.

'I know perfectly well what you mean,' he said eagerly. 'Philosophy to you, and to me, too, isn't science at all! It's life winnowed and heightened. It's life *framed* . . . framed in room-windows . . . in carriage-windows . . . in mirrors . . . in our "brown studies", when we look up from absorbing books . . . in waking dreams—I do know perfectly well what you mean!'

Christie drew up her feet beneath her on the sofa and turned her head, so that all he could see of her face was its delicate profile, a profile which, in that particular position, reminded him of a portrait of the philosopher Descartes![4]

This "atmosphere" of which Christie speaks not only mediates between the tangible and the intangible but evokes the landscape the mind actually inhabits, in which both the concrete and the abstract lose their precision and merge their boundaries. In his 1960 Preface to *Wolf Solent* Powys maintains that "the purpose and essence and inmost being of this book is the necessity of opposites. Life and Death, Good and Evil, Matter and Spirit, Body and Soul, Reality and Appearance have to be joined together, have to be forced into one another, have to be proved dependent upon each other, while all solid entities have to dissolve, if they are to outlast their momentary appearance, into atmosphere." The mind thus moves from the language of philosophy to the awareness, as Christie puts it, of "life going on outside" and then gropes for the poetic language needed to unite its diverse perceptions. Powys humorously but not fortuitously compares Christie as her precise speech becomes groping and impressionistic to Descartes, who hoped with his hard logic to illuminate areas of experience that instead need to be dissolved into the atmosphere of poetry.

In a chapter of his *Dostoievsky* entitled "Nature versus Doctrine" Powys praises the Russian for remaining faithful to the vagaries of nature, "the Supreme Novelist," rather than rounding off his philosophical themes too neatly: "since his first great purpose is to convince his readers that his invented world is a world of 'real reality,' a world intimately, psychically and magnetically connected with the immediate actual world that these same readers know only too well in their own experience," the great novelist "must deliberately as a good craftsman in the most subtle craft that exists, obscure and side-track his ideal thoughts, saw, hack lop, and disfigure the beautifully balanced branches of his long-cherished meta-physical *entelechies*, and, above all, never allow his own passionate, mystical, secret, personal vision of life to sail prosperously with all its flags flying and its masts unbroken into the haven where it would be."[5] There remains underlying the work of Powys a penchant for metaphysical speculation, and one remains aware of the abstractions that are being trans-formed into atmosphere. With his rhetorical skill Powys has a genuine aptitude for presenting intellectual argument and debate in his fiction, and sometimes his efforts to "obscure and sidetrack his ideal thoughts" with natural interruptions seems more artificial than the philosophizing itself. Usually, however, individual philosophies are subsumed into the play of "life-illusions" that constitutes his fiction, and his own philosophy is a pluralistic one that allows full scope to this sense of play that is also his sense of life. Philosophy is for him essentially fictive, and in his work philosophy and fiction merge into atmosphere, just as does the intermingled imagery of solid integrity and fluid multiplicity which corresponds to his vision of the self as well as nature.

Still, his desire also to communicate his view of life more directly and explicitly than through the poetic atmosphere of his fiction induced him to write the books of popular philosophy which he liked to call his "lay-sermons." But in 1920 he had published *The Complex Vision*, in which he attempted to articulate his philosophy in a more sophisticated and systematic, as well as more artful, way than he was to do in the subsequent "lay-sermons," and in a prose rather less hortatory and flamboyant. This volume of 370 pages, published only in America, has been all but ignored even by Powys's admirers, yet in its elaborate explication of his metaphysical vision it sheds valuable light on the novels, only two of which preceded it, and is itself a notable product of his imagination. In the following discussion of the book I shall attempt not to evaluate its arguments as philosophy, but to see them as providing the perspective and underlying mythology of the fiction. No summary, however, can do justice to the subtlety and richness with which Powys deploys and elaborates his themes in this remarkable book.

*   *   *   *

In *The Complex Vision* Powys makes it clear that his aim is not to supplant reason as a tool of human perception but to harmonize it with other means of insight. He objects to Bergson's exaltation of instinct over intellect and declares that "to intellectualize instinct is one of the profoundest secrets of the art of life" (49).[6] As a good Worsdworthian he likes to speak of "imaginative reason" whose "synthetic activity . . . in the long run alone satisfies the soul" (318). Imagination at once includes and transcends mere reason: it is "the half-creative, half-interpretative act by which the complex personality seizes upon, plunges into, and moulds to its purpose, that deeper unity in any group of things which gives such a group its larger and more penetrating significance" (37). He freely admits that *The Complex Vision* is fundamentally a product of his imagination rather than a revelation of absolute truth, but he suspects that other works of philosophy differ from this only in their authors' unwillingness to make such an admission. He repeatedly takes James and Bergson, whose work in many respects seems to have provided the impetus for his own, to task for their "pseudo-scientific, pseudo-psychological methods of thought" which fail to take into account man's "aesthetic sense" (Preface, xxiii; 302). "Philosophy," he suggests, "is so closely dependent upon the activity of aesthetic sense that it might itself be called an art, the most difficult and the most comprehensive of all the arts, the art of retaining the rhythmic balance of all man's contradictory energies" (304). His own approach is in this book far more deliberately aesthetic than in his other works, and his "speculative system" with its carefully organized structure at times seems a more disciplined work of art than many of his fictions.

In order to construct this speculative system. Powys needs to discover a fundamental reality that is free from doubt upon which to build, and, not unlike Descartes, he finds this in the indubitable reality of his own self. He postulates a unified core of personality which is contained by his body but which is somehow distinct from it, which "must inevitably be associated with what might be called 'the vanishing point of sensation'." This irreducible hard core of personality, always a central image in Powys's work, is here termed the "soul" for philosophical rather than religious connotations, and its "concrete reality" is declared to be the only "axiom" in "the philosophy of the complex vision". The soul then is the integral self which he repeatedly visualizes in his fiction as alternatively capable of reducing itself to the solidity of stone or diffusing itself into the insubstantiality of mist; it partakes of both mind and matter but is something different from both.

This use of personality as the keystone and central truth of his philosophy reflects Powys's conviction that a philosopher can lay claim to no absolute or universal reality, only to a personal and imaginative vision. Communication between diverse personalities is possible because objective reality does exist, and so the philosopher may plausibly attempt to persuade others of the truth of his vision, but since each personality is unique and inevitably creates its own reality out of the "object-ive mystery" by means of its own "complex vision", perfect communication is difficult. However, Powys ultimately suggests the possibility of the individual soul momentarily attaining and thereafter preserving through memory glimpses of the "eternal vision", in which the creative tensions of the complex vision are harmonized and the objective mystery is resolved. His ultimate conclusion is that "when subjectivity is carried to the furthest possible limit of rhythm and harmony, it transforms itself, of necessity, into objectivity. The subjective vision of all mortal minds, thus rendered objective by the intensity of the creative energy, is nothing less than the eternal vision" (361). Thus, in *The Complex Vision* Powys outlines a movement from the isolation of self to the creation of a cosmos in which the self becomes a medium for comprehending a multitude of other lives. The philosophical work, therefore, is a kind of blue-print of the process that begins with the storyteller and culminates in the tale. The blue-print is no less revealing for being ex *post facto*.

In formulating his *cogito* Descartes broadly interpreted thinking to include feeling and imagining, but in reconstructing the world after his initial doubt he concluded that the mind's abstract powers of conception and judgment, as manifested in mathematics and logic, provide a clearer and more distinct, and therefore truer, picture of reality than do the senses and the imagination. To Powys this kind of emphasis presents a distorted view; true perception can only come from a fusion of the various aspects of man's "complex vision". He recognises that "the aspects of the complex vision may be separated from one another according to many systems of classification," but he himself, while encouraging the reader to make his own list if dissatisfied, notes eleven aspects which "may be summarized as consisting of reason, self-consciousness, will, the aesthetic sense, or 'taste', imagination, memory, conscience, sensation, instinct, intuition, and emotion," and he cautions that these "are not to be regarded as absolutely separate functions, but rather as relatively separate 'energies' of the one concrete soul-monad" (20).

Powys is deliberately vague about how these attributes ought to be synthesised in formulating a viable philosophy; his fundamental quarrel with other philosophers seems to be based upon their failure to recognise the need for such a synthesis and their tendency to over-simplify the complex nature of our "instrument of research." But he clearly prefers imagination to reason as the primary agent of synthesis because of its tendency to avoid abstraction and seize upon the concrete; his temperament is at the opposite pole from Descartes, who preferred reason for its abstract clarity and freedom from the delusion of the senses. Furthermore, he indicates that "the abnormal individual whose complex vision is distorted almost out of human recognition by the predominance of some one attribute, is yet, in his madness and morbidity, a wonderful engine of research for the clairvoyance of humanity," while "the kind of balance or sanity which some average persons, as are commonly called 'men of the world' possess is in reality further removed from true vision than all the madness of these debauches of specialized research. For the consummation of the complex vision is a meeting place of desperate and violent extremes; extremes, not watered down nor modified nor even 'reconciled', certainly not cancelled by one another, but held forcibly and deliberately together by an arbitrary act of the apex-thought of the human soul" (22, 23). This then is the dynamic vision of the dramatist rather than the static vision of the philosopher.

The Complex Vision repeatedly conveys Powys's sense of the essentially dynamic relationship between self and non-self, as the soul, unable to plumb its own mysterious depths, struggles to illuminate the ever-receding and ever-enduring mystery of external reality. The inevitable subjectivity of the soul's vision precludes materialism, but he also steadfastly refuses to follow the lead of idealism in either denying the existence of external reality or declaring it unknowable, or in reducing it to the monistic unity of an absolute mind. Like William James he instinctively rejects both the absolute unity of a "block universe" and the absolute disunity of chaos, and he instead postulates a "pluralistic universe" in which there is both continuity and a measure of independence for every living entity. He cannot remain content with "the first revelation of the complex vision," which is the reality of his own soul; he must embrace the "second revelation," which is "the objective reality of the outward visible universe" (80). Pure reason in its isolation may doubt this reality and is indeed incapable of logically proving it, but the soul's "instrument of research" is not limited to reason, and other attributes of the "complex vision"—instinct, intuition and imagination—not only assert the truth of external reality, but confirm it. This recognition that the "objective mystery" really exists and is not a subjective illusion is for Powys "the act of primordial faith":

> This act of primordial faith is the active belief of the soul not only in an objective universe outside itself, but also in the objective existence of other individual souls. Without this primordial act of faith the individual soul can never escape from itself. For the pure reason not only reduces the whole universe to an idea in the mind; but it also reduces all *other* minds to ideas in *our* mind. In other words the logical reason imprisons us fatally and hopelessly in a sort of cosmic nutshell of our own mentality. (81)

Personality is thus not only the starting-point of Powys's philosophy, but, after the leap of primordial faith which corresponds to imaginative desire, it is seen as the fundamental reality of the entire universe. Just as his own body contains an irreducible soul-monad which consists of both mind and matter without being either, and which exists at the "vanishing point of sensation" and perceives by means of its complex vision, so every body in the universe must similarly be inhabited by a soul which possesses in some form the attributes of the complex vision. To Powys these souls are not restricted to human beings but are possessed by "all living entities whether human or non-human" (82). This intensely animate universe in which every living entity participates in consciousness is essentially the universe of his fiction, although there even apparently inanimate objects are sometimes seen as conscious entities. Here Powys is content to regard inanimates as parts of the body of the earth, which, as a living body, has its own consciousness. But unlike the pantheism of Fechner, in which lesser consciousnesses are compounded into greater—from man to planet to solar system to God, the ultimate container of all consciousness—Powys posits a multiverse in which each separate consciousness "half-creates and half-discovers" its own private universe from the "objective mystery" that confronts it and retains its own integrity as long as it lives.

Bergson saw existence as a dualistic struggle between the volatile life-force that is "spirit" and the inert resistence of "matter", but Powys, although obviously influenced by the Frenchman, stubbornly rejects such efforts to sum up life in terms of lifeless abstractions inimicable to the imagination. Instead, he firmly locates a similar dualism in each living personality. He contrasts himself with Bergson by saying that while the latter "seeks to interpret human life in terms of the universe", he seeks "to interpret the universe in terms of human life" (164). One of the attributes of the complex vision is emotion, which Powys sees in somewhat Bergsonian terms as perpetually divided between "creation and what resists creation, or between love and malice" (163). Well aware of the wide and various connotations of the word "love," he is careful to indicate that he means it as the "creative apprehension of life" (195) and therefore virtually equates it with creation. Its opposite is "not so much 'hate' as a kind of dull and insensitive hostility, a kind of brutal malignity and callous aversion," and so he prefers to call it "malice," which conveys "a more impersonal depth and wider reach of activity than the word hate and has also a clearer suggestion of deliberate insensitiveness about it" (34). Similarly, the true opposite of creation is not destruction, but an essentially inert and passive resistence to creation. The *act* of destruction "must necessarily, by reason of the passionate energy in it, be a perversion of

67

creative power, not the opposite of creative power." Further-more, "creative power, even in its unperverted activity, must always be capable of destroying. It must be capable of destroy-ing what is in the way of further creation" (35).

This fundamental emotional duality can also be explained in terms of the struggle between life and death and between good and evil that exists in every living soul. Not surprisingly in view of his characteristic emphasis on sadism Powys asserts that "the most concentrated and energetic opposite of love" is cruelty (34), and that "the complicated mood resulting from this association of sadistic cruelty with inert malice is perhaps the most powerful engine of evil that exists in the world; although a pure unmitigated condition of unsensualized, unimpassioned, motiveless malice is, in its inmost self, more essentially and profoundly evil" (171). He points out that "cruelty, profoundly evil as it is, has a living intensity which makes it less dull, less thick, less deliberately insensitive, less coldly hostile, than the pure emotion of malice" (35). Indeed, for Powys neither pure love nor pure malice exist, for if either love or malice were to triumph absolutely, personality as he knows and conceives it would itself cease to exist; he requires the "living intensity" of their struggle. Therefore, in his fiction he cannot portray characters who are exclusively good or evil, and even his sadists and wielders of worldly power are treated with creative sympathy; his life-haters are as alive as his life-lovers. Life in itself implies a relative triumph of love over malice, and though his characters may sometimes perversely allow malice to gain the upper hand, they manifestly partake of their creator's love. For him personality and creation are virtually synonymous: "The power that creates must be regarded as embodied in personality, for creation always implies personality. But the power that resists creation—though present in every living soul—cannot be embodied in personality because personality is the highest expression of creation" (127). Similarly, "directly evil becomes personal it ceases to be evil, because personality is the supreme achieve-ment of life" (229).

Since Powys repeatedly emphasizes that his philosophy is a "creative" one whose method is closer to that of art than of conventional philosophy, and insists that truth is not knowledge but a "creative gesture" (69), it is inevitable that *The Complex Vision* should ultimately provide an imaginative rationale for his own deep creative need to participate in the animation and vitality of a world outside of himself, to create living personalities rather than yield to the lifelessness of the inanimate. In the remarkable chapter which he calls "The Illusion of Dead Matter" he revealingly speaks of "the peculiar psychological melancholy which sometimes seizes us in the presence of inanimate natural objects, such as earth and water and sand and dust and rain and vapour, objects whose existence may superficially appear to be entirely chemical or material." However, he concludes that this "impression of complete soullessness" is "a melancholy which descends upon us when in any disinterested moment the creative energy, the energy of love in us, is overcome by the evil and inertness of the aboriginal malice. Under the influence of this inert malice, which takes advantage of some lapse or ebb of the creative energy in us, the rhythmic activity of our complex vision breaks down; and we visualize the world through the attributes of reason and sensation alone" (248, 249). He strikingly evokes a man at a "moment of visionary disintegration," standing "on some wet autumn evening, watching the soulless reflection of a dead moon in a pond of dead water; while above him the motionless distorted trunk of some goblinish tree mocks him with its desolate remoteness from his own life". Though gripped by "unutterable loneliness" and feeling himself "an exile in a dark and hostile assemblage of elemental forces," such a man, Powys declares, has the imaginative power to "resist this desolation": "He then, by a bold movement of imagination, restores the balance of his complex vision; and in a moment the spectacle is transfigured."

> The apparently dead pond takes to itself the lineaments of some indescribable living soul, of which that particular portion of elemental being is the outward expression. The

apparently dead moonlight becomes the magical influence of some mysterious "lunar soul" of which the earth's silent companions (sic) is the external form. The apparently dead mud of the pond's edge becomes a living portion of that earth-body which is the visible manifestation of the soul of the earth. The motionless tree-trunk at his side seems no longer the desolate embodiment of some vague "psychic life" utterly alien from his own life but reveals to him the magical presence of a real soul there, whose personality, though not conscious in the precise manner in which he is conscious, has yet its own measure of complex vision and is mutely struggling with the cruel inertness and resistence which blocks the path of the energy of life. (250, 251)

This conflict between seeing the world creatively and seeing it maliciously occurs frequently in the fiction, most notably perhaps in *Ducdame* and *Wolf Solent*, the two novels which followed *The Complex Vision*. One thinks of the fatal struggle between Rook Ashover and Hastings in *Ducdame*, and, of Wolf's internal fluctuations between the consolation of a "life-illusion" and the horror of his "malice-dances" or the suicidal impulses inspired by Lenty pond.

Powys also maintains that we must not be dismayed by death itself, for at the very instant a body loses its individual soul "it is at once 'possessed' by the soul of that planetary globe from whose chemistry it drew its elemental life and from whose chemistry, although the form of it has changed, it still draws its life" (257–258). For him, as for one of his favourite poets, Whitman:

All goes onward and outward, nothing collapses,
And to die is different from what any one supposed and luckier.

As to the continuation of the individual soul after death, he here professes agnosticism, although in old age he often indicated that he did not expect to survive his body. But he insists that to yield to the "illusion of dead matter" means that through "a perverted use of the imagination" the soul has been "driven by the power of malice to relinquish its centrifugal force and to become the very mud and slime and excremental debris which it has endowed with an illusive soullessness." He acknowledges the anthropomorphism of his position and asserts that "in this way we are doing the only philosophical thing we have a right to do—namely, interpreting the less known in the terms of the more known" (262).

Despite Powys's close identification of love and creation, he is careful to distinguish both from ordinary sexual passion. He emphasizes that his "creative philosophy" is based essentially on contemplation rather than action. Since "life is an art towards which the will must be directed" and "the larger portion of life manifests itself in interior contemplation and only the smaller part of it in overt action" (339), " 'the art of philosophy' consists in the attempt to attain the sort of 'contemplation' which can by the power of its love enter into the joy and the suffering of . . . living things" (369). Therefore, a curious but significant omission in *The Complex Vision* is the absence of any discussion of the actual creation of personality that can result from the sexual act. Similarly in the fiction, although Powysian protagonists occasionally have children and even idealize them (cf. *Rodmoor* and *Ducdame*), they remain dissatisfied with ordinary sexuality. Powys's romantic imagination with its onanistic bent is concerned rather with that alternative creation in the mind wherein the materials of the external world are at once utilized and transformed. Although he insists upon the ultimate reality of the external world, he is far more interested in what the mind makes of the sexual object than what the body does with it and fathers from it. In sexual passion "there is a savage instinct of cruel and searching illumination," but it is dangerously allied to hate and in itself is "directed towards death rather than towards life, because it is dominated, through all its masks and disguises, by the passion of possession" (196). Unless sexual passion is transformed by the creative power of love, it is liable to be corrupted by the malicious power that resists creation and become "a vampirizing force of destruction" (286). It may become indeed the sadistic impulse which he constantly recognized and feared in himself. In old age he was even to go so far as to reject the imperative of love itself . . . because "love is too involved with sex and with nerves and with many other dangerous and unstable things in life" and to declare that "we are under an obligation to be kind, considerate, tolerant, indulgent, and sympathetic towards all . . . but not to love them."[7] But in *The Complex Vision* love is the name he gives to the creative impulse whereby sexual passion is transformed and transcended by the imagination; passion for the body becomes love for the soul:

> It is only by associating itself with love and malice; it is only by getting itself transformed into love and malice that the sexual instinct is able to lift itself up, or to sink itself down, into the subtler levels of the soul's vision. The secret of life lies far deeper than the obvious bodily phenomena of sex. The fountains from which life springs *may flow through that channel* but they flow from a depth far below these physical or mental agitations. And it is only the abysmal cunning of the inert malice, which opposes itself to creation that tempts philosophers and artists to lay such a disproportionate stress on the thing. The great artists are always known by their power to transcend sex and to reduce sex to its relative insignificance. In the greatest of all sculpture, in the greatest of all music, in the greatest of all poetry, the difference between the sexes disappears. (363)

The Complex Vision then tends toward bisexuality, and the love affairs between Powys's sexually ambiguous heroes and his boyish girls reflect the difficulty of achieving personal integration and harmony as well as the difficulty of sexual fulfilment. Although bisexual consummation is continually sought in these stories, it is rarely achieved, and what is most powerfully realized in them is the yearning and dissatisfaction of contradictory sexual impulses.

Just as Powys postulates the possibility of bisexual consummation wherein isolated souls are joined and integrated,
he argues that the isolated complex vision which half-creates
and half-discovers its own universe can obtain glimpses of an
"eternal vision" wherein subject and object, creation and
discovery, universe and multiverse are merged and made one,
and the objective mystery, if never completely solved, is at
least banished beyond the periphery of immediate perception.
The fact that the isolated universes can communicate with
each other indicates that their isolation is not complete;
"language itself is founded upon that original act of faith by
which we assume the independent existence of other souls"
and also "that the vision of other souls does not essentially
differ from our own vision" (130). Powys notes that in our
interchanges with others we assume the existence of an "invisible standard" of truth, beauty, and goodness. He cannot
relate this standard to any creator of the universe because the
universe itself is so deeply and fundamentally dualistic that he
can only conceive of the creator or parent of the universe as
dualistic too. Such a creator is "a stopping-place of all thought,"
an "unutterable mystery out of which the universe originally
sprang" (122). This is the abstract and amoral First Cause of
A Glastonbury Romance, pouring out its perpetual duality of
good and evil; the conception probably derives from the
Immanent Will of Hardy's *The Dynasts*, which also is conceived
as not only uncaring but unconscious of what it brings about.
We owe "this thin simulacrum, this mathematical formula,
this stopping-place of thought" no awe or reverence; it is
"beneath contempt" (123). Our ideas of truth, beauty, and
goodness are projections not of this hardly conceivable parent
of the universe, but of children of the universe like ourselves.
Certainly, since everything in the universe is related to personality, these ideas cannot be mere abstractions. The difficult
question is whether they are "the projections, upon the evasive
medium which holds all human souls together, of such beauty
and such truth and such goodness as these souls find that they

possess in common," or whether they are the projections of superhuman gods, "invisible watchers" of our human destiny (132).

Powys makes no effort to prove the latter alternative logically; instead, he attempts to overwhelm us with a sense of its inevitability. He evokes desperate moments when we cannot be satisfied with the duality of love and malice, when "the soul seems to rend and tear at the very roots of this duality" and so, "roused to a supreme pitch of rhythmic energy", the complex vision attains the perfect harmony of all its elements and achieves "a music which is so intense that it becomes silence." The struggle is transcended, and the soul becomes aware that love is "the secret of the whole struggle and the explanation of the whole drama," that beauty, truth, and goodness "are only varying facets and aspects of one unfathomable secret which is the activity of love . . . the creative principle of life itself." This rather Pateresque realization of the condition of music toward which all art aspires "requires the revelation" that the emotion of love exists in "a far greater completeness in these silent 'watchers' and 'companions' whom we name 'the immortal gods.' " Also, it requires that "these immortal ones should be regarded as conscious and living 'souls'; for the ultimate reach of the complex vision implies the idea of personality and cannot interpret life except in terms of personality" (134–135). Ultimately then, creativity is seen as an imperfect form of revelation, and, of course, inspiration is basic to both romanticism and religion. In this "revelation" of the eternal vision of the immortals Powys, the son of a line of Anglican priests, unmistakably reveals the fundamentally religious nature of his imaginative faith; unable to accept the God of his fathers, he constitutes himself secular priest of his own pluralistic religion. His gods are neither omnipotent nor omniscient; like the pagan deities of his beloved Homer, these superhuman personalities are far more powerful and knowing than men, but their attributes remain distinctly human. Their vision, only relatively more perfect than men's, is continually created from the same duality and the same unfathomable "world-stuff" that they share with human souls. Beyond even their vision lies the ever-receding objective mystery which they continually strive to illuminate.

However, as much as Powys is temperamentally attracted to pagan pluralism, his own soul is too imbued with the "Christian Conscience" he found in the far more desperate paganism of Nietzsche to accept it wholly. What Powys wrote of the pseudonymous Claude Silve in an apparently unpublished review of her *Eastward in Eden* applies to himself as well: "The very difference between Christianity and Heathenism comes NEAR to being left behind in this non-mystic, sub-realistic breaking down of barriers; but though this nearly happens, it never quite happens, for the author has a soul 'naturaliter Christiana.' "[8] Although he rejects Christ's God— the early poem *Lucifer*, which was originally titled *The Death of God*, described His demise—Christ retains a special significance in Powys's pantheon. Dissociated from the historical Jesus, Christ becomes the "Intermediary between the transitory and the permanent" (224), a concrete tangible symbol of the inevitably obscure "sons of the universe" who are Powys's superhuman gods and who embody in the completest form the creative love of his "eternal vision." Christ is the consummate, though still relative, triumph of life and personality over malice and death, and reflects the insatiable human need for such a symbol. Powys explains that "no symbol arbitrarily invented by any one man, even though he were the greatest genius that ever lived, could supply this want or satisfy this desire. And it could not do so because it would lack the organic weathering and bleaching . . . of the long panorama of time" (230). Christ, therefore, is released from the specific dogmas of Christianity and made to stand for "all that is most beautiful and profound, all that is most magical and subtle, in the gods of the ancient world" (241). This attempt to retain the figure of Christ as a synthesis in whom "all mythologies and all religions must meet and be transcended" recalls Lawrence's contemporaneous efforts at synthesis in *The Man Who Died* and Eliot's in *The Waste Land;* one senses the pervasive influence of Frazer as common to all.

Powys's reduction of his immortals to the symbolic figure of Christ suggests that complementing his desire to revel in multiplicity was a need to relate his pluralism to a single and integral personality in whom objectivity could be incarnated. He does not speak of the visions of the immortals but of the *vision*, because "all the unfathomable souls of the world, and all souls are unfathomable whether they are the souls of plants or animals or planets or gods or men, are found, the closer they approach one another, to be in possession of the same vision." Since the gods are closest to a complete comprehension of reality, their vision "is not broken up and divided but is one and the same; and is yet for ever growing and deepening" (246). Thus, in the figure of Christ dramatic diversity is reconciled with a unity that is at once objective and personal. Christ is only one of "an immeasurable company of immortals," yet he also "has become the supreme and solitary embodiment of the Ideal to which we look" (244). The emphasis in Powys's fiction moves subtly and by no means consistently from a fascination with the unity symbolized by Christ—most emphatic in the first novel, *Wood and Stone*—to the celebration of diversity for its own sake. Wolf Solent associates the coming of Christ with the desired unification of his inner and outer worlds, but the multiplicity and complexity of life continually overwhelms his aspirations. Christ is tangibly present in Glastonbury, but we are more conscious of the dramatic interplay of diverse attitudes toward him than of his specific actuality. In the pagan worlds of *Porius*, *Atlantis*, and *Homer and the Aether* the synthesis he represents is either distrusted or altogether ignored. But Powys can never really reject Christ, and in "Two and Two", one of his last, and unfortunately still unpublished, fantasies, Christ actually appears and is given the final word—even here Powys remains faithful to the fundamental dualism of his imagination, for the devil is present in the background while Christ speaks.

In addition to its religious aspect Powys also includes a chapter in *The Complex Vision* on "The Idea of Communism" in which he argues that the application of his philosophy to politics and economics inevitably leads to an awareness of the need for communism. The possessive instinct, the desire to reduce an object to private property, is seen as deriving from malice inasmuch as a dynamic universe is thereby made fixed and static, and living is converted to dead matter. The community of life and love which is the revelation of the eternal vision results in "the desire to 'have all things in common'," while "malice must naturally express itself in the desire to have as little as possible in common and as much as possible for ourselves alone" (325). Although Powys is capable of shrewd insights into the shortcomings of capitalism and its apologists, his picture of communism is predictably somewhat idealized and abstract. In *A Glastonbury Romance* (1932) he had already put "the idea of communism" and "the idea of capitalism" into dramatic conflict as part of the larger struggle between love and malice, good and evil, life and death which informs that enormous work and is resolved in the cataclysmic flood that concludes it. For him these ideas are real on a cosmic scale, and their embodiments are more convincing in their symbolic dimensions than in their social actuality.

Both "the figure of Christ" and "the idea of communism" reflect the idealizing tendencies which he readily allowed to enter his fiction, but never to dominate it. More pertinent to an understanding of Powys as novelist or romancer is his conception of the role of the ether, wherein he reconciles his desire to escape the limitations of his own personality with his need to see everything in terms of personality. This desire to escape sometimes led him to deny that he even had a personality of his own and to insist upon his protean diversity rather than admit to his personal singularity, but more frequently he liked to visualize the self as alternatively possessing the solidity of a stone and the diffuseness of mist, sometimes reduced by circumstances to a resistant hard core of personality and sometimes able to project itself imaginatively into the vastness of space. His sense of the continual intermingling of the solid and the fluid, the fundamental limitations of existence and the freedom of imagination, is given perhaps its richest imaginative embodiment in *Weymouth Sands*, but he indicates in the *Autobiography* his own awareness that he moves consistently between two poles of imaginative being, the ponderousness of Caliban and the volatility of Ariel. In *The Complex Vision* he seems to contract these Caliban and Ariel aspects as he discusses the effect of isolating sensation from the other attributes of the complex vision:

> Sensation carried to its extreme limit becomes impersonal; for in its unconscious mechanism personality is devoured. But it does not become impersonal in that magical liberating sense in which the impersonal is an escape, bringing with it a feeling of large, cool, quiet, and unruffled space. It becomes impersonal in a thick, gross, opaque, mechanical manner. (46)

Interestingly he here speaks of these not as aspects of personality but of impersonality, and he leaves no doubt that he is powerfully attracted to the idea of the impersonal as a refuge from subjective isolation. In "the loneliness of our souls," he declares, we desire not only "to invade, and mingle with, other personalities" but, more profoundly, "to break the isolation of all personalities, and to enter, in company with all, some larger, fuller, freer level of life, where what we call 'the limits of personality' are surpassed and transcended" (92). However, he confesses that his own desire for the impersonal is even more extreme:

> To some temperaments it might seem as though this reduction of the immense unfathomable universe to a congeries of living souls were a strangling limitation. There are certain human temperaments, and my own is one of them, whose aesthetic sense demands the existence of vast interminable spaces of air, of water, of earth, of fire, or even of blank emptiness. To such a temperament

it might seem as though to be jostled throughout eternity by other living souls were to be shut up in an inescapable prison. (183)

But ultimately he decides that the conception of impersonality is both unnecessary and superficial. Not only does the universe perpetually recede in its unfathomable mystery beyond the advancing vision of even the immortals so that it can never be reduced to an impersonal forumla, but "this desire for liberation from the bonds of personality" is itself "one of the profoundest instincts of personality" (185). Thus, the vastness of space to which he is temperamentally attracted is not empty and lifeless despite its atmosphere of cool remoteness; it is the medium that links all the diverse souls in the universe. Further- more, it is itself the body which contains "the material element in every living soul, the material element which binds all bodies together, and the material element which composes the objective mystery" (354). Space then is the very stuff of creation, nor can it be conceived as a merely dead body; like all other bodies in the Powysian universe, it contains its own living soul. In the main text of *The Complex Vision* Powys speaks of this only as the "elemental soul" or "elemental personality", but in his Prologue he calls it the "universal ether." Therefore, "what we name the universe . . . is an enormous group of bodies joined together by the body of the ether; such bodies being the physical expression of a corresponding group of in-numerable souls joined together by the soul of the ether" (Prologue, xii). The ether is thus the living medium that unites all living souls in the universe, but Powys cautions that "this uniting does not imply any sort of spiritual *including* or subsuming of the souls thus united. They communicate with one another by means of this medium; but the integrity of the medium which unites them does not impinge at any point upon their integrity" (367).

One is reminded that Powys frequently liked to regard himself as a medium rather than a creator, and it hardly seems fanciful to suggest that in his fictions he aimed to tran- scend the bounds of his own personality not by attaining the godlike impersonality of the Joycean artist paring his fingernails, but by assuming the ubiquitous personality of the universal ether. This identification only becomes explicit near the end of his career in *Homer and the Aether* (1959), his fascinating rendering of Homer's Iliad as a Powysian romance, but it is more or less implicit in his narrative approach to most of his tales. They are usually told in the third person by a distinctive narrative voice which, combining humorous detachment with all-embracing sympathy, reveals its intimacy with the most private thoughts of a multitude of personalities, not necessarily human. It is too facile an analysis to see this as a naive reversion to the frequently discredited nineteenth-century tradition of the omniscient narrator, supposedly made obsolete by the restricted point of view of James, the subjectivity of Proust, and the stream of consciousness of Joyce. Powys, of course, knew and respected the work of all these novelists, and his rejection of their more "advanced" techniques was both conscious and deliberate. His assumption of the personality of the ether is hardly less valid than Eliot's assumption of the impersonality of "the mind of Europe," as articulated in "Tradition and the Individual Talent" and embodied in *The Waste Land*, however much the technical implications of its working out may conflict with the modern *Zeitgeist*. It was only through the intervention of the ether that Powys was able to convey his fundamental vision of the universe as a play of individual but imperfect life-illusions, rooted in physical bodies and unified by the immensity of space. Space is the medium that embodies and links all the diverse personalities in the actual universe, and the verbal space of his enormous fictions is the medium that embodies and links the multitudinous inhabitants of his imaginary universes. This sense of diversity and largeness is vital to the realization of his spatial imagination, and he was not merely being self-indulgent when he repeatedly insisted upon his need to write on a large scale. Although late works like *Up and Out* and *All or Nothing* are shorter in length than their predecessors, in them the remotest reaches of outer space are subject to the excursions of Powysian personality as all barriers between actuality and imagination are transcended.

It is important to note that Powys in his etheric guise is never quite an omniscient narrator. It is essential to his vision to indicate the limitations of vision as well as its scope, and so, after endowing himself as narrator with cosmic insight, he is likely to remind us with subtle humour that there are things which even he is unable to tell us. In *The Complex Vision* the elemental personality is similarly not "absolute"; since "perpetual creation is the essence of life," it still must "eternally confront and be confronted by the unfathomable objective mystery of its own body" (354). In addition, it has too much of the malice of the primordial duality to be more than a demi-god: "The elemental personality would not necessarily be better, or nobler, or wiser than we are. There would be no particular reason why we should worship it, or give it praise" (355). He even insists that "Christ is far more important to us and precious to us than such a being could possibly be" (356). Similarly Powys as narrator maintains an ironic tone toward himself as well as a serene confidence in his own powers. His identification with the other might well be described as Powys's own "life-illusion." Just as Christ incarnates the vision of the immortals, Powys himself wants to incarnate the vision of the ether.

Despite his keen awareness of the limitations of human consciousness, Powys still insists upon its coherence and upon the integrity of personality. It is here that he departs most radically from the assumptions of modernism. In the fictions of Joyce, Virginia Wolf, or Beckett we are constantly aware of the instability of personality; instead of remaining essentially fixed and definable, characters not only participate in but reflect the incoherence of the flux around them, and their consciousness is impressionistic and frequently sub-rational. With the rather more traditionally presented characters of Lawrence, we are still aware of a discrepancy between the ideas they articulate and their subconscious emotions which can only be articulated by the narrator. But although Powys's characters are endowed with something of their creator's protean sensibility and a complex unpredictability rarely found in earlier fiction, they also have a capacity to articulate their impressions analytically, which is increasingly rare in the twentieth century. Powys only infrequently gives us a "stream of consciousness"; he generally prefers a more coherent sort of interior monologue. Significantly, in *The Complex Vision* he disputes Bergson's highly influential contention that the flux is within us as well as without. He argues instead that "in our normal moods of human introspection, as well as our abnormal moods of superhuman illumination, what we are conscious of most of all is a sense of integral continuity in the midst of change, and of identical permanence in the midst of ebb and flow."

> The flux of things does most assuredly rush by us; and we, in our inmost selves, are conscious of life's incessant flow. But how could we be conscious of any of this turbulent movement across the prow of our voyaging ship, if the ship itself—the substantial base of our living consciousness—were not an organized and integral reality, of psycho-chemical material, able to exert will and to make use of memory and reason in its difficult struggle with the waves and winds? (298)

Therefore, "what philosophy requires . . . is neither an absolute in whose identity all difference is lost, nor a stream of 'states of consciousness' which is suspended, as it were, in a vacuum" (311). This, of course, is a programme for fiction as well as philosophy, and it becomes clear that for Powys to dissolve either character or narration into a stream of consciousness would be to abandon them to an impersonal "vacuum."

Instead, he resolutely preserves the fundamental personal integrity of both his multitude of characters and of the narrator who brings them all together. He ultimately admits that he, like all philosophers, can only know directly the inner life of his own soul, and that we apprehend others "by an inevitable act of the imagination" wherein "we assume to reproduce in their interior reactions what we ourselves experience in ours" (317). And so Powys imagines his stories from the viewpoint of the ether which fills their narrative space and in turn populates it with fresh imaginative life. Creative emotion is for Powys a "sort of psychic fluidity or out-flowing," but this ultimately becomes inseparable from the soul's role as medium, just as the complex vision ultimately becomes the eternal. The ether then is not really an escape from the self, but the self's furthest imaginative reach: "The 'objective' . . . is the supreme attainment of the 'subjective' " (217). It is the self diffused into the fluidity of space rather than concentrated into the solidity of matter, yet penetrating and informing matter too. It provides the distance and perspective that transforms introspection into drama, tragedy into comedy, and endurance into enjoyment. The etheric perspective was sought in the fiction from *Wood and Stone* onward, but Powys repeatedly had to descend to confront the subjective anguish of Adrian Sorio, Wolf Solent, Dud No-man and all the other isolated souls who reflect aspects of his own before he could attain the serenity of the late fantasies and become one with the "eternal vision" of his immortal Aether.

NOTES

[1] *The Meaning of Culture*, New York, 1929, pp. 8 and 13.

[2] *A Pluralistic Universe*, New York, 1909, p. 10.

[3] Powys notes James's approval of Fechner's animism in *The Complex Vision*, New York, 1920, p. 294; he also notes in passing "Fechner's planetary spirits" as material for his own lecture in *Autobiography* (1934), 1967, p. 286.

[4] *Wolf Solent*, 1929, pp. 87–88; 1961, pp. 78–79.

[5] *Dostoievsky*, 1946, p. 100.

[6] Numerals in parentheses throughout refer to pages in *The Complex Vision* New York, 1920.

[7] *Obstinate Cymric*, Carmarthen, 1947, p. 176.

[8] Quoted from a typescript in the collection of Mr. E. E. Bissell.

IV

JOHN COWPER POWYS:
LANDSCAPE AND PERSONALITY IN
THE EARLY NOVELS

Glen Cavaliero

John Cowper Powys possessed at least one advantage as a late-starter: except for the early poems there are no juvenilia among his published writings. The early novels, *Wood and Stone* (1915), *Rodmoor* (1916) and *Ducdame* (1925), are mature work, distinctively their author's own, and full of the richness of sensory response and the sympathy for human aspiration and weakness that characterise *Wolf Solent*, *A Glastonbury Romance* and *Weymouth Sands*. Their inferiority to those books is an inferiority of confidence: the author is not yet fully sure of himself. The extravagance that is an essential part of his finest work is here being held back. These novels relate to the later work as the bud to the flower.

This can be seen when one considers the use they make of landscape. Powys was to take in turn as backgrounds to his fiction the various towns and villages in which his boyhood had been spent, and in his first novel the last of them, Montacute, appears under the thin disguise of "Nevilton". The images of wood and stone which control his presentation of the opposing forces of love and the will to power are related to the two hills which dominate the Montacute scene—the Tor, and Ham Hill. The latter is here called "Leo's Hill", and its quarries symbolise the power of capitalism. Powys's attempt to introduce a political aspect into his study is, however, a failure: neither here, nor in *A Glastonbury Romance*, the novel most clearly foreshadowed by *Wood and Stone*, is he able to make his political agitators convincing. More significantly, the quarries are the place where the neurotic stone mason, James Anderson (an obvious portrait of the young self described in the *Autobiography*), falls to his death. Already we can see Powys's characteristic use of landscape to point his themes. Similarly, the Tor ("Nevilton Hill") with its associations with a legendary piece of the True Cross, is associated in one remarkable scene with virginity and sexual frustration, as the tormented young vicar simultaneously watches below him on one side of the hill the first of the Powysian saintly old maids pacing to and fro, and on the other a young couple making love. It is an early example of the author's interest in voyeurism; and in this scene, with its intensely realised physical actuality and masterly juxtaposition of images, he fuses psychological insight with physical intimations of an unusual kind. The hill and what happens on the hill reflect and control each other; man is seen as being at once a part of nature and as transcending it.

Although Powys is frequently described as a great delineator of landscape, it is only in these early novels that we find objectively descriptive passages, though detailed pictures of weather and cloud persist until the end. At his best he could write with graphic particularity, in a style clearly influenced by Hardy—to whom this novel is dedicated.

> It was one of those sinister days that have the power of taking all colour and all interest out of the earth's surface. The time of the year lent itself gloomily to this sombre unmasking. The furze-bushes looked like dead things. Many of them had actually been burnt in some wanton conflagration; and their prickly branches carried warped and blighted seeds. The bracken, near the path, had been dragged and trodden. Here and there its stalks protruded like thin amputated arms. The elder-bushes, caught in the wind, showed white and metallic, as if all their leaves had been dipped in some brackish water. All the trees seemed to have something of this dull, whitish glare, which did not prevent them from remaining, in the recesses of their foliage, as drearily dark as the dark dull soil beneath them. The grass of the fields had a look congruous with the rest of the scene; a look as if it had been one large velvety pall, drawn over the whole valley.[1]

This sombre note sounds persistently through the book, and the heavy soil of Somerset is pictured in a sinister light; images of death and decay recur. Indeed at times it seems as though Powys were positing some collusion between nature and the powers of evil; but in the last resort he remains sceptical, is a shade ambiguous, as to the reality of spiritual forces.

There is a certain play upon supernatural dread—or rather dread of the preternatural—in the chapter called "Auber

Lake", in which Powys's admiration for Poe overlays his own gifts: the episode seems bookish and contrived. But in Lacrima Traffio's compassion for the mad girl, a compassion that conquers her own fears, we have the kind of confrontation which is handled with greater subtlety in the Lenty Pond episodes of *Wolf Solent* and the visit of John Geard to Mark's Court in *A Glastonbury Romance*. In each case the final affirmation is of human values, of the power of love and sanity over fear and superstition. Powys recognises the awareness of the supernatural as being an aspect of man's awareness of nature; but he never isolates it from its context. His taste for gothic romances may lead him to the brink of attempting something in the same kind himself; but his commonsense always gets the better of him. This conflict can lead to bathos, a bathos that he learned to deploy deliberately. In *Wood and Stone* the prevailing mood is speculative and, where human motives are concerned, disenchanted. All the characters have to settle for the second best. Though not Powys's most tragic book, this is arguably his most bitter one.

Rodmoor is written with greater spontaneity and force. Alone among the novels, except for part of *A Glastonbury Romance*, it is set in East Anglia; and in it Powys distances his theme by putting to a tragic purpose a landscape with happy associations for himself. For the book is a tragedy, though it includes elements which the author was to push on to other, more affirmative conclusions. The landscape harmonises with the bleakness of the tale. Rodmoor itself is a decaying port backed by immense salt-marshes and eroded by the sea, and the novel is haunted by a feeling of isolation and menace. The geographical notation of *Wood and Stone* is here reversed. Now it is the woods and orchards and gardens of the inland country which are friendly, and the sea which is the enemy and destroyer: agraphobia replaces claustrophobia. The huge marsh skies, the swirling turbulent river, the dikes and withy beds and sand dunes are evoked with great power, and the novel suggests a landscape by Ruysdael. It is notable that when, as here and in *Ducdame*, Powys is describing a landscape that is not so much specific as distilled from a general impression, he is far more vivid than when depicting a place whose appearance he is familiar with and thus takes for granted.

The plot of *Rodmoor* relates to those of *Ducdame* and *Wolf Solent*, and it is in the nature of a preliminary sounding. It concerns the breakdown of the hyper-sensitive Adrian Sorio through his inability to come to terms with his own life, and through his love for two very different women. Here in embryo we have the dominant Powysian themes—the relation of man to his own self-consciousness, and the relation of his necessarily self-protective private world to those of others. Adrian finds sanity and freedom from fear with the loyal and simple Nance Herrick, but his spiritual affinities with the capricious Philippa Renshaw. The latter is native to Rodmoor and to the wild and dangerous elements that surround it, and she and her gigantic brother Brand are presented as members of a doomed race. (The Herricks come from the outer world, just as in *A Glastonbury Romance* the Crows are aliens in Somerset.) *Rodmoor* is dedicated to "The Spirit of Emily Bronte", and a kindred contrast to that between the Earnshaws and the Lintons is clearly contemplated. But *Rodmoor* is far more ambiguous than its great original. Adrian's dilemma is unresolved, and the book ends on a note of complete agnosticism, though not, as in the later novels, an agnosticism cheerfully accepted.

In it we find the oblique Powysian method of presentation. While being a master-hand at the evocation of the atmosphere and undertones of drama, Powys is less successful at working out its logical development. He is no master of plot. But his novels are not so much stories as portraits of a view of life: the various dramatic scenes have their symbolism stressed less within the scene itself (as, for example, in Lawrence's account of the struggle with the mare in *Women in Love*) than in their relationship with each other. Powys's novels are pictorial rather than dramatic in conception, and need to be interpreted in this way if their force is to be appreciated.

This is exemplified in his use of landscape for the mediating of his themes. Adrian has been describing his imaginative horror of the bodies of men and women when these are divorced from their personalities (one might call it his horror of pornography):

> There began to fall upon the place where they sat, upon the cobble-stones of the little quay, upon the wharf steps, slimy with green sea-weed, upon the harbour mud and the tarred gunwales of the gently rocking barges, upon the pallid tide flowing with gurglings and suckings and lappings and long-drawn sighs, that indescribable sense of the coming on of night at a river's mouth, which is like nothing else in the world. It is, as it were, the meeting of two infinite vistas of imaginative suggestion—the sense of the mystery of the boundless horizons seaward, and the more human mystery of the unknown distance inland, its vague fields and marshes and woods and silent gardens— blending there together in a suspended breath of ineffable possibility, sad and tender, and touching the margin of what cannot be uttered.[2]

This passage is characteristic of its author, moving as it does from the close particularity of the opening, with its clearly felt physical objects (the cobble stones, the slimy steps) to things clearly seen (the rocking barges, the pallid tide) and then through an increasing fluidity and subjectivity into an invocation of another dimension of reality altogether. Powys's characters are a part of nature not only in their physical senses but in their imaginative intuition.

The vision is further developed in *Ducdame*, Powys's most compact and tightly constructed novel. In none of the others is he so responsive to the moods and rhythms of nature, and none of them leaves so vivid a recollection of their setting: the woods and coverts and hill slopes of central Dorset are described with passionate love and sensitivity; indeed the human drama is so dominated by them as to be almost secondary in its effect. Like *Rodmoor*, *Ducdame* recounts the destruction of a man whose inner desires seem to be at war with the forces of nature. Rook Ashover, an introspective young squire, is trapped between his love for his forlorn lower-class mistress and the need to propagate a son to carry on the family line: the machinery of the book is partly that of the nineteenth century novel. The theme is handled with a good deal more assurance and clarity than in *Rodmoor*, and with a greater feeling of hope. The book's final conclusions are not negative: Rook comes to accept his nature as itself a part of the life force which urges him to continue his family into the future. Once again the setting gives the tone; but instead of the open spaces of the world of *Rodmoor* we are in a world of seclusion akin to that of Hardy's *The Woodlanders*.

> Dead leaves that had lain softly one upon another in the mouths of old enmossed fox holes or under clumps of fungi at the edges of woods were now soldered together, as if by tinkling metal, with a thin filigree of crisp white substance. The wet vapour distillations clinging to the yellow reeds down by the ditches began to transform themselves into minute icicles. Birds that had reassumed their natural thinness fluffed out their feathers again as they hopped about searching for sheltered roosting places. In every direction there were tiny rustlings and tightenings and crackings as the crust of the planet yielded to the windless constriction, crisp and crystalline, of a gathering hoar frost.[3]

Along with such meticulous precision is a frequent resort to what Professor Wilson Knight calls "etherealising", the suggestion of other dimensions opening out of space and time. A good example of this is the description of the swan seen by Rook and his brother Lexie.

> The bird was so beautiful that the vision of it passed beyond the point where either of them could share the feelings it excited with the other. It seemed to bring with it an overpowering sense of awe; for both the Ashovers regarded its advance in spellbound silence. It was as if it were floating on some mysterious inner lake that was, so

to speak, the platonic idea, or the ethereal essence, of the actual lake which they were contemplating. It might have been swimming on an estuary that had suddenly projected itself into our terrestial spaces from a purer level of existence, some tributary of the Eternal and the Undying, that flowed in for one ineffable second of time, converting the watery element it mingled with into its own ethereal substance.

But Powys never loses touch with physical reality: so the account proceeds.

The spell of its approach was broken as soon as the bird itself realized that the Ashover brothers were not two motionless tree-trunks, but alien and disturbing invaders. It swung round with a proud curve of its great neck and an eddy of the blue water about its white feathers, and sheered off toward the centre of the pond.

Rook and Lexie regarded its departure with concentrated interest; but now that the magical moment had passed they were able to note the almost humorous effect of the swan's attempts to retain his impassive dignity, to show appropriate indignation, and at the same time to put a good clear space of deep lake water between himself and the onlookers.[4]

It is a measure of Powys's inclusiveness that the one kind of experience is not cancelled by the other. He can move from intensity to humour without a jarring note.

Chapter XIX of *Ducdame* is one of the finest things in all of Powys's fiction; and an analysis of its development brings one very close to the heart not only of this novel but of his work as a whole. It is, quite simply, the account of a walk; but in it Powys achieves a perfect correspondence between outward and inward action.

The time is Midsummer: nature is at her full flowering and Rook's life is at its nadir. His mistress has left him, and he is now unhappily married to his cousin Ann, at the urging of his mother, who wants an heir for the house of Ashover. Only his brother Lexie is left to him, and Lexie is slowly dying. The chapter describes Rook's journey to meet Lexie for a picnic at an old manor house called Comber's End. The accounts of the foliage and scenery are supplemented by Rook's thoughts as he gives way to his depression and remorse.

> He felt responsible at that moment for the unhappiness of all the lives within his reach . . . He saw life at that moment in a different light from any that he had seen it in before. He saw it as a place where not to have become involved in any other existence was the only cause for real thankfulness to the gods; in any other existence than such as was organically linked with his own.[5]

These thoughts lead on to a more generalised conclusion, as he follows the course of a long lane lined with pollard willows.

> The world was full enough of "honourable men" struggling frantically to get the advantage of one another in this race for success, for fame, for recognition, for achievement. What did it matter? Far, far better, to live harmlessly in some quiet untroubled place, watching season follow season, month follow month, aloof and detached; leaving the breathless procession of outward events to turn and twist upon itself like a wounded snake![6]

But this conclusion, natural to one with an assured income, is not allowed to stay at that. Its logical outcome is despair.

> He began to walk more slowly and driftingly along that interminable lane. He felt as if he had already been following it for half a day; and it still stretched straight in front of him, without any sign of an end or of a turning.[7]

The length and straightness of the lane, the almost hypnotic power of its direction, permeates the whole of this passage. There follows an acute description of the condition of the passive man, of the unassertive character whose delineation Powys excelled in.

He stopped for a while, leaning over a gate and gazing into the green slime of a cattle-trodden ditch, across which three orange-bodied dragon flies were darting with as much arrogance as if it were a Venetian lagoon.

He had a feeling that some deep inarticulate grievance, much less clearly defined than these other causes of misery, was obscurely stirring within him. He tried to plumb the recesses of this emotion and he came to the conclusion that it was a blind repulsion at the idea of being married to Lady Ann. He suddenly found himself actually trembling with a convulsive fit of anger against his wife; and not only against his wife. It was as if he had never realized before how profoundly his life illusion was outraged by his marriage . . . He had drifted into this cul-de-sac in a sort of anaesthetized trance. Something very deep in his nature had always preserved an absurd faith in his power of extricating himself from any trap. This faith no doubt depended on his emotional detachment; on those remote translunar journeys of his mind that seemed to reduce all human relations into a misty puppet show, seen through the smaller end of a telescope!

He cast about in his brain until his mind trailed its wings and sank huddled and drooping from sheer exhaustion in the attempt to find some outlet from his dilemma.

To and fro those orange-bodied dragon flies darted. To and fro across the oozing footprints of the cattle, between great heaps of dung, clouds of infinitesimal midges hovered and wavered; while in a corner of clear water a group of tiny black water beetles whirled round and round, as if they were trying to outpace their own small shadows which answered to their movements, down there on the sunlit mud, in queer radiated circles like little dark-rimmed moons.[8]

The relation of reflection to observation is delicately indicated by the use of the phrase "mind trailed its wings"; and the assimilation of Rook's mind to what he sees has already been prepared for by the "arrogance" of the dragon flies and the likening of human affairs to a puppet show—something watched as Rook is watching the midges and beetles. But a further development of his feeling comes with the assimilation of his mind with what he is half-consciously observing. His detachment recoils upon itself; he becomes what he is looking at.

> His vision of things would go on to the very end drawing its quality from just such vignettes of the ways of nature as he was staring at at that moment—those casual heaps of cattle dung, those dancing midges, that green pond slime, those revolving jet-bright beetles!
>
> He was sick and weary with the effort of thinking; of thinking round and round in the same circle. He was like a hunted gladiator who, in his blind race for life, keeps seeing the same impassive faces looking down upon the same heart-breaking circuit of the arena.[9]

Self-pity is placed in perspective by a kind of imaginative sleight of hand: the image of the gladiator is an image of how Rook feels to himself; but since it arises from the circular movement of the insects in relation to Rook's fixed gaze we are aware of its fundamental falsehood. Powys is able in this way to dissect Rook's feelings without sitting in judgement upon them: he simply indicates by his use of imagery their place in the over-all reality.

Rook's thoughts of his wife lead him to a dread of the feminine principle, to feelings of drowning and of suffocation. These emotions are furthered by his almost hypnotised staring at the muddy stagnant pool; and this in turn affects his exterior vision:

see Scummy Pond in Maiden Castle

> ... the hedges ceased to be green under that halcyon sky. They became grey like the colour of wood ashes. The trunks of the willows, too, became grey; and the lane itself under his feet, its deep clay-stiffened cart ruts and its

margins of silverweed and feverfew, became grey as the face of some enormous dead creature upon which he was treading.

A paralysis of dizziness seized him, mingled with an abysmal loathing for he knew not what. He staggered as he walked and he found himself feebly shaking his head as if to make some overt protestation against a vision of things that his reason still assured him was unreal.

It is at this point that Rook is joined by a young horseman who is his unborn son.

He was not in the least surprised to detect in his companion's face a certain unmistakeable resemblance to his own, nor was he startled or in any way shocked when the youth addressed him as "Father".

"It is just dizziness," Rook found himself saying. "It has nothing to do with what I have been suffering."

"You must not suffer, Father," the youth said gently, stroking his horse's neck with a light hand.

"I thought just now," Rook retorted, "that there was no human being in the world unhappier than I am . . ."

He placed his hand on the edge of the rider's saddle and the boy laid his own upon it and began caressing it.

"There's no need for you to tell me, Daddy," he murmured. His voice became so low and faint just then that Rook glanced at him anxiously. And it was not only that his voice seemed to sink away like a wind that sighed itself into silence among feebly stirred grasses. His very form and face grew shadowy and indistinct.[10]

The encounter is described with great tenderness; but what clinches its effect is the way in which interior vision is fused with the external setting in a manner which convinces one that this is, in the strictest sense, a supernatural experience. And in his dialogue with the boy, or rather his revelation of himself to the boy, Rook comes to a self-acceptance which is at the same time a vindication of his desire for freedom as well as a defeat of his self-pity.

> "It was the green slime," the man began again, in a hurried husky voice, his brain full of the one obstinate desire to make a very difficult point clear. "And the cattle dung," he added, pressing the horseman's hand against his saddle.
>
> "What they made me think was that no one who makes any effort to change his nature or to change any one else's nature has any right to be alive upon the earth." His voice subsided but he was still driven on by that desperate impatient sense that he *must* make everything plain before the lad cantered off.
>
> "Slime—dung—not one grey feather—" he gasped wildly; and then, in a sudden burst of exultant freedom: "No one is worthy to live," he cried with a loud voice, "who doesn't know—who doesn't know—"
>
> "What, Daddy?" whispered the voice at his side.
> He flung the words into the air now with a ringing triumphant voice.
>
> "Who doesn't know that all Life asks of us is to be recognized and loved!"
>
> The young rider suddenly snatched up the hand with which Rook had been so desperately retaining him and raised it to his lips. Then he gave him a smile the penetrating sweetness of which diffused itself through every fibre of the man's body.
>
> "Good-bye, Daddy," he murmured gently; and whispering some quick word to his horse he gave the bridle a shake and cantered away down the lane.[11]

The ghost is a ghost from the future; and in due course, at the time of Rook's own death the child is born. What Powys is doing in *Ducdame* is to suggest a mystically apprehended unity between man and the natural world of vegetation and seasonal change; and to assess its significance for human relationships.

Rook in his inner isolation is both sympathetically presented and yet analysed unsparingly in terms of the havoc that he wreaks on others: and in *Wolf Solent* the process is carried still further. In *Ducdame* the problem remains relatively in the background, and subordinate to the depiction of the natural setting. Nature is therefore not presented as sinister: this only happens as it reflects Rook's own feelings. But *man* in nature is often a disturbing element, as, for instance, in the character of Binnory, the idiot boy, or the twin monsters begotten by Rook's father on a gipsy girl—an example of Powys's use of the grotesque to stress the unity of all forms of life and the need to recognise it. But there are no absolute judgements to be made: Binnory knows the monsters affectionately as "the half-beasties", and of Binnory himself Powys comments, "This child, whose half articulate utterances and facial distortions would have been horrible in a city, fell naturally into his place among wilting hemlocks and lightning struck trees and birds eaten by hawks and rabbits eaten by weasles."[12] In its context the comment is not a bitter one.

And it is the grandmother of the monsters, Betsy Cooper, (named after an old gipsy woman known to the Powyses at Montacute[13]) who tells of Cimmery Land, the kind of dream world of escape for which Rook longs, a world of impersonal existence as part of earth and water, "the land where folks do live like unborn babes."

> As (Rook) listened to the old woman and watched the smoke of her pipe floating up into the illuminated sun-ray where it broke at once into a hundred silver-blue undul-tions, it came over him that this Cimmery Land of which she spoke was the thing that he had so often vaguely dreamed of; dreamed of on lonely roads at twilight; dreamed of lying on his bed listening to the sounds of the morning; dreamed of under the walls of old buildings

in the quiet places of historic cities, where the noons fell
hotly and the shadows fell darkly, and from hidden
fountains came the splash of water.[14]

In this passage we have the first appearance of one of Powys's
central concerns, the cult of sensations, sensory and imaginative,
as a way of life. In *Ducdame* it is regarded with a certain
mistrust. The imagery used in speaking of Cimmery Land
relates to the water meadows where Rook meets his unborn
son and where he is shown to be in revolt against the natural
forces of birth, death and rebirth, as symbolised in his marriage
to Lady Ann. But in accepting his part in the natural order
he has to accept also the peculiarity of his own nature. In
Ducdame, through his portrait of Rook (and indeed of several
of the other characters as well) Powys is depicting another,
more personal, life of super-sensory perceptions to which some
people are more sensitive than others. It is here that he shares
the same territory as Proust, of whom he wrote, "(his) *real
theme* . . . has to do with the most evasive element in our secret
personal life, namely with those obscure feelings of delicious
ecstasy which are as hard to arrest or analyse in their swift
passage as it is hard to explain why such small, slight, trivial
and casual chances are the cause of their rising up out of the
depth."[15]

Powys analyses these states repeatedly in his work, but
nowhere more thoroughly than here. Following his meeting
with his son, Rook arrives at Comber's End, and in the beauty
of the scene finds the confirmation of his inner life. Powys
goes on to remark that "in addition to the ordinary gregarious
human life, led by us in contact with others and in the stress of
our normal pursuits, there is another, a more intimate life,
solitary and detached, that has its own days and months and
years, such as are numbered by no measurings of common
time, by no computation on any terrestrial almanac."[16] In the
Autobiography he describes the central part played by such
sensations in his own consciousness, and in his philosophical

books recommends their systematic cultivation as a key to happiness. But it is in the novels that they are treated dynamically in relation to their context.

In Rook Ashover Powys achieved his fullest portrait to date of the kind of man who is among his unique contributions to fiction, the man who fails to achieve his fulfilment in normal human contacts and who seeks oblivion in the impersonal forces of nature. The character is not romanticised. Rook sees his plight and limitations clearly, and is granted the oblivion he craves; but there is a goodness in his death and, before it, a reconcilation with what has oppressed him. This reconciliation, however, remains at a mental level and is not worked out dramatically, so that the novel, despite its pictorial vividness, has a slight feeling of unreality. It lacks the author's normal preoccupation with the day-to-day details of ordinary life (is this the result of the cuts advised by Llewelyn Powys?) and the action goes on more through the minds of the characters than in dramatic conflict. But for all these shortcomings *Ducdame* is a significant and rewarding novel, and a haunting portrayal of the interaction between a man's private fears and self-distrust and the physical world which he inhabits.

As such it looks forward to *Wolf Solent*. Distinguished in many ways though the early novels are, they do not possess the amplitude, the complexity and the continuous undertide of humour that mark the great novels. But Powys was a writer who continued to change and develop; and in the slow growth evident in these early books we see part of the secret of his greatness. His work was never manufactured: it evolved, an integral part of his evolving personality. In the characters of James Anderson, Adrian Sorio and Rook Ashover we see the vulnerable young man portrayed so memorably in the *Autobiography*, the young man whose weakness provides the challenge met by the superior energies of the books of Powys's creative maturity. He made of his youth a growing point for a triumphant old age; and if we are to look for juvenilia in Powys's work they are to be found not in the early novels but in the final fantasies. Powys delighted in his self-styled second childhood, and with justice: its serenity had been earned. And there is a singular consistency in this. Powys knew from the beginning what he wanted his own fiction to effect, and at the outset of his career as a novelist he provided a definition of what was to be his own achievement when he wrote in the preface to *Wood and Stone* that the business of art is "to keep the horizons open . . . She must hold fast to poetry and humour, and about her creations there must be a certain spirit of liberation, and the presence of large tolerant after-thoughts." The description fits his own work perfectly.

NOTES

[1] *Wood and Stone*, New York, 1915, pp. 370–371.
[2] *Rodmoor*, New York, 1916, p. 203.
[3] *Ducdame*, 1925, p. 136.
[4] *Ibid*, pp. 330–331.
[5] *Ibid*, p. 300.
[6] *Ibid*, p. 301.
[7] *Ibid*, p. 302.
[8] *Ibid*, pp. 303–304.
[9] *Ibid*, p. 304.
[10] *Ibid*, pp. 307–308.
[11] *Ibid*, pp. 309–310.
[12] *Ibid*, p. 36.
[13] See Llewelyn Powys, *Somerset Essays*, 1937, "Nancy Cooper".
[14] *Ducdame*, p. 265.
[15] *The Pleasures of Literature*, 1938, pp. 625–626.
[16] *Ducdame*, p. 315.

V

WHITENESS

Diane Fernandez (translated by Eileen Cottis)

As early as his first autobiographical essay *Confessions of two brothers*, John Cowper Powys stresses his search for the neutral and the formless; these confessions brim with a longing to dissolve into an impersonal state free from all suffering, whether inflicted or received:

> The thought of the large free expanses of the desert, whether in its hot noons or under its glittering stars, makes me realise what it is that I require from natural scenery. I require an escape. I require an escape from all disturbing and distracting objects—objects and people. I want to be liberated from everything that 'sticks out', from everything that calls attention to itself by its colour, its form, its challenge.[1]

Associated with this absence of colour one finds a desire to be enfolded, protected, curled up as if in the womb, a desire which Powys, just like Amiel, expresses by the static life of a jellyfish.

> I suppose my ideal existence, out of the human circle, would be that of some happy irridescent jelly-fish, expanding its sunlit body in placid warmth at the bottom of a rock-pool, hurting nothing and being hurt by nothing— and living entirely for sensation . . . I like the sensation of being 'created'. I do not at all like the responsibility of 'creation'.[2]

This impulse to retreat towards non-existence, which, to start with, was for Powys no more than a withdrawal and a fear of competing, but became in the course of his work a principle of creation and a poetical process of identification, goes together with all sorts of variations on the theme of whiteness.

Rodmoor, which was published at the same time as the *Confessions*, is suffused with a cruel and blinding white glare; the poems of his youth (1896–99) like the later poems (1916–22) offer a symphony of whiteness; *Ducdame*, where the hero Rook is haunted by a feeling of guilt and a puritanical rejection of earthly and sensual metamorphoses, is pervaded with the chill of the moon, the hard purity of frost, with suffocating snow, and Cimmerian mists. The *Autobiography* itself shows how

far the imagery of coldness is developed in Powys: he speaks
of his thoughts "heavy as frost",[3] his saurian love, his arctic
heart; he is a Polar bear, or an ichthyosaurus. Why are whiteness and coldness so essential in Powys's work? We shall
attempt to discern some of the hidden reasons for these variations on whiteness.

I. WHITE, THE COLOUR OF FIDELITY TO THE DEAD

In 1893 John Cowper Powys's favourite young sister,
Nelly, died following an attack of appendicitis. What he
loved in his sister was her detachment, her ability to keep
different aspects of her life apart from each other. Brother and
sister were bound together by powerful affinities despite the
years that separated them. John Cowper was twenty-one when
his sister, who was fourteen, died so tragically. "My ideal
future", he wrote in an unpublished letter to his sister Philippa
in 1950, "was to be a famous actor living with Nelly and always
acting with Nelly for she and I were alike exactly in our mental
life, our aesthetic or artistic life, our emotional life, our imaginative life, and our erotic life. We turned from one to another of
these and kept them apart".[4] But this detachment which he
loved so much in Nelly was only the echo of another detachment, that of the imaginative and morbid Mary Cowper, the
author's mother. In another unpublished letter of 1939 to
Philippa Powys, John Cowper wrote: "It's certain that your
elder brother—and maybe lucky for him and maybe not!—is
an exact mixture of our mother and father over death—mother's
detachment . . . and father's tough earthy ash-root, or oak-root,
going on . . ."[4] But these two people who meant so much to
Powys were dead before he really started to write, Eleanor
Powys in 1893, and Mary Cowper in 1914. To his coldness
which echoes the detachment of these beloved women, to the
absence of colour significant of a wish not to suffer, to the
desire of regressing towards non-existence, of merging with
death, is added the cold whiteness of a pure and destructive
sorrow which kills all that is not itself, excluding for a long
time the possibility of loving anew without being haunted by a
sense of guilt, by voices and faces rising from the past.

In the *Poems* the obsession with whiteness rules the choice of images.[5] Thus in *Whiteness* the word "white" is found no less than sixteen times in the five stanzas that compose the poem, and everything named in it evokes this colour which is both virginal and mortal: marble, moon, sand, and also silver— shutting out the red of blood:

> Then all red things shall fade away—
> Red flame, red roses, and red blood.[6]

Other poems are concerned only with places, animals or objects that have some element of white or silver: a haunting face mingled with moonlike pallor and with death, whiteness suggesting virginity and childhood (*Obsession, Exiles*)[7], white arms beckoning from beyond the grave (*Piety*)[8], the moon's presence reviving a passion for a dead woman (*The Book*)[8], a white ghost with whom the spirit travels along a river until it merges with the sea (*Euthanasia*)[9], cries of wild swans, an exchange of sighs between water-lilies and grasses that conceal other, human, laments, the laments of one who is dead (*The Cry*)[10], a wan face appearing at the window above an ethereal, misty, wraith-like body (*God*)[11]. The common theme in all these poems is nostalgia for a relationship brutally cut short by death. Sometimes this love is felt for a child-woman, inno- cent and virginal:

> And a white wraith-figure of you—
> White arms, white hands, white breast—
> Drifts by my side, and alone we two
> Drink of the river of rest.[9]

Sometimes it is for a woman with a mature and tragic face, upon which the sorrow of the world is concentrated, a face foreshadowing the agonising visions of *Rodmoor* and *Wolf Solent* ("the face on the Waterloo steps"):

> The wreckage of the whole damned race,
> As I go whistling to my white bird,
> Is in that wavering ghastly face
> That speaks no word![12]

Sometimes the poem goes so far as to express the wish to be reunited with a "wraith" even before the poet's death, or the compulsion to reject life in order to enter the dance of death in a ghostly ring of moths (*The Malice-Dance*),[13] or the pain of that long-known feeling of betrayal when the poet has had to pretend he loved and lived (*The Traitor*)[14]. It is not at all surprising that these poems, which according to Kenneth Hopkins's preface[15] explain many of the silences and reticences of the *Autobiography*, fill the reader with the impression of a tortured loyalty to what was and is no more, a loyalty reminiscent of the world of love and death in Edgar Allan Poe's *Ulalume*, which one of Powys's poems, *The Castle of Gathore*,[16] recalls by its sonority and rhythm. This citadel of death, has only one pilgrim, who worships for ever in loneliness the "Black morgues of leafy doom" of his phantasy, the Castle of Gathore from which the odours of death are "wafted", driving away all "true love from (his) bed".

The world of these poems, where the memory of a dead woman is continuously present through apparitions and laments, foreshadows that of the visions which in *Rodmoor* and *Wolf Solent* overwhelm the hero with remorse. It comes as no surprise that Powys's essay on Poe shows such insight, when one understands their deep affinities. "Here", Powys writes,

it is no more the human, too human, tradition of each man 'killing' the 'thing he loves'. Here we are in a world where the human element, in passion, has altogether departed, and left something else in its place; something which is really, in the true sense, 'inhumanly immoral'. In the first place, it is a thing devoid of any physical emotion. It is sterile, immaterial, unearthly, ice-cold. In the second place, it is, in a ghastly sense, self-centred! It feeds upon itself. It subdues everything to itself. Finally, let it be said, it is a thing with a mania for Corruption. The Charnel-House is its bridal-couch, and the midnight stars whisper to one another of its perversion. There is no need for it to 'kill the thing it loves', for it loves only what is already dead.[17]

This absence of living loves is also characteristic of Powys's early novels and poems. Moreover Powys is fully aware, in Poe's work, of the desire to make the past recur, of that "Death-hunger, our eternal craving to make *what has been* be again, and again, forever!"[18]. This love of the past, this "deliberate 'petrifaction' of the human soul in us", this "glacial detachment",[18] this same insane wish to make things live again, this faculty of discovering only that which has already been discovered, this quest for what is past and lost, is the very key to Powys's work. The icy hand which freezes Poe's loves is the same as that which, in *Maiden Castle*, compels Dud to sacrifice his human love for the circus-rider Wizzie to the phantasm of Dor-Marth, the wooden head symbolic of his dead mother. And when Powys underlines how much sex is present even in Poe's icy coldness, where "dead lips remain woman's lips still" he emphasises how great is the difficulty of new love and justifies the fears of Psyche before Astarte in *Ulalume* (fears of which Marie Bonaparte, like Powys, has written so well) and that long line of bloodless forms, so much more alluring than the Faustinas and Juliets whom Poe and Powys disregard, forms that are incarnations of a single Figure:

> But a few among us—those who understand the poetry of Edgar Allan—turn away from them, to that rarer, colder, more virginal Figure; to Her who has been born and has died, so many times; to Her who was Ligeia and Ulalume and Helen and Lenore—for are not all these One?—to Her we have loved in vain and shall love in vain until the end—to Her who wears, even in the triumph of her Immortality, the close-clinging, heavily-scented cerements of the Dead![19]

Poe's fidelity to that One Primary Figure, whom Marie Bonaparte has shown to be his mother who died so early,[20] is also found in Powys's works, whether as fidelity to his mother, felt so achingly after her death in 1914, or directed towards a younger image, as it were his mother made young again, the virginal figure of his sister and soulmate who died just as she had learned, perhaps thanks to John Cowper, the full enjoyment of a tender brother-sister relationship.

II. WHITENESS AND SELF-DESTRUCTION IN *RODMOOR*

The nostalgic white of the *Poems* becomes a blinding light in the novel *Rodmoor* (1916). Here whiteness hardens into violent self-destruction through the maternal figure of Mrs. Renshaw. This woman, both strong and masochistic, casts herself before suffering, no longer to endure it, but to become an integral part of it: merging with suffering itself, she can no longer suffer. We remember her agonisingly resigned words: "We were made to bear, to endure, to submit, to suffer".[21] and later: "What we suffer seems to me like the weight of some great iron engine with jagged raw edges—like a battering-ram beating us against a dark mountain."[22] Sorio, describing his book which is devoted to destruction, expresses himself in words similar to Mrs. Renshaw's, transmuting her fatalistic, sombre statements of the necessity of sacrifice into a dazzling white light:

> "What I'm aiming at in my book is a revelation of how the essence of life is found in the instinct of destruction . . . Out of destruction alone—out of the rending and tearing of something—of something in the way—does new life spring to birth . . . Pure destruction . . . 's a burning and devouring flame. It's a mad, splendid revel of glaring whiteness like this which hurts our eyes now . . . What the saints and mystics seek is the destruction of everything within reach—of everything that sticks out, that obtrudes, that is simply *there*."[23]

Thus for Sorio destruction implies the absence of "everything that sticks out" which was already rejected as galling in the *Confessions of two brothers*, where the same expression was used. Destruction, for Sorio, implies the death of sex, the abolition "of one's own body and the passions of the body",[24] in the same way as Mrs. Renshaw considers one must endure and suffer whatever the wounds inflicted upon the body. To

Sorio's image of a "rending and tearing" corresponds Mrs. Renshaw's terrible image evocative of rape, when she imagines "a battering-ram". Just as in *Ducdame* Rook Ashover and his mother share the same lunar detachment, so Sorio and Mrs. Renshaw both reject the life of the body as they communicate in a destructive and puritanical whiteness. There are no less than three deaths in *Rodmoor*; this repetition of violent death is found in another "angelistic" novel, Gide's *André Walter*. The self-inflicted sacrifice of suicide in *Rodmoor* allows the characters' secret sexuality to remain voluptuously fixed on the past, freeing them of unknown ordeals. Passive in the *Confessions* the desire for annihilation has become an active search; it is no mere longing for an absolutely negative state, but a quest for ecstasy. Sorio experiences this ecstatic "mad splendid revel of glaring whiteness" as the supreme stage where destruction becomes creative: only in ecstasy can the sensual man die as his sharpened sensuality reaches its climax.

III. LUNAR COLDNESS AND ECSTASY IN *DUCDAME*

In Powys's novels, ecstasy and contemplation coexist in sterile love. The whole of *Ducdame*, extolling the refusal of procreation, is imbued with a strong inter-connection between lunar whiteness and death. The first sentence immediately places us in an unreal, ghostly atmosphere: "Some of the most significant encounters in the world occur between two persons one of whom is asleep or dead".[25] So Rook muses at the bedside of a sleeping woman, Netta, his sterile but human love. Soon, by dint of gazing at this woman's face, Rook loses himself in the landscape outside, bathed in moonlight. He chooses the landscape rather than the face. He chooses "a cold, remote, detached tenderness", an "inhuman detachment",[26] rather than love. While there is no communication between the sleeping body and Rook, there is, on the other hand, an encounter and a coalescing between the man and this new world formed by the moon:

> It was almost as if, just behind all this etherealized chemistry, there really did exist something corresponding to the

old Platonic idea of a universe composed of mind-stuff, of mind-forms, rarer and more beautiful than the visible world.[27]

Thus for Rook (rather as in *Wolf Solent* the hero feels estranged from Gerda "rounded with a sleep"[28] at the top of Poll's Camp), the sleeping woman is merely a means of establishing communications with the reflection of his physical universe in the world around: with the deep waters of Saunders' Hole where the fish "moved rapidly to and fro as if under some lunar ecstasy", with the ancestral tombs, "shimmering group of white objects, objects more congruous with the moonlight than they were with anything else in the world"[29], with the spell-binding moon beckoning to him, "immense silver disk, . . . round illuminated lake that drew him toward it, that drew him into it"[30]. The visible world below is progressively drawn up towards the invisible world above, and already one can foresee that in this ascent, the spiritual climate of a haunted soul, the sleeping Netta, like Poe's virgins, will be sacrificed. Rook undergoes a petrifaction such that "if some nocturnal bird had been circling above him the creature might easily have mistaken his face for some inanimate piece of whiteness".[30] The whole novel, whose main elements are snow and frost, those waters which by their crystalline appearance recall stars or moon, is one long variation on the theme of detachment from human, fruitful love. The Cimmerian mists, the crystal ball of the clairvoyant in which Rook sees the forewarning of his own death, the comparison between the Cimmerian Land and Limbo ("Cimmery Land", says Betsy Cooper, "that be the land where folk do live like unborn babes"[31]), all combine to reveal in the character of Rook a nostalgia for a prenatal world where, as Powys wrote in the *Confessions*, one is content to "be created" rather than to "create".

From the very start of the novel it is quite clear that the vampire-like power of the moon is hostile to what is human. If Rook submits only too willingly to its magnetism, his brother Lexie, a solar being with a passion for life, finds that the moon "has never been really friendly to the human race".[32]

And no doubt it is not mere coincidence that immediately after the description of a malefic moon, Powys stresses the solitude of Netta, whom Mrs. Ashover persistently ignores. Under the gaze of Rook's mother his mistress feels shattered, broken, disowned; and we suspect that there are cruel concealed connections between the hostile lunar world, the oppressive mother and the dominated son, since Rook is no more aware of his forsaken mistress than Mrs. Ashover is. Hidden affinities link Ashover mother and son in the white detachment of a destroyed sexuality.

IV. WHITENESS AND CREATION IN *WOLF SOLENT*

Thus from the *Poems* to *Rodmoor*, and from *Rodmoor* to *Ducdame*, whiteness runs like a pure Ariadne's thread of fidelity to the past, to a Mother Image, and to death. As the red of suffering was already rejected in *Whiteness* ("Then all red things shall fade away"),[33] in the two novels, red and blood inseparable from feminine nature, flowering, and procreation are scorned and denied.

Whiteness is also to be found in *Wolf Solent*. But here it is filtered, its quality is less cruel and offending, it has an inner iridescence, forerunner of the "friendly whiteness" which covers the fields watched by the hero of *Porius*, a whiteness where green predominates, evoking "the mother-of-pearl glimmerings in the hollow curves of some vast green-veined sea-shell".[34] The self-punishing colour that ruled the guilty puritanical hearts of Powys's early heroes melts into that soft glaucous green which ceaselessly bathes *Wolf Solent* with its undersea prenatal hue, the hue of seashells, ferns and mosses, the gentle light that shines from Christie's lamp.

But one poem here brings out the importance of whiteness in a series of images that show how its destructive force has grown into a creative urge. The poem, written by Jason, is called *White Seaweed* and describes how the bodies of the drowned float,

> White as the foam in the track of a whale
> As he spouts and sports for a thousand miles.[35]

This image recalls another whale, the one that looms up, white and disquieting, in Wolf's mind when he is on his way to fetch his mother from the station and guesses the future failure of his love for the earthy Gerda ("It's odd . . . it's funny . . . it's just like the spouting up of a great white whale . . .").[36] In *White Seaweed*, the drowned float on the swell, while fish and seagulls stare and wait, but the sea gives them a tomb where they can sleep in inviolate peace. Whiteness here is the preserved colour of virginal beings whose chastity is prolonged by the sea which has engulfed them. The foaming ocean itself is pure as the drowned. It is lonely, without "masthead" or "sail". From the dead:

> A seaweed grows that is soft as silk,
> White as the moon on St. Alban's Head,
> Moss-like, fern-like, white as milk—,
> The fingers of Mary are not more white![35]

A real hymn to whiteness and the purity of bodies sheltered and entombed in the sea (where Powys himself chose to have his ashes strewn), this poem to seaweed celebrates the joint creation of the dead with a sea as enfolding and chaste as a mother. Jason is a poet and as such a reflection of John Cowper himself. Other features also make him a double of Powys, for he and Darnley make up the fraternal couple, already found in *Wood and Stone* and in *Ducdame*, of John Cowper and Llewelyn. In Jason's verses whiteness no longer expresses annihilation of the self as it did in *Rodmoor*, it is no longer a vampire-like power as in *Dudcame*, but becomes the very matter of the poem. Jason, by linking the drowned body with the maternal theme of water, succeeds in celebrating the trinity that is extolled by the whole of Powys's creation, that of the son, the mother, and the written work which, even beyond death, unites them.

NOTES

1   *Confessions of two brothers*, 1916, pp. 87–88.
2   *Ibid*, pp. 66–67.
3   *Autobiography* (1934), 1967, p. 265.
4   Letters kindly lent to us by Francis Powys.

5 The reader should consult the remarkable analysis of J. C. Powys's *Poems* by Professor Wilson Knight in his recent book *Neglected Powers* (1971), especially the chapter entitled "The Ship of Cruelty" (pp. 197–227).

6 In *Mandragora* (1917); *John Cowper Powys. A Selection from his Poems*, ed. K. Hopkins, 1964, p. 178.

7 *Ibid*, pp. 176–177.

8 *Ibid*, pp. 170–171.

9 *Ibid*, p. 172.

10 *Ibid*, p. 162.

11 *Ibid*, p. 139.

12 "The Face" in *Samphire* (1922); *Poems*, p. 194.

13 *Ibid*, p. 183.

14 In *Mandragora* (1917); *ibid*, p. 137.

15 *Ibid*, p. 16.

16 In *Samphire* (1922); *ibid.*, pp. 190–191.

17 *Visions and Revisions* (1915) 1955, "Edgar Allan Poe", p. 199.

18 *Ibid.*, p. 202.

19 *Ibid.*, p. 208.

20 Marie Bonaparte, *Edgar Poe, sa vie, son oeuvre*, Paris, 1958.

21 *Rodmoor*, New York, 1916, p. 252.

22 *Ibid.*, p. 428.

23 *Ibid.*, pp. 111–112.

24 *Ibid.*, p. 111.

25 *Ducdame*, 1925, p. 1.

26 *Ibid.*, p. 2.

27 *Ibid.*, p. 3.

28 *Wolf Solent*, 1929, p. 325; 1961, p. 309.

29 *Ducdame*, p. 4.

30 *Ibid.*, p. 7.

31 *Ibid.*, p. 264.

32 *Ibid.*, p. 17.

33 *Poems*, p. 178.

34 *Porius*, 1951, p. 4.

35 *Wolf Solent*, 1929, p. 380; 1961, p. 362.

36 *Ibid.*, p. 134; p. 123.

VI

JOHN COWPER POWYS AND KING LEAR
A Study in Pride and Humility

Frederick Davies

It is possible, with many writers, to recommend certain of their books as the epitome of their achievement, and a reader's appreciation of them will not be greatly diminished by his not having read other books by those writers. This is not so with John Cowper Powys. The full impact of *Wolf Solent* or *A Glastonbury Romance* cannot be appreciated by a reader unacquainted with, at least, the *Autobiography* and *A Philosophy of Solitude*.

Powys is unlike any other writer in that, from the age of about forty and for nearly fifty years, he wrote in almost alternate annual sequence novels and philosophical books, all of which are intricately-interwoven variations on one theme: how it is possible to find happiness, "the pleasure there is in life itself", by discovering the essential nature of oneself and of the world in which one lives.

> Here we are—confronted by this sublime and horrible universe—with only one brief life at our disposal, and what must our bemused, bewildered minds do but rush blindfold over the crude surface of experience, taking everything for granted and finding nothing extraordinary in what we see. Extraordinary? We are surrounded by things that are staggering; by things that are so miraculously lovely that you feel they might dissolve at a touch; and by things so unbearably atrocious that you feel you would go mad if you thought of them for more than the flicker of a second.

> Something is wrong with us and it goes deeper than our pathetic docility towards a vulgarised public opinion. We have come to the point of taking life for granted. So much do we take life for granted and so little does life in its larger, simpler aspects interest us any more, that in order to titillate our jaded senses the very arts of our time have to crack their whips, have to spout bloody flukes like hysterical whales, have to "make trumpets of their rumps" and skin themselves alive for our delight.[1]

We, and he, have lost the art of living: to rediscover it, in his books and in his private life, was the life-long task which Powys set himself. And to appreciate his novels more fully, one needs some understanding of Powys's complex personality and temperament, and of his psychological-philosophy—his insight into the human mind and the unconscious, which, as George Steiner has said, is "no less subtle, no less comprehensive, no less radical than that of Freud".

It would be quite impossible to explain briefly Powys's philosophy. Any attempt to do so would inevitably lack the Rabelaisian humour of Powys. It would also ignore that caution which Powys himself remembered to observe when writing about Goethe. Powys reminds us of Goethe's reply to Eckermann when the latter was teasing Goethe for interpretations: "Do you suppose that a thing into which I have put the Life-Blood of all my days is able to be summed up in anything so narrow and limited as an Idea?" And because all men and women who read Powys will react to a different facet of his "Complex Vision", each will find his or her own uniquely necessary vein of precious ore in this quarry of cosmic life which is the mind and philosophy of John Cowper Powys.

Here then are two of the many facets of Powys which have contributed to my own understanding of his philosophy. To others, they may not seem so important—simply because, to use Powys's own frequently-used expression: their "I am I" is not my "I am I". These two facets of Powys are his pride and his humility.

It is of the greatest importance to realise that Powys began his literary career, not as a writer writing to be read, but as a lecturer speaking to be listened to. He is primarily a Teacher.

It is also of the greatest importance to remember that, as a lecturer, he was extremely successful. Many of those who heard him lecture in America and in England forty to seventy years ago have testified to the effect he had on them. Henry Miller has written:

I remember most vividly the way he wrapped himself in his gown, closed his eyes and covered them with one hand, before launching into one of those inspired flights of eloquence which left me dizzy and speechless . . . Leaving the hall after his lectures, I often felt as if he had put a spell upon me . . . it was my first intimate experience, my first real contact with the living spirit of those few rare beings who visit this earth . . . Powys fulminated with the fire and smoke of the soul, or the depths which cradle the soul . . . He pierced the veil time and again.[2]

A reporter on his lectures, in the American *Little Review,* wrote:

Powys is for those possessed enough of their imaginations to fall for a miracle when they see one. Who goes to hear a lecture on Nietzsche and Dostoievsky to find out what Powys thinks of those men? You go—hoping through the gloom of Nietzsche and Dostoievsky to catch a glimpse of Powys. Powys is the best thing that has come to us—that mad wolf! I always feel sorry for Velasquez that he never had a chance at him.[3]

Louis Wilkinson (Louis Marlow) wrote:

He was the most powerful public speaker that I have ever heard. Eloquence, imagination, force of life, and a complete freedom from the usual cautions and conventions and deferences and meannesses were what most strongly impressed me in John Cowper Powys when I first met him.[4]

Powys's brother, Littleton Powys wrote:

He was a most brilliant lecturer; without a note of any kind in his hand, by the gift of sheer eloquence he held his audience under a sort of magnetic spell. On the dais he might well have repeated the saying of his childhood: "I am the Lord of Hosts!"—if by that he meant: "I am the Great One, the Lord of Words and of this Assembly!"[5]

And equally important for the present purpose is what John Cowper Powys himself has said about his own ability as a lecturer:

> I must confess that it often seems to me as though I were swept away, out of my own methods and consciousness, on the tide of some invisible force. . . . My own personal motives are transcended; I forget the occasion, my author, and my friends, and am driven on from utterance to utterance, like a man speaking under the influence of some drug or hypnotic suggestion.[6]

Consider now this power and success of Powys as a lecturer in conjunction with the intellectual and spiritual pride which made such a deep impression on so many people during his early career. His brother, Littleton, refers in his book *Still the Joy of It* to John Cowper as a boy at Sherborne School being "full of his own importance" and conscious "that he possessed qualities of an unusual order". Llewelyn Powys's wife, Alyse Gregory, in her Introduction to *The Letters of Llewelyn Powys* speaks of "my brother-in-law, John, who is always too proud or too indifferent to defend himself." Louis Marlow, in his *Welsh Ambassadors*, wrote, "He (John Cowper Powys), then in 1901, was twenty-eight and unknown . . . He had written nothing but a few lecture syllabuses and a little verse. But he had complete faith in his own genius . . . That he was megalomaniac, and outrageously flamboyant, seemed evident to me even in 1901."[7]

And again equally important for the present purpose is what Powys himself has said. Speaking in the *Autobiography* of "the extreme slowness of (his) development as a writer", he says:

> I had for so long to satisfy my pride, which for all my superficial humility is fathomless, by my own secret knowledge . . . of the value and depth of my imaginative perception.[8]

So here we have a man who, on the evidence of his friends and by his own testimony, was temperamentally as proud as

Lucifer, a man who was highly conscious that he was intellectually and imaginatively superior to his fellowmen, who was aware that he was able to cast a magnetic spell over huge audiences by his great gift of oratory. And this man then spends the major part of his long life as a writer expounding a philosophy the essence of which is the practice of a humility "delivered from ambition, aiming at interior peace rather then glory or success".[9] And during the last thirty years of his life he put that philosophy into practice by living in seclusion amongst the mountains of North Wales.

These two facets of John Cowper Powys, his former pride and his subsequent humility, find an irresistible parallel in King Lear. And add to them the fact that he himself said that of all novelists Dostoievsky influenced him most and many things become clear:

> (In the novels of Dostoievsky) the everlasting tragedy of absolute penury, the existence of the tramp, the beggar, the desperate wayfarer, is never long allowed to be forgotten.
>
> Dostoievsky's imaginative awareness of the feelings of these wanderers, as the worm i' the bud of all our well-being, is as Shakespearian as it is Homeric and Biblical, and brings us down, as Lear was brought down, to the basic level.[10]

"*Dostoievsky's imaginative awareness . . . brings us down, as Lear was brought down, to the basic level.*" Was it Powys's own imaginative awareness which turned his pride to humility? "*The existence of the tramp . . . the desperate wayfarer*". What is that but the face on the Waterloo Steps which so haunts Wolf Solent?

> "The day I left London, from Waterloo Station, I saw a tramp on the steps there . . . It was a man," Wolf went on; "and the look on his face was terrible in its misery. It must have been a look of that kind on the face of someone

> ... that made Ivan Karamazov 'return the ticket' ... It
> (that look) has become to be a sort of conscience, a sort
> of test for everything I—"[11]

And Powys's "Ninnyisms", his continual clowning, his
eccentric idiosyncracies, which so annoyed Louis Wilkinson
and puzzled his brother Llewelyn, what are they but Powys
playing the Fool to his own Lear? For Powys is Lear and the
Fool in one. He has to be, because the qualities which give
him the stature of Lear are supernormal, superhuman, supernatural. And in order to remain normal, human and natural,
he has to become as a Fool. And it was, perhaps, this intrusion
of deliberately (and maliciously?) exaggerated idiosyncrasy
which so largely militated against true and valid assessment of
his work during his lifetime.

Since the first statement of his philosophy appeared in 1916
in *Confessions of two brothers*, it is there we should expect to
find the first evidence of this bringing down of himself to the
basic level. And it is there in abundance. Indeed it was so
unexpectedly there to his brother Llewelyn, that Llewelyn wrote
rebuking him: "They (J.C.P.'s part of the *Confessions*) are
also too modest ... what is all the coil about not loving yourself?"[12]

In Powys, an arrogant pride in his unusual intellectual and
rhetorical gifts found itself allied to the sensitivity of an unusual
imaginative awareness. The result was a deep spiritual and
moral conflict which Powys resolved and overcame by writing
his books.

> For me, work is the supreme escape—from myself, for
> there madness lies.[13]

There, once again, appears the parallel with Lear:

> O, that way madness lies: let me shun that: No more
> of that.

And more clearly still:

Poor naked wretches, whereso'er you are,
That bide the pelting of this pitiless storm,
. . . . O, I have ta'en
Too little care of this! Take physic, pomp;
Expose thyself to feel what wretches feel,
That thou mayst shake the superflux to them
And show the heavens more just.

(*King Lear*, Act 3, Scene 4)

Thus can a reading of the *Autobiography* and *A Philosophy of Solitude* lead to a fuller appreciation of the novels, especially of *Wolf Solent* and *A Glastonbury Romance*. For the novels are all complex variations on the same theme—how Powys made his own arrogant pride "take physic" and how he actually did, in practice, in his own life, expose himself to feel what wretches feel.

Certainly, knowing what I know of myself, I will deal gently with every type of perverse and arbitrary egoism . . .[14]

It was perhaps this determination of Powys's to "deal gently with every type of perverse and arbitrary egoism" that made him so generously assailable to the intrusion of strangers, so ready to expend himself in encouraging the ambitions of young writers, and which caused him to remain all his life outside all the literary cliques and coteries, puzzling and confusing the more academic critics by his loneness and remoteness.

NOTES

1   *A Philosophy of Solitude*, 1933, pp. 46–47.
2   *The Books in my Life*, 1952, pp. 136-137.
3   *Little Review*, I, 11 (February 1915), pp. 61–62.
4   *Seven Friends*, 1953, pp. 68–69.
5   *Still the Joy of it*, 1956, p. 164.
6   *Confessions of two brothers*, 1916, p. 136.
7   *Welsh Ambassadors*, 1936, pp. 43–45.
8   *Autobiography* (1934), 1967, p. 388.
9   *A Philosophy of Solitude*, 1933, p. 61.
10 *The Pleasures of Literature*, 1938, "Dostoievsky", pp. 93–94.
11 *Wolf Solent*, 1929, pp. 470–71; 1961, p. 448.
12 *The Letters of Llewelyn Powys*, ed. L. Wilkinson, 1943, p. 58.
13 *The Letters of John Cowper Powys to Louis Wilkinson*, 1958, p. 355.
14 *Confessions of two brothers*, p. 171.

VII

THE MODUS VIVENDI OF JOHN COWPER POWYS

Timothy Hyman

In surveying Powys's achievement, I want to focus on his work as being, above all, representative of a certain way of life.

If we take *Wolf Solent*, for instance, we see that the book is mainly about one man's method for living, and that the whole shape of the book is expressive of this method. Wolf is a man unable to accept any single reality, or any certain stable belief. Wolf conceives the world as a "multiverse" in which he will contrive to live by "no system at all". Wolf's passage between different versions of reality is the central theme of the book. The reader is therefore shown, in the course of the book, one reality, only to have it broken and substituted for another, which, it is implied, may itself transpire to be no less delusory. What should be emphasised is that, although it does resemble one, *Wolf Solent* is not a dialectical novel (on the lines of Thomas Mann's *Magic Mountain*, for instance). Wolf's passing from one reality to another is not a passing upwards, to wisdom or knowledge. Even at the end of the book, all values remain uncertain.

This is not the uncertainty of youth. *Wolf Solent* was Powys's first major work, yet Powys was almost sixty when he wrote it; and in each of the five long prose romances that followed over the subsequent twenty years he exhibits the same ambivalence. At eighty he was still uncertain.

It seems to me that in this apprehension of a fundamentally uncertain world is the essence of what Powys has to offer us. But it is also this ambiguous, anticlimactic element that makes his books such uncomfortable works of art, and that must probably bear the chief responsibility for his neglect.

Powys may have defined "Art" and "Life" by his own polarity of poet and philosopher. He had spent his earlier years mainly as a popular lecturer, travelling the length and breadth of the United States. Especially as a young man, he had written a good deal of verse; but parallel to this he had begun to develop a popular philosophy which he published under titles like *The Art of Happiness* and *A Philosophy of Solitude*.

Powys's verse had been somewhat derivative and aestheticis-
ing. Writing to a friend in 1909, when he was already thirty-
seven, he asks:

> Have I, I wonder, been all this while on wrong tracks?
> asking of myself what do you admire most in literature
> and what therefore would you like to go further with?—
> instead of what do the secret boy-maids of your inner
> Self—the beautiful, coy Diapheneites of your hidden
> thoughts, of your real, native, unalloyed, untampered-with
> sensations—whisper, when you try to lay all 'literary'
> influences away and listen to them?[1]

Although they are unstructured and repetitive, Powys's
philosophical writings do convey a personal apprehension of
life; and, for better or worse, this was the kind of achievement
that was to interest Powys most. As he was later to write in
his *Autobiography:*

> My writings . . . are simply so much propaganda, as
> effective as I can make it, for my philosophy of life.[2]

It was, I think, a mistake for Powys to have attempted to
present his "untampered-with sensations" in the form of
philosophic discourse, which cannot really convey the kind of
sharply contradictory and complex experience that we have
seen to be characteristic of him. But by the time he had
discovered the all-inclusive form of the long prose romance,
a form that had "no system at all" and could reconcile all his
previous activities, the balance had already turned against
"Art".

*   *   *

The underlying values that make Powys's fiction, for all its
convincing density of texture, so uncomfortable, can best be
introduced by surveying his *Autobiography.*

The earlier chapters often recall *The Prelude* recording the
"growth of a poet's mind" through a series of intimate, solitary
experiences:

The greatest event in my life at Cambridge was a very quiet event . . . it was a sort of Vision on the Road to Damascus. I remember the exact spot where it took place. Not far from Trumpington Mill—somewhere in the umbrageous purlieus to the rear of the Fitzwilliam Museum —there stands an ancient wall; and as I drifted along . . . I observed, growing upon this wall, certain patches of grass and green moss and yellow stone-crop. Something about the look of these small growths, secluded there in a place seldom passed, and more seldom noticed, seized upon me and caught me up into a sort of Seventh Heaven.

A few seconds ago, before touching my pen . . . I felt all that I have ever felt, of the burden of this extraordinary moment . . . I would call it a *beyond sensation*, and it lies in my consciousness now, like a sunken ship, full of fathom-deep treasure . . . *that* impression, that vision of "Living Bread," that mysterious meeting point of animate with inanimate, had to do with some secret underlying world of rich magic and strange romance. In fact I actually regarded it as a prophetic idea of the sort of stories that I myself might come to write.[3]

It was exactly this kind of moment that was to form the foundation for Powys's doctrine, expounded first in the philosophic books like *In Defence of Sensuality* (where "sensuality" is only of his diffuse and private kind), and later in the romances, where the breaking through to some such insight is the recurrent and central experience. The sensation is not easy to pin down, but it often occurs in Powys together with the epithet "Saturnian": that is, it is a sensation which seems to hark back to a former age, now vanquished, when all nature was reconciled, an Age of Gold. Powys knew that one of the central questions that must form about his work was that of evaluating this kind of sensation. It could so easily seem too personal or too euphoric. But Powys never lost his belief that such moments were universally felt and were of enormous power and value.

> I know perfectly well that everybody born into the world has the feelings I am describing, is visited by these indescribable and apparently causeless transports. I am not in the least suggesting that I am peculiar in this. But why, in the Devil's name, then, do we go on making a cult of everything else except these?[4]

Powys's "cult" was, accordingly, a cult of these sensations, and it becomes clear as the *Autobiography* progresses that Powys's great aim in life is the day to day harvesting of such moments. The self of the *Autobiography*, the peripatetic lecturer whose life is vested not in any single person or activity but in the "diffusion" of his emotions across the face of the Earth, is the perfect embodiment of the way of life Powys is proposing.

> What I wanted was that kind of romantic struggle with things and people, things and people always yielding as I advanced, *but not too easily*, a struggle which takes place in an ideal region, hewn out of reality and constantly touching but never quite identified with reality, such as might be most conveniently described by the expression, *a Quest*.[5]

The development of the *Autobiography* is the steady intensification of this sense of Quest, with a correspondingly increasing frequency of those "transporting" moments that are the most real fruits of such a Quest. In the final chapter, entitled "There's a Mohawk in the Sky!", Powys is at last actually airborne and is able to see some pattern as he hovers above the "unrolled map" of his life.

Powys's emphasis on "Quest", rather than on any "real" goal, on diffusion, rather than on focus, results in some extraordinary omissions. As with Rousseau in his *Confessions*, an apparent candour and intimacy deceives us into accepting a thoroughly selective and manipulative record.

There is very little mention of himself as a creative artist, let alone any discussion of individual works (although *Wolf*

Solent and *A Glastonbury Romance* had already been written).
More enigmatically, it is an *Autobiography* "without women".
I believe that implicit in this mutilation of an experience that
had included marriage as well as frequent women friends was
the conviction that ordinary sexual activity was of small
consequence, set beside "Saturnian" pleasures, and that unless
sex eluded both the concrete and the domestic it would actually
get in the way of these more valuable sensations. In his *Autobiography* Powys is attempting (like Rousseau) to construct a
philosophic myth from the elements of his own life in order to
preach what he calls elsewhere "the Gospel of the Aquarian
Age".[6] He could perhaps *imagine* an equivalent sexuality; but
his own *experience* of women did not fit this Aquarian rôle.

*   *   *

In his fiction, however, Powys is able to accommodate
sexuality as a central theme, and the sexual attitudes of his
"Aquarian" characters are the most direct expression of their
attitude towards the world in general.

What is confirmed in the romances is that sexual relations
are indeed the "danger-area" for Powys's life-way. All the
major novels share a basic pattern, a cycle in which a life-illusion
is first betrayed, and then lost, and the chief agent of this
betrayal is invariably some kind of sexual involvement. The
sexual theme is especially clear in *Wolf Solent* and in *Maiden
Castle;* and here, as in all the romances, the broken world is at
the end of the book integrated anew by a "Saturnian" vision
of the kind already described.

Experientially, then, sexual failure is the precipitate of the
Saturnian vision; and this is, I think, part of the justification
of Powys's tendency to evade the commitment involved in
genital love. Freud, indeed, ascribes those Saturnian sensations
of "universal" love (so important also to Traherne and to
Wordsworth) to "infantile narcissism", and Powys never
presents a "diffusionist" without a full critique accompanying
him. But he simply believed the rewards of such a way redeemed
its inadequacies.

But there is also another, "Aquarian", justification. In these individuals the sense of yearning for love in the most spiritual-ised sense remains ever present; and there is always the possi-bility that from such a yearning may yet be born what Rimbaud calls "un nouveau corps amoreux", a new amorous body that can be held without any of the deadening or destructive effect of most partnership. In *Maiden Castle*, Powys suggests there is a basic confusion in genital "lust": there is the "lust" that is "excess of tenderness", but there is also "the "lust" in a lover's embrace that is alien to love, and indeed may be *the opposite of love*".[7] It is only by the consciousness of such a dissatisfaction that the human race might evolve to some new solution, or even some new mutation.

* * *

Wolf Solent is a man whose reality is almost entirely inward and archetypal. Wolf gives this inner life a corporeal identity, calling it his "mythology": it is the image of a plant that lives within him and is fed mostly by the "sensations" he collects on his long solitary walks (which may be seen as a ritualisation of his yearning).

At the outset, then, Wolf is a picaresque hero, armed with a walking stick, wandering into a world of mystery. To his detachment, each character presents himself as embodying some principle of Good or Evil. The obvious lack in Wolf's life, of any personal or sexual focus, is the whole source of its intensity.

Wolf then becomes entangled with two women, Gerda Torp and Christie Malakite, whose names signify clearly enough their polarisation. Gerda he sleeps with, and marries, but it is the far more elusive Christie who alone stirs his "mythology". Christie and Wolf can certainly share a great deal of one another's experience; but in a very harrowing episode, when their consummation seems already underway, Wolf discovers that he is paralysed. The obstruction is from the mythology itself tugging at him "like a chain fixed to a post",[8] refusing to be trapped in such a decisive act. Subsequently, under terrible pressure from various kinds of failure, Wolf's "mythology" withers and dies.

The novel ends with Wolf's being cuckolded; but, at the moment when he has apparently lost everything, he enters at sundown a field transformed by the horizontal rays of the sun into a "golden sea", releasing an enormous wash of pleasure and illumination.

> What he longed to do was to plunge his own hands into this Saturnian gold, and to pour it out, . . . All . . . all . . . all would reveal some unspeakable beauty, if only this Saturnian gold were sprinkled upon them![9]

It is in the light of this vision that he can accept the environment revealed by the loss of his mythology, a world less dramatic, but more complex, than the patterns he had imposed upon it. The loss of the mythology is revealed as the only road to a complete perception of the world.

* * *

The Powys novel commits suicide, so to speak, in order to gain more life. It is the suicide of Prospero, a renunciation of "rough magic", of the polarities, a deliverance from the "barren island". And yet the taste Powys leaves in the reader's mouth is so different from that finality with which *The Tempest* comes to a close. Powys's ending is in some way abject: the reader feels cheated, he had been led to expect a solution. Like the typical Powys-hero, like Dud No-man in *Maiden Castle*, the Powys novel is impotent.

I have no doubt that this cheating of the reader is conscious and deliberate. Significantly the novel written just before *Wolf Solent* was entitled *Ducdame:* the cry of barren, melancholy Jacques in *As You Like It* (Act II, Scene 5).

The scene opens with two stanzas of "Under the greenwood tree", treating of the simple life, to a chorus of "come hither". Jacques declares he has written a third verse; he sings:

> If it do come to pass
> That any man turn ass
> Leaving his wealth and ease
> A stubborn will to please
> Ducdame, ducdame, ducdame.

As he sings this outlandish word, the others begin to gather around him, peering at the paper from which he reads; he then walks out of their circle.

"What's that *ducdame*?" asks one of them; and Jacques explains:

" 'Tis a Greek invocation to call fools into a circle."

In such a way does Powys draw us into Glastonbury or Weymouth or Dorchester, and in just such a way, when we ask: "What's that *Grail*?" or "What's that *Mythology*?" we discover the author outside it all, mocking us, telling us it was but a trick, so he could draw us together; so he could show us that any such simple meaningful world was a fraud, and that all escape would end in the chaotic complexity of Nature.

*   *   *

This conception of Nature is the theme of *A Glastonbury Romance*. The whole book is set up as an equivalence to Nature's balance between affirmation and negation. The reader is obliged to share in Powys's uncertainty, because those beliefs and doubts that were Wolf's in the earlier novel are here presented as concrete realities. Parallel to the explicit suspense, as to whether those within Glastonbury will be vouchsafed the Grail, is the uncertainty of the reader, as to whether the Grail, or any of the other enormous metaphysical powers the author so coolly introduces, have any existence at all. Our belief is immediately challenged when we encounter in the book's opening sentence the personality of the First Cause. (How many potential readers must simply have put the book down at this point?) But let this work from our knowledge of the individual, and the role of these powers will become obvious.

The obvious successor to Wolf, in Glastonbury, is John Crow. Both are determinedly detached in their experience. Says Wolf:

> "I'll live in my own world to the end, . . . Nothing shall make˛me yield."[10]

Says John, in an image that is often repeated:

> "I'm a hard, round, glass ball, that is a mirror of everything, but that has a secret landscape of its own in the centre of it."[11]

They both conceive themselves as able to escape commitment to any of the conflicting beliefs that surround them, by a process they call "dissolving". Says John:

> "I'll steer my life in a religion of values totally unknown to any of them! . . . I'll become air, water, fire. I'll flow through their souls . . . I'll possess them without being possessed *by* them!"[12]

Their life method depends on a constant motion between their secret landscapes and their dissolving. As we hear of Wolf:

> What he lived in was not any compact, continuous sense of personal identity, but rather *a series of disembodied sensations*, some physical, some mental, in which his identity was absolutely merged and lost.[13]

Their metaphysic is equivalent to this; as Wolf sums it up:

> ". . . anything suggestive of metaphysical unity is distasteful to me. It must be that my world is essentially a manifold world, and my religion, if I have any, essentially polytheistic! And yet, in matters of good and evil . . . I'm what they'd call a dualist . . . Directly one comes to putting feelings into words, one is compelled to accept hopeless contradictions in the very depths of one's being!"[14]

Wolf's and John's is the individual metaphysic externalised in the *Romance*. So long as he retains the "hoplesss contradictions", Powys can introduce representatives of every conceivable shade of belief.[15] Man gods, sun, moon, or star gods, stone gods, a First Cause, Greek, Celtic, or Christian gods, even "invisible watchers"—

> As in that crystal orb—wise Merlin's feat,—
> The wondrous 'World of Glass,' wherein inisled
> All long'd-for things their beings did repeat[16]—

amid so many symbols of order, the suspicion is always present in the reader's mind that there is really "no system at all". But it is clear what the Grail represents in such a world. It is that "distasteful" metaphysical unity which would resolve these "hopeless contradictions".

The Grail is described frequently as a "morsel", a "piece", or a "fragment of the Absolute". When Evans asks himself of the Fisher Kings:

"For what did (they) . . . seek . . . when they fished?" he answers:

"the Amalgam of the Is and Is-not."[17]

The Grail retains this identity with the Fish throughout the book;[18] that is, with the symbol of the Messiah, but also the symbol of Leviathan, the World Fish, who underlies all existence, and whom the Messiah will catch and divide among the Faithful at the Apocalypse. The appearance of a Messiah, and the commencement of the Apocalypse, are the ultimate hopes and expectations in the *Romance*. But just as any "metaphysical unity" would have destroyed the experience of the Powys-hero, so the appearance of the Grail would end the book.

Powys therefore builds into it a chaotic and undermining element. Much follows from his stance of reproducing a Natural process, rather than "artistically" telling a story.[19] Squire Urquhart had explained to Wolf Solent:

> "What I want to do is to isolate the particular portion of
> the earth's surface called "Dorset"; as if it were possible
> to decipher there a palimpest of successive strata, one
> inscribed below another, of human impression. Such
> impressions are for ever being made and for ever being
> obliterated in the ebb and flow of events; and the chronicle
> of them should be continuous, not episodic."[20]

But the attraction of such an impressionism, for Urquhart as
perhaps for all others, is that it undermines any hierarchies of
experience. Urquhart's is clearly a mocking and ironic book, in
which equally, nothing or everything is holy.

The fundamental horizontality of the *Romance*—its length,
its multi-centredness, the concreteness of thoughts and feelings
within it—is a constant threat to any development of plot or
action. Powys's narrative method resembles in its evasiveness
the *modus vivendi* adopted by John and Wolf. On the brink of
any resolution, Powys contrives always to "dissolve", and the
reader finds himself transported into the "secret landscape" of
one after another of his characters. A chapter begins to resemble
a relay race—against the episodic, against meaning.

Powys likens human minds to "unknown planets, encountering and colliding",[21] and we may relate these planets to John's
"hard, round, glass ball" that is a mirror of everything, but
that contains within itself a secret world. The penetration of
that inner landscape by something from outside becomes the
pattern of all mystic experience.

Glastonbury's name signifies the form, or island, of glass,
and it is often felt as being enclosed beneath a roof of water;
while Geard talks in his final speech of "the dream-world
whose margins overlap ours". He explains of the Grail that,
"Out of this deeper dream there fell of old upon our Glastonbury Something that bewilders and troubles us unto this
day."[22] Similarly, Sam describes Christ as "the Thing Outside
breaking into our closed circle";[23] and both he and John
experience their vision as the entry of some sharp thing from
outside.

Powys's characters thus become at once a polarity to and an extension of his abstract themes. They afford a solidity, and a relief from his questioning, but eventually they reveal at their centre the identical problems. Dissolving from the cosmic to the human scale, and then to the microscopic of thoughts and feelings, the image remains the same. All this activity, this constant flight through space, exists only so that Powys can perform a kind of jugglery, can keep his hard, round, glass balls in the air, through a thousand pages.

The action covers exactly a year, the first part beginning on March 5th, the day of the Spring Solstice, and ending on Midsummer's day, on a rising note, with all kinds of promises still in the air. When the second half opens, it is already autumn: and the last three chapters enact a wintry betrayal of all the reader's hopes.

It has been seen that the revelation of the Grail is that which would end the book (because it would resolve the doubt on which it rests); but, when (in the chapter called "The Grail") Sam sees the Grail and tells people of his vision, there is no relief for us. Sam's vision is too personal an experience to have any public resonance. No-one is excited, much less do they disbelieve him.

The senseless melodrama of "The Iron Bar" continues this anticlimax. It mercilessly rids the book of nine of its characters, including the "Aquarian" lovers, the cousins John and Mary Crow, whose love is to some extent a flowering of the Grail. They had met in Norfolk, in the uncertain consciousness that they were reliving a childhood romance (uncertain because John suspects it was a boy, Tom Barter, and not Mary, who initiated him in the bottom of a boat). Barter is Mary's closest friend in Glastonbury.

What John and Mary really did was to make love like vicious children; and this was due to the fact that they were both very nervous and very excitable but not in the faintest degree tempted to the usual gestures of excessive human passion.[24]

John follows Mary to Glastonbury; far into the book we ascertain that she is still a virgin. The melodrama concerns the attempted murder of Sam; but in the event the victim is only Barter, the archetype of banality in the book. There is no satisfaction for the reader either in the crime, or in its result. John and Mary return to a normal domestic marriage in Norfolk's flat fields, carrying

> not only the corpse of Tom Barter but the corpse of their stillborn, never-returning opportunity of touching the Eternal in the enchanted soil where the Eternal once sank down into time![25]

In the final scene in a monstrous anticlimax every hope is overwhelmed, with Geard drowning in the midst of a flood. One feels the heart-sinking described (a great many pages earlier) as being felt by poor Barter:

> It was just a day dying out; of no more interest, of no more importance, than a bonfire of cabbage stalks, over which some one has thrown a bucket of water.[26]

There is however a last all important complexity. Just as the book dies on the day it was born, the day of the Spring Solstice, so, it is implied, will something be born from this wreck. For Geard could be said to have *drowned himself*,—recalling Merlin's vanishing into "Esplumeoir",

> some "Great Good Place," some mystic Fourth Dimension, or Nirvanic apotheosis, into which the magician deliberately sank, or rose; thus committing a sort of inspired suicide; a mysterious dying in order to live more fully.[27]

Moreover, Geard drowns in sight of the Tor, and we seem to understand that in his final moments he sees the hill metamorphosed to a swelling chalice, to the Grail itself . . . But the novel is already ended. The Duality that has dominated the book is already leaving Glastonbury Tor for some other "particular spot", and the revelation of her presence is only the prelude to her passing, and the book's ending. She

> moves through the generations from one twilight to another . . . until she finds the land that has called her and the people whose heart she alone can fill . . .

> For She whom the ancients named Cybele is in reality that beautiful and terrible Force by which the Lies of great creative Nature give birth to Truth that is to be . . .

> Thus she abides; her Towers forever rising, forever vanishing, Never or Always.[28]

*   *   *

Weymouth Sands is much briefer than *A Glastonbury Romance*, but it conveys far more convincingly the multi-centred and communal experience that the earlier book attempted. It is a world bound in a consciousness of romantic love, the kind of romantic love I have already called "Aquarian", whose watery essences find a marvellously literal projection in the actual landscape of beach and pier, island and causeway, saltmarsh and harbour and cliff, all the various forms water has brought into existence.

Of this love the archpriest is Sylvanus Cobbold, who preaches on Weymouth Esplanade, of whom we hear that:

> He was always trying to make clear to himself what he really was after in his dealings with women; but this seemed to be the evasive point in his days. He could not formulate it or define it. In fact he could not understand it. He only knew that he was driven more and more obstinately by some secret urge within him to do what, as he actually experienced it, he felt to be a gathering up of women's most secret responses to life; as if some half-crazed Faust had found the magic oracles of those Beings he called 'the Mothers' in the nerves and sensibilities of every ordinary young Gretchen he encountered.[29]

A succession of ordinary young Gretchens thus become his disciples and supply a half-comprehending audience for his mystical monologues (in which Powys parodies his own nature-mysticism). In his distant house on Portland, Sylvanus communes with the Absolute all through one night, holding to him, like Mephistopheles' key, the sleeping body of Marret Jones, the Punch and Judy girl who has followed him from the sands. Marret explains later,

> "We sleep together, you know, and he presses me to him, . . . but *he never does anything.* He never seems to want to, and I don't think he ever will."[30]

In one form or another, the use of unconsummated sexuality as the means of "breaking through" is common to most of Powys's central characters. Across all Powys's fiction, whether in Wolf's vision of gold "behind the pigsty", or Cordelia's vain vision in Carbonek, or Sam's vision of the Grail by the old post, we hear again and again the echo of Powys's experience at Cambridge. The intensity of yearning experienced by young girls, or in a one-sided passion; the solitary craving of the sadist; the sexual mortification of the religious ascetic: all these are shown as having their due rewards, and are to some degree equated, because in Powys the reward always takes the same form.

But the issue of responsibility is not avoided, and Sylvanus's kind of love, which catches up its objects in a game which they are not equipped to play, is shown in all its social imperfection. Marret leaves him in a fury at his essential selfishness; but while Sylvanus attempts to sleep away his disturbance, another resentful one steals in and clips off his moustaches, which were as important to his life-illusion as Wolf Solent's stick to his. Thus weakened, Sylvanus, like Samson, is led into captivity; he has to face society in the role of public nuisance, and, more seriously, corrupter of young girls; and he is confined in an asylum.

But however society may act against it, it is clear that the kind of love of which Sylvanus is a prophet is present *all over*

Weymouth. Every character shares in it, and every character is rewarded with some kind of vision.

On Weymouth Sands, on August Bank Holiday, on his lonely forty-seventh birthday, walks Magnus Muir, the stolid Latin tutor, who even in the act of mentally undressing and possibly raping his beloved, is yet paralysed by the purity of his ideal. Spread over an entire chapter, Magnus's vision is perhaps the greatest sustained achievement in all Powys's work, marvellously objectifying in the panorama of the beach, the conflict in the Latin tutor's mind, so steeped in Homer and in classical history, so wrapped in a vague "Saturnian" allusiveness, yet invaded, as it repeatedly is, by the "brazen, goatish, rammish cry" of the present, of Mr. Punch, with his alarming: "Judy! Judy! Judy! Judy!"

These sands have been the scene of much of Magnus's (and Powys's) childhood, and

> That difference . . . between the *dry* sand and the *wet* sand, which had remained in the memory of Magnus as a condensation of the divergent experiences of his life, heightened the way everything looked from the esplanade till it attained the symbolism of drama . . .

> There, above, on the *dry* sand, there were forever limning and dis-limning themselves groups and conclaves of a rich, mellow Rabelaisian mortality, eating, drinking, love-making, philosophising, full of racy quips, scandalous jibes, and every sort of earthy, care-forgetting ribaldry.

Yet below was the wet sand, of the children,

> imprinted by the "printless" feet, light, immortal, bare, of what might easily have been the purer spirits of an eternal classical childhood, happy and free, in some divine limbo of unassailable play-time.[31]

It is Magnus's ability to discover some deeper meaning that redeems the pathos of his experience. We are referred at one point[32] to the words from *Faust:*

"Alles vergangliche
Ist nur ein gleichnis."
"All appearance is but a symbol."

A little later, Magnus sees Sylvanus preaching on the beach to "a pair of the most uninteresting young women he had ever seen" (Sylvanus will be arrested that very day); and Magnus seats himself on the stern of a boat,

> not without noticing the boat's name, which was Calypso. Like a magic touch, through all his worries and obsessions, this classical word swept the mind of the teacher to the far-off realms he loved, and in a flash between that glittering bay, flecked with darting gulls, airy yachts, gaily loaded rowing-boats, and the vaporous cloud feathers of that halcyon sky, the tall figure of Sylvanus struck him as the eternal recurrence of some undying "gleichnis".

> . . . Magnus took not the smallest notice of what the man was saying, but he felt peaceful and happy as he sat on the Calypso's stern. All the fussiness, all the fretting life-worry of his usual expression left his face. The lines of his mouth grew formidable, almost majestic, his nostrils quivered like those of a proud horse.

> "Water and Sand," he thought, "are what I want. The inanimate, not flesh and blood. I am *really* happier at this minute, than I am with Curly!"[33]

Thus Magnus wanders along the beach, imagining himself for a moment as Teiresias among the "sad troops of the enfeebled Dead", or seeing in others the likeness of Belisarius, or of Marcus Aurelius and Faustina, and yet rising again and again, above any failure with Curly, to illumination:

> It sometimes happens that a contemplative person, whose head is full of contrary thought-currents, receives, in a quick, unexpected revelation, a view of the world as it exists when many separate, far-off moments of insight,

140

that have caught our landscape under a large and recon-
ciling light, melt and fuse themselves together.[34]

* * *

Maiden Castle marks the uncomfortable transition from the
novels written with the premise of "modern life" as a framework
to those in which archetypal emotions are presented within an
historical setting.[35] Against the banal domestic scene of modern
Dorchester are set a procession of characters with bizarre
archetypal names, names that breed an unreality and disturbance of their own. The central character we have to accept by
the name he gives himself, Dud No-man, a reference to his own
impotence, as well as to the uncertainty of his fathering. Dud
eventually discovers his father (though it does not cure his
ailment) in a local man, named Uryen Quirm. Next door to
the Quirms live the Platonist Teucer Wye and his daughter
Thuella.

Between Dud No-man and Thuella Wye, he a writer, she a
painter, he impotent, she lesbian, takes place the most uncom-
promised of all Powys's sexual encounters, an extended,
"purely cerebral" love-making, above a "scummy pond".

> The ungodly pleasure the girl was giving him began
> actually to take the shape of this wavering edge between
> greenness and blackness; and this congruity went so
> deep that the satisfaction of his mental desire seemed to
> him then like a delirious worm feeding upon the vegetation-
> roots of the world, a worm rising up from that black
> water—that was the primal gulf of space—to feed forever
> upon celestial duck-weed![36]

These pages are, however, no more than a fleeting episode
in a book whose characters for the most part supply a merciless
critique of the Powysian techniques for living, of which Dud
No-man is a particularly pathetic representative. Dud conceives
himself as "a good, quiet man, working at (his) book, going on
(his) walks, enjoying (his) sensations, being kind to the girl (he)
rescued."[37] The reader is alerted to the presence in Dorchester
of many old men and babies, "absolutely harmless and abso-

lutely selfish". Dud is at one point set on by all the main characters and is told that minds like his are inward-turned" and "maggotty, like cheeses." His cyclic experience is all too transparent: "It's round and round with you, isn't it?" And when, having lost his girl, Dud still works his usual trick of finding her in the landscape-sensations of one of his walks, he has to realise that;

> It meant nothing to her that there was in this a proof of the intensity of his feeling, a proof of its etherealized sensuality, of its all-pervasiveness and absorbing diffusion.[38]

Dud's father, Uryen, who believes himself to be a reincarnation of Brân, the Crow, the Welsh equivalent of Cronos or Saturn, and Maiden Castle to be the ruin of some lost Saturnian city, lives by an even more precarious method. He attempts to use as *his* method of "breaking through", the power of *another person's* yearning for yet another (in this case, the yearning of Thuella for Dud's girl). *Faust* is again recalled as "frustrated love" is identified with the "key" Mephistopheles gives Faust to reach "the Mothers".[39] The ending is as bleak as in any of Powys's works, with Uryen dead, and Dud alone, as the two girls run off together to America.

* * *

In growing old (and perhaps in moving to Wales), the focus of Powys's imaginative energy gradually passed from a condition of yearning, within our world, to the projection of a substantial "Saturnian" reality, excluding our world altogether. *Porius* for instance, is conceived largely in terms of those "patches of grass and green moss and yellow stone-crop", on that Cambridge wall; and the action of the book unfolds in vague dream-like tableaux of "rich magic and romance". The archetypal dreams of mankind are, in the final works, re-enacted in a vision of the distant past, which is clearly intended also to suggest a vision of the future.

Both the central figures of the historical romances are Saturnian heroes. Owen Glendower, making his rebellion as the last king of the ancient Welsh, and Merlin (in *Porius*), counsellor to Arthur, as the last Emperor of the Romano-Britons, both are fighting for an age which is already past, for a cause which is already lost. In the last chapter of *Porius*, Merlin is concretely shown to be Cronos himself, in some Eternal Recurrence, "forever plotting a second Age of Gold".

These later Saturnian quests take place in a world where there is no longer much doubt or modesty about Saturnian values. Both Merlin and Owen are able to escape, even after apparent failure, into some kind of inner, or other, dimension; and it is somehow felt in this Saturnian Wales, that failure in the outer world is almost an achievement.

> Over your body . . . our people will pass to their triumph; but it will be a triumph in the House of Saturn, not in the House of Mars.[40]

Wales itself is identified with this sly Saturnian victory:

> Its past is its future, for it lives by memories and in advance it recedes. The greatest of its heroes have no graves, for they will come again. Indeed they have not died; they have only disappeared.[41]

Wales is said to live by a "Mythology of escape":

> Other races love and hate, conquer and are conquered. This race avoids and evades, pursues and is pursued. Its soul is forever making a double flight. It flies into a circuitous *Inward*. It retreats into a circuitous *Outward*.[42]

But in both these books, the absence of a concrete, social context, of the matrix provided in each of the earlier books by the microcosms of small West Country forms, makes for a slackening of tension. This everyday reality had provided a kind of critical chorus against which Powys's philosophic voice could be measured. Without such criticism, Saturnian values begin to be too obviously delusory.

In *Porius*, for instance, Prince Porius appears very much in the line of introverted and sexually indecisive heroes; but we are told that he has within him giant's blood. One of the climaxes of the book is Porius's sudden encounter with the two last aboriginal giants of Wales, a beautiful giantess and her father. In the subsequent scenes, all Porius's indecisiveness is forgotten, he behaves like a hero; it is made explicit that in finding a giantess he has found his true dimension. Are we then to reach this meaning back, through Dud No-man, to Wolf Solent: that if only they had found something large enough they would have become fully potent and responsible beings? The reader who has followed this survey thus far will see that it cannot be so; the Saturnian stance, as practised in any real context, cannot allow of any such satisfaction. Nothing but "the Whole" will serve, and no giantess will be large enough.

Despite occasional suggestions of "oracular wisdom" in some of the later books, Powys is really presenting only a method for living, not a system of values. As Christie explains to Wolf:

> "I regard each philosophy, not as the "truth", but just as a particular country, in which I can go about".[43]

It was possible for Powys to regard himself as a philosopher, and yet to take as his central tenet the avoidance of any focused commitment to belief, because he viewed both Plato and Nietzsche as fellow-travellers in uncertainty. Dud observes of Plato:

> "I take him as an absolute sceptic, so uncertain about everything that he could afford to turn God and Immortality into poetry, and the Soul and Love into fairy-tales."[44]

While Powys in a letter summarises Nietzsche's stance:
There is no God. There is Nothing. Therefore fight![45]

Plato and Nietzsche thus provided a kind of tradition for Powys. They work within essentially literary forms, constructing philosophic myths around the figures of Socrates and Zarathustra, in order to project their own particular philosophic visions. Both combine a romantic idealism with a profound irony; and they both convey a cyclic experience in which "pain and pleasure grow on the same tree", so that experience goes "beyond good and evil". Socrates is proclaimed the wisest of men by

144

Apollo's oracle, only because he knows that he does not know. Plato and Nietzsche are both, above all, intent on exhorting the reader to a particular method for living, the Socratic, or the Zarathustran, and the question of any ultimate meaning is bypassed, or else simply overlaid with words that form themselves into a world, or a rhythm, an artistic equivalence to experience.

*   *   *

I have used the word "romance" throughout this survey, because Powys's fiction does not really respond to most of the expectations a reader might bring to a novel. The books that were always most in Powys's mind were what are sometimes called "Worldbooks", works which attempt to convey a total picture of life; for example: Cervantes' *Don Quixote;* Rabelais' *Gargantua; The Anatomy of Melancholy; Tristram Shandy;* Wordsworth's *The Prelude;* Nietzsche's *Zarathustra;* Ibsen's *Peer Gynt;* Goethe's *Faust.* Each of these books defines its own eccentric form and expectations.

If Powys deserves to join that company, it is because one discovers in his works a particular apprehension of life, that is not to be found elsewhere, and yet seems so universal in its application that once seen, it has to be included. He is one of those fortunate artists who find themselves in possession of an authentic originality, that is, of access to a dimension that had always been present in experience, but that was waiting to be isolated and embodied.

Powys's achievement is to have projected his method for living as a genuine alternative. The quest for which a Saturnian is striving leaves on either side many other great paths, and has all the limitations of his temperament. Yet, like Prince Porius at the end of that book, Powys could say at the end of his life, "There are many gods; and I have served a great one." The loose ends of the romances are linked by that unifying presence, who in *A Glastonbury Romance* is called "Cybele", and is elsewhere "Saturn". Powys's most grateful readers will always be those people "whose heart she alone can fill". It is Saturn's traditionally contrasting potentialities[46] that are ingredients of Powys's vision: his tenderness matched by such a shrewdness of human observation as to be indiscreet and almost malevolent, his unusually concrete descriptions overlaid with the sense of the unfinished and an unpredictable creation, his pathos so shot through with humour—and all these elements as contributing to, and included within, the vast spiritual cycle that has to be accomplished by those born beneath Saturn's enormous orbit.

This cycle does not include everything. Only by vision, never by reason, can the Saturnian hope to gain a totality of meaning. At the end of each of Powys's romances the archetypal world has been broken and the "real" world has been accepted; but accepted essentially in the golden reconciliating light of the archetypes, and with their lost beauty as the ultimate to which he must hope to penetrate again.

NOTES

1 Louis Marlow (Wilkinson), *Welsh Ambassadors*, 1936, p. 123.
2 *Autobiography*, (1934), 1967, p. 641.
3 *Ibid.*, p. 199.
4 *Ibid.*, p. 194.
5 *Ibid.*, p. 66.
6 *Rabelais*, 1948 (a book dedicated to Rousseau), p. 320.
7 *Maiden Castle*, 1937, p. 121; 1966, p. 133.
8 *Wolf Solent*, 1929, p. 465; 1961, p. 442.
9 *Ibid.*, p. 642; pp. 612–613.
10 *Ibid.*, p. 181; p. 169.
11 *A Glastonbury Romance*, 1933, p. 381; 1955, p. 370–371.
12 *Ibid.*, p. 382; p. 371.
13 *Wolf Solent*, 1929, p. 225; 1961, p. 211.
14 *Ibid.*, p. 310; p. 294.
15 See *Weymouth Sands*, 1963, pp. 98 and 158, for Richard Gaul's "Philosophy of Representation".
16 S. T. Coleridge, "The Pang More Sharp Than All" (*Complete Poetical Works*, ed. E. H. Coleridge, Oxford, 1912, Vol. I, p. 458).
17 *A Glastonbury Romance*, 1933, pp. 771–772; 1955, p. 740.
18 Sam sees a fish inside the chalice in his vision of the Grail.
19 *A Glastonbury Romance*, 1933, p. 694; 1955, p. 666.
20 *Wolf Solent*, 1929, p. 41; 1961, p. 33.
21 *A Glastonbury Romance*, 1933, p. 407; 1955, p. 395.
22 *Ibid.*, p. 1137; p. 1085.
23 *Ibid.*, p. 265; p. 260.

[24] *Ibid.*, p. 12; p. 70.

[25] *Ibid.*, p. 1113; p. 1063.

[26] *Ibid.*, p. 275; p. 270.

[27] *Ibid.*, p. 169; p. 179.

[28] *Ibid.*, pp. 1172–1174; 1955, pp. 1118–1120.

[29] *Weymouth Sands* (1934), 1963, p. 271.

[30] *Ibid.*, p. 334.

[31] *Ibid.*, p. 456–457.

[32] *Ibid.*, p. 477.

[33] *Ibid.*, pp. 477–479.

[34] *Ibid.*, p. 467.

[35] Malcolm Elwin, in a letter, commenting on this observation in my essay, has pointed to the biographical background to *Maiden Castle*, "the complement to (J. C. P.'s) Autobiography 'without women'", saying there was not "any 'transition' between his modern and his historical novels. He had suffered from libel threats with *Glastonbury and Weymouth Sands* (which had to be published in England as *Jobber Skald*), and having satirically called the hero of *Maiden Castle* Dud No-man because no bloody fool was likely to come forward and identify himself with a character so named, he reverted to historical settings (so Phyllis Playter has told me) to avoid risks of libel."

[36] *Maiden Castle*, 1937, p. 199; 1966, p. 211.

[37] *Ibid.*, p. 374; p. 386.

[38] *Ibid.*, p. 473; p. 486.

[39] *Ibid.*, p. 482; p. 495.

[40] *Owen Glendower*, 1942, p. 823.

[41] *Ibid.*, p. 890.

[42] *Ibid.*, p. 889.

[43] *Wolf Solent*, 1929, p. 88; 1961, pp. 78–79.

[44] *Maiden Castle*, 1937, p. 130; 1966, p. 143.

[45] *The Letters of John Cowper Powys to Louis Wilkinson*, 1958, p. 282.

[46] See R. Klibansky, E. Panofsky and F. Saxl, *Saturn and Melancholy*, 1964.

VIII
STYLE AND THE MAN

Bernard Jones

I

The discussion of style has become an old fashioned kind of occupation and a writer nowadays who knocks on a publisher's door with a typescript entitled *Style*, or *The Problem of Style* under his arm should not expect to be asked to step inside. John Cowper Powys, however, was in some ways an old fashioned kind of writer and it may be that an old fashioned way of looking at what he wrote, a way that is in keeping with some of the ideas of literary appreciation which held the field during the first half of his life, would not be a waste of time.

The stumbling blocks are obvious. Powys ambled through a five hundred page romance as comfortably as through an evening walk. In *A Glastonbury Romance* there are over a thousand pages and there are over nine hundred in *Owen Glendower*. Besides, the long nineteenth century novels of which Powys's romances are an aftermath did not lend themselves easily to discussion in terms of style. They have been appreciated in many ways and often with much sensitivity but it was not until the middle of the twentieth century that careful critical attention was paid to, for example, Dickens's prose. In Powys's early life the comments on its style were, apart from a few pages which were written by Gissing after Powys had already become a lecturer, mostly Chestertonian. Dicken's prose, like that of Kipling and certain other novelists, has a texture which can yield itself to the disciplines of practical criticism. But on the whole, in Powys's youth long novels were seldom read for the sake of the style of their prose. The novelists were probably thankful for such luck for, as Powys's brother Theodore wrote in the nineteenthirties,

> You might go on improving a short story for a year, or a novel for a life-time, and there would still be ample room for improvement, whereas in poetry it is just possible, now and then, to 'capture with the magic hand of chance' a perfect phrase, a line that is matchless for its purpose beyond all hope of improvement. I could imagine happiness in that. But the prose writer, even if he experiences these

flashes of pure inspiration, cannot possibly sustain them throughout a four thousand word story, much less throughout a novel.[1]

After reading the witness of so skilled a hand as Theodore Powys it must seem no more than folly to embark on a discussion of style in his brother's romances. Moreover Powys himself wrote:

> comparing my own way of expressing myself with that of both my brothers, Theodore and Llewelyn, I would say unhesitatingly that though plenty of my *thoughts* are my own and not a few of my *images*, this far rarer quality, which is the essence of what we call *style*, has been denied me,[2]

and it might seem best to give up the game.

None the less, Powys always believed that the style is the man. "The style[s] of all writers, worth as we say their salt," he wrote in the 1953 preface to *A Glastonbury Romance*, "differ basically, fundamentally, inherently from one another." He knew that sensitive readers can recognize the distinctive styles of Theodore and Llewelyn. Each wrote a prose that was fitted to achieve the ends which he had set himself. Powys also knew that in his romances he had been able to do some things which Theodore and Llewelyn had never wanted to do. He seems however—out of kind heartedness perhaps—to have overlooked the possibility that a prose which struck a note of personal distinction such as is sounded in the prose of his brothers might have been not only no help to him in the writing of the kind of romance that he wanted to write but even a hindrance.

There are, of course, many people who knew that Powys spoke with easy distinction and in his miscellaneous writings the personal note can be heard often enough. But as he wrote "from my own point of view the fiction I have written is worth much more than my lay-sermons,"[3] concentration on the prose of his romances is not unfair, even if it means leaving out of the reckoning his autobiographical writings also. Nor can the prose in all of the romances be looked at, for it is not easy to represent by brief quotations. Its Schubertian, or Brucknerian, heavenly length, indeed, leads friends to talk of Powys as one of the great sprawlers of literature, and they speak happily of his rascally old style. However, there will always be some readers who find it hard to believe that length is heavenly and for them these amused terms, which are affectionate and endearing for those who know Powys, may seem either to beg questions or to be merely a defensive smoke screen.

In fact the prose of the romances needs no such screening and repays careful reading. Here is the beginning of *Wood and Stone*, which was published in 1915:

> Midway between Glastonbury and Bridport, at the point where the eastern plains of Somersetshire merge into the western valleys of Dorsetshire, stands a prominent and noticeable hill; a hill resembling the figure of a crouching lion.

> East of the hill, nestling at the base of a cone-shaped eminence overgrown with trees and topped by a thin Thyrsus-like tower, lies the village of Nevilton.

> Were it not for the neighbourhood of the more massive promontory this conical protuberance would itself have stood out as an emphatic landmark; but Leo's Hill detracts from its emphasis, as it detracts from the emphasis of all other deviations from the sea-level between Yeoborough and the foot of the Quantocks.

The qualities which are to be found in these early paragraphs of Powys's fiction were to alter little over a span of more than fifty years. The paragraphing is a little uncertain—Powys was sometimes happy to leave such things to his publishers and printers. By the fashions of the second half of the twentieth century the prose is a little ponderous. Its portentousness, however, is in keeping with the romancer's purpose. The pace is slow—slow enough to enable the writer to reach out for any detail that might enrich his meaning. The book was written when a war was raging and when Powys had become an exile and the setting is his boyhood world in the country around

Montacute. The description of this setting calls out for comparison with Hardy, to whom the book was dedicated, and its first chapter should be looked at as a whole and compared with the opening chapter of *The Return of the Native*. Powys caught exactly the cadence of that well known tract of carefully wrought prose. Leo's Hill, he wrote, "like a couchant desert-lion . . . overlooked its prey; and would continue to do so, as long as the planet lasted." A further passage from the first chapter of Powys's romance confirms the point:

It is in the Nevilton churchyard, when a new grave is being dug, that this sinister peculiarity of the earth-floor is especially noticeable. The sight of those raw, rough heaps of yellow clay, tossed out upon grass and flowers, is enough to make the living shrink back in terror from the oblong hole into which they have consigned the dead. All human cemeteries smell, like the hands of the Shakespearean king, of forlorn mortality; but such mortality seems more palpably, more oppressively emphasized among the graves of Nevilton than in other repositories of the dead. To be buried in many a burying ground one knows, would be no more than a negative terror; no more than to be deprived, as Homer puts it, of the sweet privilege of the blessed air. But to be buried in Nevilton clay has a positive element in its dreadfulness. It is not so much to be buried, as to be sucked in, drawn down, devoured, absorbed. Never in any place does the peculiar congruity between the yellowness of the local clay and the yellowness of the local stone show so luridly as among these patient hillocks.

The tombstones here do not relieve the pressure of fate by appealing, in marble whiteness, away from the anthropophagus earth, to the free clouds of heaven. They are of the earth, and they conspire with the earth. They yearn to the soil, and the soil yearns to them. They weigh down upon the poor relics consigned to their care, in a hideous partnership with the clay that is working its will upon them.[4]

One would not look for such prose from Wells, or Bennett, or Galsworthy. In cadence it is nearer to some of the prose of Phillpotts. Powys, however, always worked within a frankly literary context. He often said that he was a bookish man and such allusions as those to Homer and Shakespeare in the last passage can be found almost anywhere in his work. As a twentieth century romancer—it is easy to overlook the fact that he must be one of the earliest to bring what are euphemistically called 'industrial disputes' into his stories—Powys carries on the trade of Homer and Shakespeare without expecting his readers to think him clever on the strength of his wide acquaintance among fellow makers. The concern with clay hints at a general paradox of relativity in Powys's work. Clay is one of the ultimate inanimate realities that experience comes up against, and yet a certain kind of life has been given to it. Likewise the hill has been imaged as a crouching lion.

The beginnings of the romances are not always as good as the first chapter of *Wood and Stone*. *Wolf Solent* moves into the action of the story more quickly, but the actual writing is comparatively undistinguished and promises less than that fine novel performs. As in *A Glastonbury Romance* Powys used the device of a railway journey, which allowed him wide scope for evoking a physical and imaginative context. A variant of this device was used at the beginning of *Weymouth Sands*. Here the outward happening is the arrival and tying up of the Cherbourg packet. The leisurely approach of the steamer allows the writer to interrupt the description with episodes which introduce characters. The whole of the opening chapter, however, is conveyed as the subjective narrative of the down at heel teacher of Latin, Magnus Muir:

> The vessel he was keeping his eye upon blew a prolonged whistle at this moment. Magnus could never hear that particular sound without a certain gathering together of his mind to meet a crisis, as if some angel of Judgment were blowing a trumpet.
>
> On this occasion that sudden whistle of the Cherbourg steamer produced a very queer impression on his mind. It

was an impression as if the whole of Weymouth had suddenly become an insubstantial vapour suspended in space. All the particular aspects of the place known to him so well, the spire of St. John's Church, the rounded stucco-façade of Number One Brunswick Terrace and of Number One St. Mary's Street, the Jubilee Clock, the Nothe, the statue of George the Third, seemed to emerge gigantically from a mass of vapourous unreality. This hallucination, or whatever it was, lasted a very short time. A second blowing of the vessel's whistle dissipated it completely; but not before it had been borne in upon him that if he really was such a coward he would have to sink back upon some philosophy that included and completely allowed for such grotesque treacheries . . .

Still that steamer remained motionless between the pierhead and the Weymouth breakwater! What was the matter with it? It was surely long past the time when Mrs. Cobbold told him it would dock. It didn't need a tug, did it? These Channel Isle steamers always came in on their own steam. He had seen them come in in that way all his life. Well, he must be stirring. He must find some shelter where he could wait, if the ship stayed out there.[5]

Apart from some jerkiness, which is in keeping with the occasional impatience of the thinker, the prose moves with easy strides which hardly differ from those of *Wood and Stone*. The seeming solidity and lastingness of external objects is matched against the fleetingness of impressions upon the mind which sometimes fall short even of full articulateness.

There is a likeness of texture in the writing at the beginning of *Maiden Castle:*

The morning of All Souls, November the second, opened in a not very remote year of Our Lord, for the town of Dorchester with a sunrise out of a clear sky.

But such complete freedom from clouds at that early hour was not a sign of a day without rain. As the sun rose over the roof of Fordington Church experts in the weather predicted at once what sort of day it was to be. It was to be what is called a "pet" day, that is to say a day that must quickly be made the most of, a pettish day, a petulant day, a day prepared to fall into a "pet" the moment any atmospheric event occurred that threatened the obscuring of its glory.

The old thoroughfare called High East Street descending the incline from the centre of the town to the London Road bestirred itself slowly as befitted the dignity of its long history, to meet this beautiful but treacherous morning. One by one the great chimneys above the old brick roofs, many of them fronted with massive slabs of stone, sent forth their smoke. One by one the prentice-boys appeared, opening the shop-doors and sweeping the pavement. Milk-carts made their pleasant clatter; while the sound of the hoofs of the horses that drew these reassuring equipages, echoing between the walls, seemed to gather the centuries together with a familiar continuity of unbroken tradition that was not disturbed when an occasional bus or car came down the street.

The homely sense of a recurrent satisfaction of old human necessities found another expression in the pleasant chiming of the clock in the tower of the Corn Exchange situated at the head of the street, a chiming that seemed in its perennial cheerfulness to purge the very mystery of Time of its tragic burden and divide the hours to the tune of some secret knowledge of its own that "good hope," in spite of all evidence to the contrary, still abode "at the bottom."[6]

More than twenty years after the writing of *Wood and Stone* the prose is almost unchanged and the same point could be made time after time simply by quoting further passages. In *Maiden Castle*, for instance, one could refer to the accounts of Dud's ritual with the kettle, of the house called Glymes, of the outing to Maiden Castle on midsummer's eve, of the statue of Hardy, of Wizzie's response to the statue of Barnes:

. . . she happened to glance through the iron rails of the church at the statue of William Barnes.

She had often passed this statue before, but never till this moment had its mellow charm and the majestic benignity of its expression struck her as they did now. Wizzie's aesthetic taste was totally undeveloped but there was in this venerable old poet's look something beyond all "art," an effluence of peace, a spirit of benediction, a promise of comfort and of healing, that seemed to rise up in the centre of Dorchester life as if it sprang from some level of goodness in the deep earth below the town's oldest foundations.

So deeply did the mystical benignity of this hushed figure affect her that as she stood there, frowning and pondering, with that weird wrapped-up object in her gloved hands, for one passing second she actually forgot everything in a rush of melting sympathy for all the people in her confused life.

But the moment vanished as quickly as it came, vanished indeed in a sudden dread of encountering Nance, and of having her as a companion all the way to Glymes; and under the pressure of this fear, which quickly became something like a panic, she fled into North Square, hurried past the prison gate, and ran down the hill to the river-path at the bottom.

All the way to Hangman's Cottage, as she went along munching her chocolate, the image of that old poet by the church accompanied her, soothing her troubled mind. Everything she had come to like best in Dorchester seemed to be expressed in that calm figure.[7]

The bringing together of such passages shows that Powys has one of the most coveted gifts that any romancer or novelist could desire—a way of writing that moves in an unbroken flow, that informs and qualifies as it goes along, and that always takes the mind forward. Dickens had this gift—or blessing, as a novelist might wish to call it—in a highly developed form, and so too had Kipling. Gissing, whose prose often moves as slowly as Powys's, also had it. The knack of making a narrative run smoothly from beginning to end seems to be such a basic requirement that it might be thought that anyone who did not have it must be disqualified from the ranks of the leading novelists. Yet neither Scott nor Hardy can always ensure that a story will move forward in an evenly flowing progress. Both, of course, have qualities which persuade their readers to follow what they write in spite of unevennesses. But many fine novelists must envy Powys his gift.

It might be thought, however, that the deliberateness of movement in Powys's prose, to which attention is perhaps drawn unfairly when one given a series of quotations, would lead to some sameness of impression. But that the prose is not wanting in suppleness can easily be shewn. The drunken brawl at the Three Peewits in *Wolf Solent*, for instance, is conveyed with all the unpleasantness of such an incident. Local wags have been bandying scandalous gossip about the bar and Wolf is eager to get to the bottom of it:

> "I don't know whose feelings you are so careful of, Mr. Manley," he said. "But since I happen to be myself one of these unfortunate 'educated' people, and since Mr. Solent, my father, came to grief in this neighbourhood, I should be very glad indeed to hear anything else you may be anxious to tell us."

> His voice, heard now by the whole company for the first time, had a disquieting tone; and everyone was silent. But Jason Otter rose to his feet, and, in the midst of that silence and under the startled attention of all eyes in the room, walked with short quick steps across the floor till he came close up to Farmer Manley, who was leaning his back against the little counter and who had his hands in his pockets; and there he stopped, facing him. No one but Wolf could see the expression on his countenance; and there were all kinds of different versions afterwards as

to what actually happened. But what Wolf himself knew was that the excited man was no longer under the restraint of his natural timidity.

His own intelligence was so clairvoyantly aroused at that moment that he could recall later every flicker of the conflicting impulses that shot through him. The one that dominated the rest was a categorical certainty that some immediate drastic action was necessary. What he did was to take Jason by the shoulders and fling him backwards into an old beer-stained chair that stood unoccupied against the neighbouring wall. In the violence of this action an earthenware jug of water—and Wolf had time to notice the mellow varnish of its surface—fell with a crash upon the floor. There was a hush now throughout the room, and most of the company leaned excitedly forward. Jason himself, huddled limply in a great wooden chair, turned his devastated white face and lamentable eyes full upon his aggressor.

"I . . . I . . . I didn't mean . . ." he gasped.

"It's all right, Solent," whispered Darnley, accepting a chair by Jason's side, which its owner willingly vacated. "You couldn't have done anything else."

"I don't know about that, Otter," Wolf whispered back. "I expect we're all a little fuddled. Sit down, won't you, and when he's rested we'll clear out, eh? I've had enough of this."

All the patrons of the private bar were gathered now in little groups about the room; and before long, with sly inquisitive glances and many secretive nudges and nods, the bulk of the company drifted out, leaving the room nearly empty . . .

Half an hour later they were all four making their way past the last houses of Blacksod. Darnley and Jason were walking in front; Wolf and T. E. Valley about six paces to the rear. They were all silent, as if the contrast between the noisy scene they had just left and the hushed quietness of the way were a rebuke to their souls.[8]

From Chaucer's time onwards English literature has been rich in tavern scenes which have usually been the occasion of mirth even among water drinkers. In *Wolf Solent* the writing conveys the experience itself—unadorned, naked, ugly. And yet there is no disturbance of the decorum of the prose. There is hardly a shift in the writing when in the same romance Powys conveys the ethereal quality of Gerda's whistling of the blackbird's song:

> Over the turf-ramparts of Poll's camp it swelled and sank, that wistful, immortal strain. Away down the grassy slopes it floated forth upon the March wind. No conceivable sky but one of that particular greyness could have formed the right kind of roof for the utterance of this sound. Wolf cared nothing that the whistler kept her face turned aside as she whistled. He gave himself up so completely to the voice that the girl Gerda became no more than a voice herself. At length it did really cease, and silence seemed to fall down upon that place like large grey feathers from some inaccessible height.
>
> Both the man and the girl remained absolutley motionless for a while.[9]

Such music floats back through Wordsworth and Shakespeare to the beginning of time. And this prose, which can be moulded to convey the crude or the ethereal, is no less effective for conveying different kinds of comedy. The sharp witticism or epigram would often be out of keeping with its pace, although there are good jokes sometimes. One such, which can be found in a scene in *Maiden Castle*, recalls Hardy's story about the painters of ecclesiastical texts who forgot to put the '*nots*' into the Ten Commandments. Dud No-man walks to the cemetery to see the grave of his wife and reads on the tomb stone: " 'Greater Love Hath No Man Than This'." But in the romances Powys's sense of comedy and irony does not often express itself in such verbal tricks. One should rather seek it in, for instance, some of the elaborately set scenes of *Weymouth Sands:*

> Had a wayfaring philosopher—if such persons still exist—rambling speculatively through Weymouth and Portland, and having just beheld the dense crowds assembled for the Cattistock wedding filling all the space in front of Trinity Church and even blocking up the Harbour-Bridge, looked casually down that path through the bushes and caught sight of this figure at the back-door, he might have said to himself:
>
> "What a peaceful time that girl in that red shawl *is* having! *She* isn't thinking about any mortal thing but 'the pleasure which there is in life itself'!"[10]

The account of the preparations for the wedding is varied by the inclusion of passages of dialogue and episodes which move forward other parts of the plot. The crowd, we are told,

> was packed so close that when once anyone was jammed into a particular vantage-ground it could only be by a violent struggle that freedom was obtained.
>
> The gipsy soon gathered from the neighbours that all the important people, except the bridegroom were already in Church. The bride had gone in, they learned, a few minutes before they appeared. In fact they could see from where they stood the helmets of the policemen who had cleared a path for her conveyance. Never, they learned, in all the history of the Two Boroughs had so many notables come together. Not another soul, they were told, could possibly get into the church.[11]

Again the coming wedding is left to build itself up in the reader's mind while the narrative echoes the irreverent gossip of the crowd and takes in passages of reflection:

> Presently there was a tremendous upheaval of the crowd and great disturbing currents swept it backwards and forwards. It became increasingly difficult to obey the gipsy's mandate, for his neighbours were flung against

him by *their* neighbours, and the whole space between Bridge and Church soon became a seething arena of anger, scurrility and indignant panic.

But the near approach of a light, open touring car that had caused all this confusion helped in a measure to allay it. The police constables on foot had now been reinforced by several more on horseback and it was by the aid of these that the machine drew up at the foot of the Church-steps . . . Simultaneously with its stopping, one of the policemen threw open its door and a man holding a silk hat was observed descending . . . When, however, the man with the silk hat paused before ascending the Church steps and began to converse with Mr. Muir and the lady with the roses, there ran through the crowd that angry murmur of disappointed expectation which is often the precursor of reckless, wild and dangerous movements. The man with the silk hat, who had been talking earnestly and rapidly to the lady in grey, now swung round and stood up very straight and very slender and handsome.

"Sippy Ballard," cried one rude humorist in a loud voice, "Why don't 'ee take thee uncle's pleäce, Sippy?"

But a much more official voice, although a much feebler voice, now made itself heard.

"Ladies and Gentlemen," it said, "the Town Clerk has something to announce."

It was then that Mr. S. P. Ballard rose splendidly to what everybody later admitted was a very awkward situation.

"Friends of the Two Boroughs," he said, "who have come to do honour to our distinguished—to *my* distinguished uncle"—he was felt at this point to indulge in a very artless and very charming hesitation—"you will all be very sorry to learn that Mr. Cattistock's wedding has—has been—indefinitely postponed—owing to—owing to—"

> But by what subterfuge, by what diplomatic euphemism, this youthful Talleyrand explained the non-appearance of his master was totally swallowed up in the clamour and hullabaloo raised by the grosser elements of the crowd . . .[12]

The relentless moving forward to something which does not happen is conducted without a slip of the face. Equally impressive and quite frightening is the sensation of mob violence. Chaos comes to town and is only just prevented from breaking loose.

Powys goes on to convey the agitation caused by the day's events in the "Servants' Hall" of Cattistock's house. The comic malignity of the old witches who come together in this scene over their kettles and under the influence of Cattistock's sherry is achieved by means which include echoes of the Bible and Prayer Book, local sayings, and a chime of Peacockian song. Some of the reasoning is unanswerable:

> "Don't 'ee mind, Lizzie dear," cried Mrs. Witchit. " 'Tis they Wiltshire ways, that's what it be! Mr. Witchit 'isself, though I'm not the one to say it, were born on Sarum Plain. 'Tis they east winds there, I reckon. 'Tis the terrible thin earth there that makes these harsh voices and these bitter tongues!"[13]

But the Dorset ladies are more merciless than the Wiltshire one and when she has gone they continue pulling Cattistock's character to pieces while drinking the wine that had been brought up for his wedding. Powys's use of dialect has sometimes been read with disbelief. Out of the dialect of Blackmore Vale at the beginning of the nineteenth century Barnes made for himself a beautiful instrument for his poetry. Hardy mostly sidestepped the problem of incorporating dialect in his fiction by working out a compromise whereby he hinted at the local speech only sparingly. There is as little dialect in Powys's romances as in the Wessex tales. Writing some fifty years after Hardy, however, Powys gives the gawky and uncouth remnant of the old folk speech as it has lumpered along into the twentieth century. It is not beautiful, but it serves Powys's ends.

It is not easy to detach passages of Powys's prose from the narratives of which they are a part and this must be the excuse for the lengthy quotations. The intricately linked sequences of clauses which Powys used in order to realize his meaning were a safeguard against mere fine writing. Generally speaking, therefore, the chosen passages can be taken to be representative.

II

If one allows that a narrative prose such as Powys's has its merits as an instrument for the writing of romances, one goes on to seek whence they derive. The prose is of a kind that was being written by no one else in the twentieth century—the possible exception of some of Phillpott's prose has already been mentioned—and it derives from the temperament and experience of the writer. Temperament responds to experience and for a writer the outcome is style. Powys's temperament was revealed at length in his *Autobiography*. One looks to his experience, therefore, and hopes to come upon some hint which may help one the better to understand his style.

Powys never tired of saying that he was a bookish man. He called himself a 'fatally bookish' man, a 'book-lover,' a 'book-worshipper.' It was hard indeed to name a book or a poem that he did not know, and on that account one has misgivings about naming one writer from among so many and suggesting that Powys's experience of his writings was peculiarly important for the creation of the romances.

None the less, something can be said for treating the writings of Walter Pater as the key to much of Powys's work. It was one of his grudges against Cambridge that he had left it without having "so much as even *heard* of Walter Pater, or Henry James, or Thomas Hardy." Taken by itself this is a puzzling statement. No one read English literature at Cambridge in Powys's youth, though, of course, one must sympathize with a novelist who had been deprived of early acquaintance with the stories of James and Hardy. Pater, however, was flourishing at the other place, although on that account he was not thought of primarily as a novelist. For Powys Arnold was perhaps the greatest of Victorian poets, and yet he could say of one part of his work:

> The airy persiflage of his prose . . . will have a place, but not a very important place, in English literature . . . when one compares him, as a sheer illuminator of psychological twilights, to Walter Pater, one realizes at once how easily a quite great man may "render himself stupid" by sprinkling himself with the holy water of Fixed Principles![14]

Much later, when most of his own romances had been written, Powys said "always I have had as regular and as recurrent a set of tags from Pater as Lulu had from Burton's Anatomy." The more one reads the romances the more one perceives that their style owes more to Pater's than to any one else's. It is essential to such a style that its pace should be slow enough to enable the rhythms to take in any elaboration or qualification, and the passages from the romances which have already been quoted show Powys's mastery of it. Almost invariably the accumulations take the mind forward. They are seldom there for their own sakes.

Of course there is a paradox. Pater is not widely read and often he is known only by his splendid sentences about Leonardo's *Mona Lisa*. Pater dated his Leonardo essay 1869 and it was printed in a book in 1873. If the tones were not echoed in *A Pair of Blue Eyes* in the latter year, there can be little doubt that in the next five years they found their way into such a passage as the chapter called "Queen of Night" in *The Return of the Native*. Pater's is almost certainly the influence that led Hardy to enrich the Wessex novels with a variety of cultural references and there were local and personal reasons why Powys should wish to continue the enrichment. Hardy once spoke to Powys of a time when he had been "feeling about for a method," and Powys had been "perhaps a little shocked" at the craftsman's way of expressing himself.[15] But Powys was also a craftsman, and there was a time when he too sought for a method of presenting his romances. Paradoxically it was because Pater was a critic as well as a novelist that Powys was so much drawn to him. He put Pater as a critic with Nietzsche. "These two critics," he said,

> are unique. They not only think, feel, and see for us, they compel us to think, feel, and see for ourselves.[16]

And it was Pater who

> was an adept long before Nietzsche's campaign began, at showing the human desire, the human craving, the human ferocity, the human spite, hidden behind the mask of "Pure Reason".

"Professional philosophers," wrote Powys, have " 'fought shy' of Pater's philosophy . . . because . . . he has undermined Metaphysic, *by means of Metaphysic.*"[17] Powys enjoyed Pater's style for its "witchery of premediated seduction" and this style was part of the key which helped him to discover and realize his own way of looking at life. Pater, he wrote,

> is able to throw the glimmering mantle of his own elaborate *sophistry of the senses* over comparatively fleeting, unarresting objects. And he is able to compel us to follow, line by line, curve by curve, contour by contour the very palpable body and presence of the Beauty that passeth not away.[18]

This is an apt description of Powys's own style and it helps one to follow, for instance, the account of the gale off Portland in *Weymouth Sands:*

> Yes, the wind seemed to set itself to force her to listen to it and to enter into its non-human passions. It forced her to follow its wild path over the whistling wave-crests and amid the flying surf. It forced her to follow it, as driving the scudding spray before it, it shrieked round those jagged rocks, while beneath it, below the sea-floor level, deep-gurgling rock-chasms drew the waves in and spewed them out. The wind made Ellen follow it when it left the turbulence of the rocks, and began whirling up the face of the cliff. Up the face of the cliff it twisted like the

166

sea-serpent. It whirled up through dead tufts of bent grass and through the wind blighted elders and ashes and stunted gorse. It whirled up over patches of samphire, and over patches of grey rock-lichen, and over whistling stalks of sea lavender and over chittering sea pods of sea thrift.[19]

The Paterian kinship of this passage is made clearer still by another of Powys's paragraphs on Pater:

Walter Pater's magnetic spell is never more wonder-working than when he deals with the *materials* which artists use. And most of all, with *words*, that material which is so strained and corrupted and outraged—and yet which is the richest of all. But how tenderly he always speaks of materials! What a limitless reverence he has for the subtle reciprocity and correspondence between the human senses and what—so thrillingly, so dangerously, sometimes!—they apprehend. Wood and clay and marble and bronze and gold and silver; these—and the fabrics of cunning looms and deft, insatiable fingers—he handles with the reverence of a priest touching consecrated elements. Not only the great main rivers of art's tradition, but the little streams and tributaries, he loves. Perhaps he loves some of these best of all, for the pathways to the exquisite margins are less trodden than the others, and one is more apt to find one's self alone there.[20]

In the year in which these words were first printed the first of Powys's romances to be published was called *Wood and Stone*. In the preface to it he wrote:

Art must prove itself able to evoke the very tang and salt and bitter-sweetness of the actual pell-mell of life—its unfolding spaces, its shell-strewn depths.

And in the light of what he wrote of Pater's description of Watteau's "happy valley" one is not surprised by his later concern with clowns and circuses:

along the borders of it and under its clipped trees, by its fountains and ghostly lawns, still, still can one catch in the twilight the shimmer of the dancing feet of the Phantom-Pierrot, and the despair in his smile! For him, too—for Gilles the Mummer—as for Antoine Watteau and Walter Pater, the wistfulness of such places is not inconsistent with the levity. Soon the music must stop. Soon it must be only a garden, "only a garden of Lenotre, correct, ridiculous and charming." For the lips of the Despair of Pierrot cannot always touch the lips of the Mockery of Columbine; in the end the Ultimate Futility must turn them both to stone![21]

Such a vision of life is in keeping with Powys's account of his lectures at the Chicago Little Theatre:

here, for the one and only time in my life, I was destined to play the Intellectual Pierrot against an appropriate *Yellow-Book* background . . . I felt as if I had become a privileged Initiate in some heavenly Alsatia, some Thelemic Cloister of Art, where the ritualistic and symbolic elements in my performances, that had hitherto only been recognized by the devoted instinct of Nuns and Communists met with a subtle aesthetic response. I've never been more like an inspired Pantaloon, in a setting designed by Aubrey Beardsley, and a Libretto composed by Ernest Dowson, than I was then; and here, while against some background put up by Raymond Jonson I interpreted such writers as Wilde and Verlaine and Heine and Blake and Walter Pater, I danced my dance before dancers, and played my act before actors.[22]

Yet it need not be thought that Powys is no more than another writer of Pater's prose. "Every Philosophy," he wrote.

has its "secret" according to Pater, its "formula," its lost Atlantis. Well! It is for us to search it out; to take colour from its dim-lit under-world; to feed upon its wavering sea-lotus—and then, returning to the surface, to swim away, in search of other diving grounds![23]

This kind of imagery comes through time after time in Powys's writing and the final gesture leads to a still deeper understanding of his art. Powys's "diving ground" might be called the 'shady side' of the positive qualities. It had already been looked upon in the past and there are hints of it in Lamb, Hazlitt and De Quincey. In the eighteen nineties it had been explored by some of Pater's followers, in a fashion, and *The Picture of Dorian Gray* is typical of such searchings. It was Powys, however, who went down into the depths of his new diving ground and embodied his new knowledge in a comprehensive vision of life. In his introduction to *Lucifer* Powys remarked that the word "poetical" could be applied to "any piece of prose," music, work of art, landscape or living creature. "For a thing to be deeply poetical," he said, "it must contain both truth and illusion, both beauty and ugliness, both good and evil." Forty years before, in the preface to *Wood and Stone*, he had insisted upon the protecting power and duty of art:

> Art . . . must defend herself from . . . the system-makers . . . She must keep the horizons open . . . She must hold fast to poetry and humour, and about her creations there must be a certain spirit of *liberation*, and the presence of large tolerant after-thoughts.

Powys was to find in Pater's books not only a manner of writing but also an insight which enabled the inner self to take on a new subject matter for literature. They help to account for both the craftsman's tireless seeking after the means for achieving his ends and for the comprehensive nature of the vision of life which he sought to realize.

III

It may be hard to believe that a writer who embarked on romance writing in 1915 made his starting ground the work of Walter Pater. It may be that much critical knitting will have to be unpicked in order to begin to enjoy Powys's romances in the way in which he meant them to be enjoyed. The facts are that both the style and subject matter of the romances owe much to Pater and that the first of the romances to be published came out during the first world war when the earlier works of Lawrence and Joyce were already well known. One would like to understand, therefore, how it came about that Powys believed that he could achieve his ends by such means at such a date.

The explanation is probably to be found in the pattern of his career. His first book, a book of poems, was published in 1896, a year which also saw the appearance of first books of poems by Dowson and Housman. In the heyday of mid Victorianism Powys would have become a full time poet like Tennyson and Browning. In the eighteennineties, however, poets had a much less friendly world to work in. Dowson died young and Housman sought distinction in the world of scholarship. Powys solved his problem by becoming a lecturer.

This calling Powys was to follow for some forty years and he gave a lively account of how he had followed it in his *Autobiography*. That book, however, was written with memories of a quarter of a century of American lecture tours in mind, and it understandably makes the most of whatever was extraordinary and ludicrous about them. Such lecturing gave free rein to the dithyrambic and histrionic propensities of his nature. After one of these American lectures Bertrand Russell summed it up as a performance—"Quite a performance." Powys did not think of lectures of this kind as work and said that the only preparation that they required was the reading of long romantic novels on long train journeys. There was more to them than that—the nature of the reader, for instance. However, the concentration upon these freshly remembered pantomimes in the *Autobiography* has been allowed to obscure the fact that in the straightforward meaning of the words Powys must have been a good lecturer.

The human form divine, indeed, was not meant to stand up to forty years of such dithyrambics and histrionics as Powys described. One seeks, therefore, to understand Powys's reasons for giving to his account of these activities the emphasis that he did. The recurrent note is one of defiance, and in the *Autobiography* it is used to cover up an underlying sense of disappointment. In some ways the extension movement was one

which afforded an ample scope to such a man as Powys and he
worked hard in the cause for many years. He was to learn,
however, that it had its drawbacks and he could not always
feel at ease in it. At some time some one had tried to hurt
him by calling him an "Extension Lecturer" and he did not
forget the wound. He recalled that the attempts of Hardy's
Jude and Sue to discuss the meaning and conduct of life had
been "held up to scorn as branded with the unscholarly brand
of 'University Extension'." *Jude the Obscure* was published at
the end of 1895 and one can imagine how such smart talk must
have irritated Powys in the last years of the old century. His
answer to it could easily have been foretold. "Personally," he
wrote,

> I have always been prepared to arise fiercely in defence of
> this sort of popular culture. You will, I believe, find on its
> side such great imaginative spirits as Pythagoras, Socrates,
> Plotinus, the Gnostic Heretics, the Scholastic Heretics,
> Montaigne, Goethe, Ruskin, Matthew Arnold, Walter
> Pater, William James.

It may seem that in finishing this sentence of the *Autobiography*
he was giving the game away—

> from Aristotle to Scaliger, and from Scaliger to the
> classical Paul Valéry, this sort of loose, irresponsible,
> careless, imaginative handling of philosophy has been
> regarded with contempt.[24]

Here Powys conflated two phases of his career. In fact once
again he shows his acute awareness of contempt for the kind
of work he was trying to do. "I had no sooner begun my life
of peripatetic philosophizing," he wrote, than

> the cry "Charlatan! Charlatan!" went up . . . But these
> people caught a Tartar when they called me as they have
> always done, and do still, by this opprobrious name . . .
>
> When they cry "Charlatan!" what they really mean is:
> "How dare this fellow talk about Dostoievsky's Christ,
> and about Plato's Eros, and about Goethe's 'Mothers,'
> and about Wordsworth's *Intimations of Immortality*, and

about the 'art' of Henry James, and about the 'critical values' of Walter Pater, and about the 'cosmic emotion' of Walt Whitman, as if these recondite subjects, complicated enough to fill the whole span of several real scholars' life-work, could possibly be lugged into an address to working-men and tradesmen's assistants!" ... To parade such topics before an unacademic audience is to give yourself away as no better than a vulgar conjuror.[25]

Resentment heightened—and repeatedly heightened—in this way naturally reaches up into comedy, and the conjuring and clowning performances link up with the concern with clowns in the romances. Affection for God's fool was widespread among the poets of the eighteennineties, and it remained a touchstone for such poets as Wilfred Childe and, of course, for Yeats, to whom Powys addressed an early piece. In looking back in the *Autobiography* over his experiences as a lecturer Powys was careful to make the most of the clowning because he wanted to shew up the limitations of the conservative academic world, the world of the "mathematical Cantabs," as he calls them, who had taken "damned good care to hide away from" him "Walter Pater, that grave Pyrrhonian monk of God." In order to do this he differentiated himself from the "real scholars" and was happy that they should think him "no better than a vulgar conjuror." Powys, however, is unfair to himself, as he was bound to be, because his code of good manners did not allow him to give an account of what he had done in academic terms for the shaded world of university extension. Besides, by the time that he wrote the *Autobiography* such things were not among his fresher and more exciting recollections.

Even in the *Autobiography*, however, his defiance leads him to write of "the admirable system of University Extension." And there is a further hint, too. Powys must be one of the few writers who have spoken sympathetically of Arnold's schools' inspecting. Like Pater, Arnold had put aside metaphysics, and

172

Powys also liked his amateurish and gentlemanly ways of nourishing and propagating culture. He saw the world, in Powys's words, a "Burlesque Show," and

> In his advocacy of what the indignant Common Rooms of Oxford would call "University Extension culture" he was as sublimely indifferent to the charge of being popular as he was of being thought priggish . . . it can never have struck him that a time would come when in our inverted intellectual snobbishness . . . our geniuses would be turning from the Loeb Classics to find—and to find with no negligible success—in gangster-saloons and bull-fights and lynchings and bombing their method of capturing the undying Protean muse.[26]

These remarks were published in *The Pleasures of Literature* in 1938 and they show that the old wound had not healed.

They also help to define Powys's point of view. By the time that they were printed *Maiden Castle* and *Morwyn* were already behind him. About the writings of the nineteenthirties he kept an open mind, but his own next imaginative step, the writing of *Owen Glendower*, though it did not take him into the Loeb Library past, took him at least into the middle ages, and so away from the immediately contemporary world which had become the dominant preoccupation of most of the younger writers. Later, after the second world war, indeed, he was to make his romantic way into the Homeric past and never tired of saying how much the Loeb Library volumes had helped him. However, open as his mind was about all kinds of writing in his own time, his extension lecturing, though it could not, of course, be confined to writers who were to be honoured by the Loeb Library, did not sink to the depths of Ally Sloper or detective stories, either. His own enjoyment of such casual reading did not tempt him to lecture about it to the people who were willing to turn out to grasp the extended hands of the universities. There was then no cloth cap and plush fours nonsense about literature. Those members of "the average intelligent public", readers, perhaps, of Everyman's Library or such as became subscribers to Boots Booklover's Library, were to be introduced to the best that has been thought and said. The five hundred and twenty of Middlesbrough and the two hundred and eighty four of Newcastle who signed up for a course in which two out of twelve lectures were devoted to Pater must be among the more surprising and admirable phenomena of the beginning of the century. Concentration upon and emphasis of later lecturing antics in the *Autobiography* have left the importance of these occasions shrouded in the mists of the past and obscured the seriousness of Powys's Arnold-like educational purpose. Later, however, he brought out an English edition of a book of essays which had first been published in America in 1915. Besides a paper on Arnold it contains an essay in which Powys states briefly and comprehensively all that Pater meant to him. It sums up some twenty years' experience of reading his books and there is not a sentence in it which does not light up Powys's critical and imaginative landscape.

Once Powys's debts to Pater's criticism and style have been allowed, however, it might still be urged that Pater's writings were not the key to Powys's romances on the ground that Powys was not sure that Stevenson as a novelist was wise to spend hours writing in the style of Hazlitt.

Yet even if Stevenson might have found better ways of spending his time, Powys's circumstances were not Stevenson's. He was early a compulsive story teller and in other days he might have become a full time poet. Most instinctive story tellers begin early and critical powers strengthen with the passing of years. Dickens and Kipling are examples of such a pattern. Powys, however, was fortytwo or fortythree years old when he first had a romance published, and by that time he had spent twenty years in lecturing which meant that his business had been that of a critic interpreter. Whatever he thought of Stevenson's imitations of Hazlitt, therefore, it would have been odd if Powys, who began publishing romances at an age at which Stevenson's life was all but ended, had not embodied in those romances the experience of his years as a critic interpreter. When allowance has been made for the circumstances of Powys's academic career, his long and serious consideration of and wrestling with the work called for in a shaded and shadowy area of education, and his consequent or fortuitous late arrival on the scene as a writer of romances, the long discipleship to Pater did him little harm. It was his grasp of and development of an instrument which Pater had already brought near to perfection that enabled him to explore with endless inquisitiveness and to realize with seemingly endless resource the whole of life in its setting of rocks, and stones, and trees.

The notion of a careless writer, therefore, gives room to the notion of a conscientious and patient craftsman who worked decade after decade to refine his means of expression in order that he might refine his insight into the ways of this unintelligible world. One could show equally clearly that Powys built up his romances chapter by chapter with the same aesthetic conscientiousness. Their shapeliness is as much the outcome of aesthetic judgment as the shapeliness of a book by Pater. For Powys as for Pater all judgments are in the end aesthetic judgments. Art is the subject most worthy of conscientiousness and if one is faithful in one's discipleship to it taste settles every question.

IV

One must go back beyond Lawrence and Joyce and the social realists of the Bennett and Wells era in order to follow the growth of the kind of romance that Powys wrote. The sway of later fashions may make such a step seem either an impossibility or at least a heavy price to pay for one's understanding. Unless one goes back to Pater, however, it is easy to miss the overall simplicity of conception which Powys achieved by showing endless respect for the merest detail of experience. "Pater's famous methods of style and treatment," wrote Powys in *The Meaning of Culture*, which was published four months after *Wolf Solent* in 1930, may

175

seem antiquated and even affected; but . . . the stimulus afforded by this noble and meticulous fastidiousness is second to none . . . No one is more of an adept than he in indicating the manner in which the various inanimate objects which touch the sensibility of exceptional minds affect the symbols of their thought. External objects of all kinds, landscapes, houses, gardens, furniture, the fabrics of dress, the qualities of food and drink, hot and cold airs, the stuff of the soil, the feeling of masonry, the way the light falls, the way the darkness flows—all these things, as he introduces them in his slow, careful, reticent, economic way, yield up their recondite essences and grow little by little to be incorporated and embodied in the shapes and contours of the particular thought for which he is seeking the precise formula.[27]

By the nineteenthirties Pater had become of little more than academic interest and it was probably on that account that Powys did not include an essay on his work in *The Pleasures of Literature*. However, his old essay on Pater was reprinted in 1955 when *Visions and Revisions* which had been published in America in 1915 was issued in London. For this new edition Powys wrote an introduction in which he again swore his allegiance. "I swear to you, my friends of the Hydrogen-Era," he writes,

that our special shelf of "Books to Live by"—and I don't mind adding "to Die by" also—*must* have at least one volume of the subtlest critic of art in our language, a language so much more poetical than it is "artistic," namely Walter Pater.

And he closes the paragraph with words which may fittingly bring to an end these remarks:

If he happens to be out of fashion at this particular epoch, don't let that worry you. He will return.

NOTES

1. *John O'London's Weekly and Outlook*, 23rd October, 1936.
2. Llewelyn Powys, *A Baker's Dozen*, 1941, Introduction by J. C. Powys.
3. *A Glastonbury Romance*, 1955, Preface, p. xiv.
4. *Wood and Stone*, 1915, pp. 6–7.
5. *Weymouth Sands* (1934), 1963, pp. 25–27.
6. *Maiden Castle*, 1937, p. 3; 1966, p. 15.
7. *Ibid.*, p. 431; p. 443.
8. *Wolf Solent*, 1929, pp. 176–180; 1961, pp. 164–167.
9. *Ibid.*, p. 103; p. 93.
10. *Weymouth Sands*, 1963, p. 406.
11. *Ibid.*, p. 410.
12. *Ibid.*, pp. 415–416.
13. *Ibid.*, p. 426.
14. *Visions and Revisions*, 1955, "Matthew Arnold", pp. 117–118.
15. *The Pleasures of Literature*, 1938, "Hardy", p. 622.
16. *Ibid.*, "Greek Tragedy", p. 139.
17. *Visions and Revisions*, "Walter Pater", p. 174.
18. *Ibid.*, p. 173.
29. *Weymouth Sands*, 1963, p. 268.
20. *Visions and Revisions*, "Walter Pater", p. 177.
21. *Ibid.*, p. 178.
22. *Autobiography* (1934), 1967, p. 513.
23. *Visions and Revisions*, "Walter Pater", p. 174.
24. *Autobiography*, p. 285.
25. *Ibid.*, pp. 285–287.
26. *The Pleasures of Literature*, "Matthew Arnold", p. 429.
27. *The Meaning of Culture*, 1930, "Culture and Literature", pp. 41–42.

IX

J. C. POWYS AND ROMANCE

Francis Berry

The title of the book, *A Glastonbury Romance*, points to a distinction between *romance* and novel, a distinction strengthened by the prefatory list headed "Principal Characters in the Romance".

Wherein does a romance differ from a novel? Or, better, 'the romance' from 'the modern novel'? *The Glastonbury Romance* may be a mixed thing, a romance containing elements we expect in the modern novel. But Malory's *Morte d'Arthur* also contains elements we expect in the modern novel. What is true of Malory's book is no less true of the French or Welsh prose romance or of later romances such as Shakespeare's sources— *Rosalyndie, The Arcadia, Pandosto*. Just as certainly does 'the modern novel', from Defoe onwards to to-day, frequently contain material or features proper to romance.

Women's Weeklies may announce 'our great new romance serial starting in the next number'. This will simply be an advertisement for a serialized novel with a strong love interest. But such a novel, in order to satisfy its readers with a love affair that ends happily is likely to fulfil wishes—the wishes of its readers which are also the wishes of the story's characters, for the readers of these Weeklies identify themselves, or so it is supposed, with the characters.

Le Morte d'Arthur, despite the craving of lovers, and their rapture, ends disastrously. Wishes may be fulfilled, but for moments in time, not for ever after. With this book, the wishes of characters and readers probably diverge. Readers probably would have the book end as it does end.

Generally though, the fulfilment of the wish may be a feature more characteristic of the romance than of the novel. And if we bring in wish and wishing we must consider the will, or whatever organ it is that wishes. Or to this extent: in the romance space and time, the dimensions to which we must submit in life, are more obedient to the will. In the romance people can be transported from place to place, as though magically, as we can seem to be transported in a dream; and since the condition of space is more obedient so—it is a corollary—is time. In a romance ballad about *Gawain* the foul old witch becomes a beautiful young bride, time has reversed. Perspective, or its absence, and the lighting of landscape are, in the romance, nearer to those we experience in dream than in waking.

In the modern novel there are phantasies and—remembering *Ulysses*—phantasmagoria, but these are usually recognised as such by the author and his readers are warned to take them as such. The wish is not allowed to have all its own way. If the wish is admitted to have its way in the romance, and if the wish can express itself in the forms of phantasy, phantasy not regarded as something delusive, false or inferior, then phantasy is proper to the romance. On occasions we might do well to call it, not phantasy, but vision.

Nevertheless, though it is the material of their study, many psychologists have made phantasies disreputable. Yet it has been established that if we are forcibly prevented from dreaming while in a state of sleep, our health will suffer: we need dreams. Whether we would readily admit to it or not, all of us have spent waking hours, having phantasies—enjoyable or hateful, consolatory or disturbing. Powys, in his *Autobiography* and elsewhere is quite unusually honest in confessing to the importance of the role of phantasies in his waking life; and, in *The Art of Happiness* he prescribes a technique for controlling them. For he has also confessed to tormenting sadistic phantasies, although all those who knew him would aver that no-one was more innocent of cruel actions. If some phantasies can be a substitute for action, and not an arousal to action then, if the action would be cruel or destructive, then such phantasies are obviously valuable. It may be that some are driven to act out their phantasies, as Mr. Evans acts out his phantasy in *A Glastonbury Romance*. But this event is in a work of literature, Mr. Evans is a fictive character, and the reading of the episode may provide readers, affected like Mr. Evans, with a vicarious satisfaction.

Since Powys was so honestly insistent upon the part that
phantasies played in his own life, it is not surprising that,
besides Mr. Evans, it is the habit or propensity of nearly all
the major characters in all his fictions to have, and to cultivate,
phantasies of the most diverse kind. These characters resemble
ourselves in this.

For many people phantasising is their only creative exercise;
only when they phantasise do they create situations, landscapes,
people, events, narratives. Of course it is desirable that these
people should always be able to distinguish between fact and
phantasy, and those that cannot are ill and could be dangerous.

If the self-evident is stressed, it is because it is generally
agreed that phantasy—or the visionary—and the prestige
attached to it is a feature more characteristic of the romance
(of any period) than it is of the modern novel. 'Phantasy—or
the visionary'. This is to risk an equation that might be held to
be unjustified. Sam Dekker has his vision of The Grail as
though he were an Arthurian seeker. To have a vision used
not to be discreditable; all have phantasies, the chosen few had
visions. But what Sam Dekker may have experienced was a
hallucination—for now it is the tendency to discredit the
visions of the past and to term them hallucinations.

*   *   *   *

The *NED* tells us that in the seventeenth and eighteenth
centuries the novel "was frequently contrasted with a romance
as being shorter than this, and having more relation to real
life". And Chesterfield is quoted, "A Novel is a kind of abbrevia-
tion of a Romance".

In 1972 we can call to mind long novels and short romances,
while acknowledging there is a tendency for the romance to be
longer on account of the moralizing digressions, and because
events, of a crudely decisive or coarsely exciting nature, are
more widely spaced. Nevertheless we see that in a romance,
and perhaps especially in *A Glastonbury Romance* there is an
abundance of adventure distinguishable from the "real life"

events of the definition. It is the "more relation to real life" part of the definition which would still be supported to-day, and held as pointing to the superiority of the novel—though, since "a faithful representation" of it in the modern novel means, to a large extent, the ignoring of those phantasies which employ so much of the time of those who live, it should make us sceptical of the "real". The novel is supposed to have "more relation with real life" however—whatever "real life" is—and in 1871 *The Spectator* declared "England has scarcely received the honour she deserves as the birthplace of the modern novel".

Besides these claims we can set the *NED's* most comprehensive definition of the *romance:* "a fictitious narrative in prose of which the scene and the incidents are very remote from those of ordinary life".

Powys may have been thinking of all "composers of fiction", but it is far more likely that he had in mind the practitioners of "the modern novel", and not—say—Malory, when, almost in the manner of an eighteenth-century critic, he pronounces on Imitation and Nature.

In a paper read to The Powys Society in 1970, Timothy Hyman quoted this passage from *A Glastonbury Romance:*

> The composers of fiction aim at an aesthetic verisimilitude which seldom corresponds to the much more eccentric and chaotic dispositions of Nature.[1]

Novelists aim at a verisimilitude ("faithful representations"), but seldom—we are to be told—achieve their aim. For

> They intersperse their "comic" and their "tragic" in a manner quite different—so hard is it to throw off the clinging conventions of human tradition!—from the ghastly monotonies and sublime surprises that Nature delights in.

Between these two passages, quoted by Hyman, Powys concedes that "composers of fiction", though "rarely", may occasionally come nearer to the truth, as though in despite of themselves, and in despite of their "aesthetic":

> Only rarely are such writers so torn and rent by the Demon within them that they can add their own touch to the wave-crests of *real actuality* as these foam up, bringing wreckage and sea-tangle and living and dead ocean monsters and bloody spume and bottom silt into the rainbow spray!

So, the charge, if we accept it, is that novelists, in their obedience to aesthetic principles, though striving to attain a *"real actuality"* (Powys's italics), commonly fail to attain what they are striving for, largely because of their aesthetic ("aesthetic verisimilitude') principles. The order they present in their novels does not approach "the wave-crests of *actual reality*".

'Of course it does not', some are ready to retort: the artist, and the novelist is an artist,[2] imposes an order—or pattern, or scheme—upon the patternless, or undecipherable pattern, the mess of *"actual reality"*. Others will protest, 'but does not D. H. Lawrence complain against those novelists who impose such mentally contrived patterns on the quick moments of life?' While others will ask, 'Does not Joyce combine or fuse "actual reality" completely with a perfected pattern?' But Lawrence hardly wrote romances; and Joyce certainly did not. Scott may have done so: among the Waverley novels, *Ivanhoe* is subtitled "A Romance".

In many ways maybe the romance, notwithstanding, is more loyal to *NED's* "real life" or Powys's "real actuality" than the novel, the birthplace of which was England.

The romance pursues The Grail even if that limited thing, the intelligence, declares that there is no Grail. Perhaps that is because the writer of *A Glastonbury Romance* realises that a quest for *something* is essential if we are to keep going; and if the object of the quest does not exist—if that is the grim truth—it is perhaps the more necessary to behave as though it did exist. Otherwise we would not keep going. The writer of a great modern romance is certainly not going to believe that woman, however delightful to the senses, *is* the Grail. He is not going to be a 'romantic fool' in this sense of romantic; nor would he inflate the value of the act of sexual intercourse to a pitch it cannot sustain as one greatly admired twentieth-century novelist has done. That is to spoil the good thing. Miss Austen never approached such folly.

The hunger is metaphysical.

The object of the quest may be illusory, remembering that Powys in his 'philosophical' writings refers often to "*our* favourite life illusions". The choice of the possessive "our" is characteristically humble. He assumes that his readers in their hearts are as certain as he is that "there is no *ultimate* mystery". What Sam Dekker saw ("a globular chalice that had two circular handles")[3] *may* have been The Grail. Does it follow that he was hallucinated if there is no "*ultimate* mystery?"

The vessel contained "dark water streaked with blood," and in this liquid was a fish.

We are told that Sam was quite unlearned in the Grail legends. He was unaware that it was essential that those who succeeded in seeing The Grail should ask the right (Powys says "crucial") question. Sam's "third thought", the one that— according to the author—"put the seal of authenticity upon his vision", was a question. The thought-question concerned the *species* of the fish: "What is that fish? Surely it is a Tench, surely it is a Tench?"

"The seal of authenticity . . . Surely it is a Tench?" Perhaps after all it was no illusion. The author here intervenes, and *he* then first echoes Sam's question and then asks his own questions:

> *Is it a Tench*? Is there a fish of healing, one chance against all chances, at the bottom of the world-tank? *Is it a Tench*? Is cruelty always triumphant, or is there a hope beyond hope, a Something somewhere hid perhaps

in the twisted heart of the cruel First Cause itself and able to break in *from outside* and smash to atoms this torturing train of Cause and Effect?

These questions are the *right* questions, but they are, of course, unanswerable.

Hardy, in his novels, did not ask the questions because he was resigned to the impossibility of such a "break in". "Crass casualty" did not admit of a "break in" of this kind: it would disturb "the aesthetic verisimilitude" if it did. Blind and cruel chance was a formula for tragedy supporting his experience. Other novelists do not admit a possibility which would upset design, falsify character, "where character is fate", and compromise their own honesty of conviction.

But the medieval romance had admitted, not the possibility, but the likelihood of such a "break in". It may or may not be the Grail; it would not have been the marriageable heroine who in the last chapter of a novel, or the magazine serial story styled a romance, is captured by the hero.

The important modification worked by Powys, in this book, in the history of the romance is this: whereas in the medieval and renaissance romance, the people—through the exercise of dream or the gift of vision or the power of magic—are rendered variably independent of the restrictions imposed by the dimensions of space and time, Powys does subject his people to the restrictions of these dimensions. In this he is a novelist; he is more than a novelist in that he is open "to the much more eccentric and chaotic dispositions of Nature" than most "composers of fiction".

*   *   *   *

In its earlier stages the reputation of J. C. Powys was fostered by loyal enthusiasts. Often intensely individualistic, though of diverse tastes and dispositions, but sharing this admiration and enjoyment, and finding in this writer a consolation, they formed no party. *A Glastonbury Romance* presents a vast array

186

of characters—some of them 'characters' in the sense of *seemingly* eccentric. Many of Powys's earlier readers may have resembled these fictional personages; attuned to the book, they would have understood it. But whereas the fictional characters congregated in a book, its warmest admirers—though numerous —were scattered. Not necessarily in communication with each other, they formed in no way a party or fashionable pressure group.

These earlier readers recognised an author who recorded hints and manifestations scarcely recorded, if at all, in the fiction of the twenties and thirties.

Since then an increasingly large number in a succeeding generation, including novelists and literary critics, have come to realize that what these previous readers had recognised was not crazy, eccentric or marginal—this refers especially to the mental life of Powys's characters—but the experience of general humanity which the author had succeeded in expressing, honouring the multifariousness of nature. Consequently his reputation has been consolidated, and continues to grow. This is indicated by the emergence of paperback editions and by the conviction, among younger academic critics, that here there is a major twentieth-century author.

Asked to write for the centenary collection, I thought there was something to be said for making a distinction between 'romance' and 'the modern novel'. It is but one of many possible starting points. If it does not go far, it is because Powys, despite his use of romance sources for a fiction set in the twentieth century, is so extremely inclusive that this book resists categories because it conjoins them.

A few years ago, in 1962, I set out, in a few lines, what this author has meant to me. It is a positive and concise statement, and I hope I may be allowed to re-print the lines here.

For a Ninetieth Birthday

Sir, what you give, we have and hold:
Magus, you kiss life into the dead stone;
The plain woman and the crazed man in the dull town
Make quick and green with loving; and make the moon
Re-act to the stretcht dog's pain and the plant's groan.

J. C. Powys has felt the thuds of the sun
Startle the wild block of wood; he has shown
Us the Arthurian sword as down it shone
Yesterday afternoon; and he has seen

Unshudderingly the livid spear; caught the sheen
Of that hovering, oval, roseate Urn
Repolished till it throbs; has made the mean
Insect thrilling and ghostly, and the dead return.

Sir, what you give, we have and hold,
John Cowper Powys, ninety years old.

NOTES

[1]   *A Glastonbury Romance*, 1934, p. 694; 1955, p. 666.
[2]   In reply to a letter in which I praised him as "an Artist", Powys rejected the attribution with vehemence.
[3]   *A Glastonbury Romance*, 1934, p. 982 ff; 1955, p. 939 ff.

X

POWYS ON DEATH

G. Wilson Knight

When on a visit to Powys in 1955 I referred to an after-life, he replied that he no longer believed in one. For long, he said, he had supported it in arguments with Llewelyn, but since his brother's death he had changed. Whether he meant that he had been disappointed by receiving no intimations of Llewelyn's survival, I cannot say. His mind seemed made up. He said something to the effect that he did not himself want to survive; he was tired.

After my visit, he wrote, on 25 April 1955: "But Beware of the occult! my dear dear friend, O beware of it! You and I have enough of the demonic in us without that! Its *effect on us* is a weakening one and a blurring one and *not* an enlightening one". I reassured him and on 14 January 1957 he wrote approvingly of my essay on Spiritualism, adding some phrases from the Witches in *Macbeth*.

Powys's views certainly changed. In *Mortal Strife*, "The Soul" (1942) he strongly supports survival; in the profound and deeply considered last chapter, "Old Age and Death", of *The Art of Growing Old* (1944) he preserves a balance just tilted in its favour; in *In Spite Of* (1953) he is against it. In his preface to the 1961 edition of *Wolf Solent* he wrote:

> Whatever death may mean, and none of us really know, I have come to the conclusion for myself that when I die it is the complete and absolute end of me. I am now satisfied that when I lie dying I shall be feeling a perfect contentment in the sure and certain knowledge that no consciousness of mine will continue after my last breath.

That sounds, in its way, definitive: at least, this is now what Powys *wants* to believe.

When we call Powys a great writer, we are thinking primarily of his imaginative works. On certain issues fiction may be more reliable than fact; if only because the fictions of genius may be supposed, as the word "genius" implies, to be in some degree inspired.

190

In Powys's most famous books we find the occult a major concern. In *Ducdame* (1925) there is a dominating emphasis on ancestral powers. Our heroes may feel themselves in contact with a dead relative, as when in *Wolf Solent* (1929; new edn. 1961) the hero talks to his father's body in its grave (XXV. 625–7 or 596–8). True, emphasis here falls on the dead and mouldering body; but that is often the way literature approaches the mystery, and in *A Glastonbury Romance* (1933; new edn. 1955) the spirit powers are explicit. The whole book is saturated in the animistic, the occult, the numinous. We receive a sense of non-human powers, good or evil, over-watching, and sometimes engaging with, the human drama: "Were there really powers of good and evil moving about in the ether and touching us all *at their own* will, not at ours, and at the strangest moments?" (VI. 168 or 177). Again:

> Above every community, above every town, there are invisible Powers hovering, as interested in the minnows, male and female, swimming about in that peculiar human aquarium, as Mat Dekker was in his fish. (XX. 647 or 622)

Here is an extended statement:

> On this particular noon-day not one of these great Elemental Powers became aware, for the flicker of a single second, of the existence by Pomparlès Bridge, between the town of Glastonbury and the village of Street, of the entity known as John Crow. But the Great Powers among the natural forces possessed of consciousness no more exhaust or fulfil the innumerable categories of the supernatural than the Great Powers among the nations of the earth exhaust or fulfil the categories of humanity. There are countless supernumerary beings— all sons and daughters of the First Cause—whose meddlings and interferences with the affairs of earth have not received the philosophical attention they deserve. (XIII. 369 or 358)

This is typical: it is what *A Glastonbury Romance* is *about*.

Spirits of the dead are active. Like Wolf Solent, John Crow expects contact with a dead parent. We hear how, when exhausted, he "prayed, calmly, fervently, simply, to the spirit of his mother" and of her we are told:

> The woman had died in a convulsive spasm of tragic tenderness for the child she had to leave; nor is it difficult to conceive how, even on the most material plane, some formidable magnetic vibration, issuing from that grave in the Yaxham churchyard, might linger upon the chemical substratum of the ether, and prove of genuine supernatural value to the child of her womb, when in his weakness he was most in need of her. (III. 79 or 95)

Here is another such occasion:

> Philip stretched out his right arm now as he lay on his left side and seized in the dark the cold rosewood bedpost at his pillow's head. Out of the dream-dimension which surrounds our visible world the wraith of his Devereux grandmother struggled frantically to give him a warning. To be able to see his small, neat, well-moulded head—for these insubstantial tenants of the etheric envelope of our material plane find physical darkness no hindrance—lying on the pillow and not to be able to attract his attention was an atrocious tantalisation to this proud spirit from beyond our palpable dream-world. (XXI. 700 or 672)

These are no facile indications. There is throughout a close earth-contact, a sense of the spirit-powers half-glimpsed or half-impinging, but nothing easy, and all fraught with difficulties.

We have a variety of approaches, of insights, on death. In the first chapter we read of the Rector of Northwold, William Crow's phantasmagoria of dream-like "thoughts" during his own burial.

> These thoughts did not include any distaste for being buried or any physical shrinking, but they included a calm, placid curiosity as to whether this dream-like state was the end of everything, or the beginning of something else. Nerves of enjoyment, nerves of suffering, both were

atrophied in this cold, sweet-sickly, stinking corpse; but around and about it, making a diffused 'body' for itself out of the ether that penetrated clay and plants and grass-roots and chilly air, all alike, the soul of the dead man was obsessed by confused memories, and deep below these by the vague stirring of an unimpassioned, neutral curiosity.

(I. 26 or 45)

These memories concerned primarily his long-dead wife and her cutting animosities. Her words are resuscitated in his mind. But it remains impervious:

It wondered too, with the same complacent indifference, whether the humming of these confused memories was going to lapse into what they called 'eternal rest' or going to prelude some new and surprising change. Whichever it was, it was equally interesting, now that pleasure and pain were both gone. Annihilation—how strange! A new conscious life—how strange! (I. 28 or 47)

At the chapter's end, when the business of the Will is concluded, the ghosts of William Crow and his wife emerge from one of the rooms in the half-living house, and she continues her envenomed complaints. What is here most interesting is the subtle treatment of these ghosts' nocturnal emergence from the already charged atmosphere of stairs and portraits, and the comparison of their words to the "sub-human breathings" of plants; as though the physical universe were itself the home of a thousand livingnesses beyond our normal perceptions.

Our most powerful ghostly chapter is that entitled "Mark's Court", in which the miracle-worker Geard sleeps in the haunted gallery, the scene where Merlin punished King Mark by turning him into dust. Geard's brain, soon after his entry, receives the word "Nineue", the name of the lady who bewitched Merlin. Alone in the room he tries to sleep. The occasion is handled in Powys's slow, unsensational, yet highly charged, manner. The word "Nineue" still beats in his brain. He sleeps. Then he is waked by actually hearing the name cried twice, and he is next aware—by a typically Powysian counter to the ghostly atmosphere—of a man making water into a chamber pot in a room below. He meditates on the million sounds, perceptible or imperceptible, active on earth and radiating into space. He hears part of a human conversation. What was that sound "Nineue"—a dream interpretation of the voice in the room below? He expects it again; is near panic; and then calls it out, himself. He is in a state of fear mixed with pity for the anguished spirit, and tells it to appear plainly. He levels all his own, vast, thaumaturgic powers against the anguish. "Christ have mercy upon you" he gasps. He becomes peaceful, with a sense of "unutterable achievement" (XV. 463 or 448). The incident is, as always in Powys, realised through a sense of the otherness as closely entwined with earth-normality, both part of a whole beyond human conception.

Twice an actual death is recorded. The first is the murder of Tom Barter:

> He was killed instantaneously, the front of his skull being bashed in so completely, that bits of bone covered with bloody hair surrounded the deep dent which the iron made. His consciousness, the 'I am I' of Tom Barter, shot up into the ether above them like a released fountain-jet and quivering there pulsed forth a spasm of feeling, in which outrage, ecstasy, indignation, recognition, pride, touched a dimension of Being more quick with cosmic life than Tom had ever reached before in his thirty-seven years of conscious existence. This heightened—nay! this quadrupled—awareness dissolved in a few seconds, after its escape from the broken cranium, but whether it passed, with its personal identity intact, into that invisible envelope of rarefied matter which surrounds our astronomic sphere or whether it perished irrevocably, the present chronicler knows not. (XXIX. 1100 or 1051)

A supreme coalition of inspiratory perception and human reason is brought to bear, with all possible precision, on the central enigma of mankind. The concluding disclaimer rounds off, but in no sense negates, what precedes: it has been definitely stated that the mind, or consciousness, can function *after* "death".

More complex is Geard's mystically conceived death in the Flood. He has already spoken a public address on death, saying that his "Christ" has told him that all existences, even insects and microbes, have immortal souls (XXX. 1136 or 1084). Now, in the Flood, he is himself purposively "set upon dying". He believes without any question in the "next world", and knows "for certain, by the evidence of personal experience, that a living Being, who might, or might not, be the Christ the Churches worshipped" awaits his arrival:

> Mr. Geard had been made to understand by the medium-ship of this Being, that conditions of life after the death of the body were immeasurably superior to those now existing. (XXX. 1157 or 1104)

His actual dying is elaborately described: the settled will, the physical contortions, the supervening peace, the "death". And next we are told that Geard's "death" was followed by un-consciousness. Geard, like Powys, was a great seer. If we remember Powys's 1961 statement on himself in the preface to *Wolf Solent*, we might almost suppose that, the greater the seer, the less is the likelihood of consciousness beyond death:

> Unlike the experience of his patron and friend, the Rector of Northwold, the consciousness of Bloody Johnny's soul suffered a complete suspension after his body was dead. Whether this suspension outlasted his burial in the Wells Road Cemetery, which happened immediately after the flood, and whether it will outlast the life of this planet, and of all other such bubbles of material substance that the torrent of Life throws up, is unknown to the writer of this book.
>
> It is certain however that Mr. Geard was not mistaken when he decided that to plunge into the bitterness of death

in order to gain more life was an action that at least would destroy what he had found so hampering to his spirit in the infirmities of his flesh. (XXX. 1172 or 1118)

Perhaps it may help us if we feel the reservations coming from Powys's normal uninspirational self, and the more mystical intimations from a less easily definable source.

The intuition may be completely optimistic:

What they were aware of was the dumb, numb, cold, heavy downward drag of the vast undersea forces that are sub-human; chemical forces, that belong to that formless world of the half-created and the half-organic whereof bodies of lower dimensions than ours are composed and which has a mysterious weight that draws down, a pull, a tug, a centripetal gravitation, against which the soul within us struggles and upon the surface of which it swims, and over which, when the process of decomposition commences, it spreads its contemptuous wings.

(XXIX. 1080 or 1032)

With which we may group a statement in the 1941 *Owen Glendower* (XX. 865) that "when our lips touch the ice-damp of a dead face we know by the feel of *that skin*, which we recognise now for the first time to be what it is, that this cast-off shell, this husk of matter, this puppet of shame, this moment of corruption, has no connection at all with the indestructible spirit we have lived with and have loved."

If these two ringing statements hold truth, then all our other, more tentative, probings are readily placed as painful strugglings against the inertia, the "weight" and "pull", of earth-conditioned understanding. If, on the other hand, such thoughts of "contemptuous wings" and "indestructible spirit" are, as so many today would assert, utterly absurd, then not only the labours of *A Glastonbury Romance*, but the greater part of our religions and literature—including in our time (as

196

I have shown in *Neglected Powers*) Yeats, Masefield and Eliot—is little better than a sham which we should do better to ignore.

Survival is a major concern in *A Glastonbury Romance*. Not all Powys's books are so impregnated. *A Glastonbury Romance* aims at a comprehensive reading of man in relation to the cosmos. That could scarcely be repeated: one such book is surely enough. It was followed by *Weymouth Sands*, or *Jobber Skald* (1934; new edn. 1963), choosing as its *locale* Powys's well-loved Weymouth, and concentrating on an imaginatively transfigured earth, rock and sea setting. Mysteries are present, and discussed (e.g. V. 154 or 159), but emphasis falls on marvels that are in, or act through, earth-nature. But *Maiden Castle* (1937; new edn. 1966) again engages the occult. In Chapter VI the question of survival is closely argued between the hero No-man and his father Enoch (Uryen) Quirm:

> "But do you really believe in all this business of spirits and powers and influences and presences? Mind you, the point is not whether there may be *something* in it . . . I think it's extremely likely that there *is* 'something' in it. But the question is—do you believe in what's in it enough to fight for it, to starve for it, to sacrifice women for it, to desert children for it? Is it as important as your lust, your glory, your peace of mind? . . . Are you just playing with these supernatural influences, with these 'Powers' as you call them, or do you take them as actually real, real as this stick, real as your cap in your pocket? (VI. 221 or 233)

Enoch admits that they do not have exactly *that* kind of reality; but they have "their own *kind* of reality". Girls, he says, understand better, as they are satisfied with the "*atmosphere of reality*" and do not insist on "all or nothing truths". His son remains unsatisfied:

> I know what atmospheres are, as well as anybody. But I can't help feeling that when you touch the supernatural it must be a clear issue—yes or no. I feel just the same

197

about life after death. There's something teasing to my mind when people blur the issue of a thing as important as that. Either we *do* survive, or we *don't* survive . . .

(VI. 223 or 235)

The discussion has penetration and urgency. *Maiden Castle* is mainly concerned with the ancient powers of its Hill, with which Enoch is in contact, but there is one peculiarly precise, "spiritualistic", event, when it seems that the hero's dead wife Mona has actually inscribed her name on a paper (VIII. 382 or 394; IX. 405 or 417, 430 or 442). The book's "cast of characters" lists "the Spiritual Presence of Mona Smith, ten years deceased".

We cannot understand Powys without entangling our mind with such categories. His grim *Morwyn* (1937) is an intensely conceived realization of an after-life. All Powys's esoteric and visionary skills are given to making this evil spirit-world, this etheric dimension, tangible.

The occult in literature is often enough, as in *Macbeth*, associated with evil and fear. *A Glastonbury Romance* is a dark book, and *Morwyn* an "Inferno". When, as in *Weymouth Sands*, nature is itself both bright and magical, we shall hear less of external powers. This is the general situation, applying to masses of our literature. There is a natural human desire to feel the spirit-powers as embodied; it is our task while on earth to assure, so far as may be, that they are; and the Christian doctrine of the Incarnation is a lever in the process.

It is within this situation that Powys's work functions; more, it is this very situation which it is always labouring to interpret.

Powys's later writings are part of what is sometimes known as the "mysticism of descent". He does not challenge us with the spirit-powers, as before; but they are nevertheless active, and activating. This comes about in various ways: mysteries may be felt within moments of paradisal recognition, as happened at the end of *Wolf Solent*, and often in *Weymouth*

Sands; magicians are active within the historical works, *Owen Glendower* (1941), *Porius* (1951), and *The Brazen Head* (1956), where their powers are, being distanced, the easier to accept, though we have more of a contemporary challenge in *The Inmates* (1952); or we have myth, as in *Atlantis* (1954); and the "fairy tale" conventions of *Up and Out* (1957), *The Mountains of the Moon* (1957) and *All or Nothing* (1960). Of all these only one, the short and not wholly successful *Up and Out*, is sceptical in tenour, and even that is only sceptical within the structure of a religious fantasy wherein God and the Devil are persons.

Powys's imaginative structures support, as structures, the affirmations, while including a number of intellectual reservations. In *The Brazen Head* Sir Mort believes in the reality of psychic presences while denying human survival (XI. 165). Three persons especially, Jobber Skald in *Weymouth Sands*, Broch-o'-Meifod in *Owen Glendower* and Zeuks in *Atlantis*, point the nature of Powys's later philosophy. They are rock-like persons for whom mysteries are irrelevant; cut, as it were, from nature's solidities, their very being invites us to make that nature our centre. Neither Broch nor Zeuks involve themselves in esoteric mysteries; the one rejects survival, the other remains dubious. Even so, each is part only of the grand design in which he occurs: Zeuks may be favoured, but he has against him the less likeable but far from unimpressive prophet of the Mysteries, Enorches.

There certainly *is* a development in the imaginative works, or in one emphatic strain of them, corresponding to that in the philosophical essays. In *Porius* Taliessin has a long statement in verse of the purely natural mysticism with which Powys became more and more content:

> The centre of all things, yet all on the surface,
> The secret of Nature, yet Nature goes blabbing it
> With all of her voices from earth, fire, air, water!

(XIX. 418)

We may call it a "super-Wordsworthianism". But it does not necessarily deny what Powys had written at the conclusion to his *Autobiography* (1934): "The astronomical world is *not* all there is. We are in touch with other dimensions, other levels of life" (XII. 652). Or in *Mortal Strife*, written during the war:

> What in this Dimension we naturally think and feel about life and death is in harmony with this Dimension. When we are dead, life and death, according to this present dimension, cease; and something else substitutes itself for them. Of the nature of this something else it is not only now impossible to obtain the faintest clue; it must of necessity always be impossible, simply because Time and Space *get in the way*. (VII. 113)

There are, surely, 'clues': in art, in mystical reports, in clairvoyance. Powys himself knows this; so well, indeed, that he fears too close an engagement, as in his letter to me (already quoted), on the dangers of the occult. This corresponds to his views in *In Spite Of*, where he rejects spiritualistic engagements, saying of his present philosophy:

> It contains an instinctive dread of being led into contact with a whole dimension of strange, unruly, disorderly forces that can be very dangerous to our natural peace of mind and to our normal human activities. (IV. 94)

He does not here deny this other dimension; it is only too real; he just regards it as dangerous, especially for those, like himself, most intellectually sensitive (IX. 293).

Death beats through Powys's writings. The seers, Enoch Quirm in *Maiden Castle* and Myrddin Wyllt (Merlin) in *Porius* are death-impregnated. Death keeps returning (*The Saturnian Quest*, Index C, 'Death'). In *The Art of Happiness* (1935) Powys had told us to replace Wordsworth's "the pleasure which there is in life itself" (*Michael*, 77) with "the pleasure which there is in life and death" (42–4, 47). In *Mortal Strife* we were told that Time and Space veil the truth. What happens in his later thought is, simply, this: he tends to reject Time, and rely on Space. In my discussion of *In Spite Of* in *The Saturnian Quest* I wrote (VI. 89):

Powys's consciousness seems to have plunged so deep and expanded so widely in mastery of space that temporal extension . . . begins to lose authority. Normally we think of space as within time; in Powys space has begun to swallow time. Insight so reduces egoism that survival becomes an irrelevance; the sky's infinity makes life so marvellous as to be utterly satisfying apart from any thought of it (IV. 91; VIII. 237). Despite his dissatisfaction with modernistic poetry (*Obstinate Cymric*, VIII), his own thought-lines are running parallel to its tendency to concentrate in depth or height on particularities without temporal reference. Such thinking presupposes a state already within a dimension wherein futurity, and therefore all questions of survival, lack meaning; a state, some would call it, of 'eternal life'. Only so can we make sense of Powys's assertion that the 'I' can feel immune from, and 'outside the radius' of, even a 'planetary disaster' (VII. 207).

Powys himself calls it a state of "eternal security". To feel so "immune" would do credit to the most fervent Spiritualist, or Christian, believer.

It will be seen that Powys's later scepticism is, even in his philosophical books, far from simple; it is nearer to an all-embracing mysticism irreducible to concepts. In so far as concepts are forced, he puts his money on "space" (*The Saturnian Quest*, Index C, 'Space'). In *All or Nothing* space assumes a major importance. The story's very title, together with its dominating symbols of Skull and Flower-bowl, indicates the ultimate nature of Powys's final survey, reduced to simplicities beyond thought, in correspondence with the end of *A Glastonbury Romance:* "Never or Always". Among such simple ultimates we cannot breathe easily, or for long. We must return to the thought-currencies of our life and their extension into the higher currencies of art.

We must beware of attending to separate pieces of Powys's explicit thinking in his philosophical books or similar strains in certain persons of his narratives, without giving our primary attention to those narratives as wholes; which, in their most powerful elements, are so consistently made from an awareness of the mysteries: in spirit-powers, in his succession of magicians, in soul-projection; in use of legend, myth and fairy-story. These all take us beyond all ordinary thoughts: we must instead respond to, and put final trust in, the imagination. Death, we are told in *The Mountains of the Moon*, "will be as your ideas and thoughts about it create it" (in *Up and Out*, 218).

All writers of genius admit (as the word 'genius' itself implies) a degree of inspiration, but only Powys has, to my knowledge, deliberately set himself to analyse it. In his *Homer and the Aether* (1959), the Aether is an inspiring deity who in an introductory statement "The Aether Speaks" explains just what she does for the poet and what she leaves him to do for himself.

Here Powys, as artist, is writing of, and fictionally creating, the Goddess of Literary Inspiration; and in so doing he may well be supposed to be, as a writer of genius, more than usually "inspired". The Aether is accordingly active behind what is being said. Though not in this context obviously relevant, Powys's obsession with death must be, on this unique occasion, contained; more, it must conclude.

First, the Aether calls mankind "lucky" to be able in death to sleep and never wake. That sounds definite. And yet the inspirer will not let us end with this. Perhaps Powys tried to, but felt uneasy; that is just the way inspiration often acts. So the Aether now follows on with (i) a brief covering of Powys-the-man's personal desire for rest and (ii) a more extended and, in a fairy-tale style, beautifully worded dream of Elysian bliss. I quote the concluding paragraph ("The Aether Speaks", 29):

> What I am going to help you to do, you old indomitable, indefatigable Homer of my heart, is to accept and enjoy to the limit all the ordinary events in that human life of yours, which, wherever it is played out, is always a magnified view, or a minimized view, of some kind of Trojan War. Yes, I want to help you to describe the

amazing life of mortals upon the earth; and when you have ushered each one of them in turn to the brink of the grave I want you to make them long to lie down in peace and sleep an unbroken sleep, or to soothe them if they are afraid of annihilation, by lovely dreams of a kindly Hermes-Angel who will guide them gently, softly, swiftly when the end comes, to some blest Elysian Field where they can meet everybody again that they want to meet, and forget everything they want to forget forever and forever and forever.

Powys cannot make the deity of poetic inspiration conclude on a denial. We are not however told that human beings survive. The statement deliberately confines itself to what they feel and think; it is addressed to the imagination, and the imagination remains, as it should, our guide. If survival be a fact, it remains, for us on earth, a fact dependent on our imagination. So guided, we shall note how half-hearted sound the few words on extinction and in contrast with what exquisite and lingering care the author draws out those concluding phrases.

XI

THE SANDS DO NOT RUN OUT

H. P. Collins

It is in an Aristotelian preference for the impossible probable over the improbable possible that one may well find the clue to John Cowper Powys's psychological penetration: for if it is to the elemental that he naturally and most creatively gravitates, he might well appear something less than our contemporary in his tone and manner if he were not something more than our contemporary in his penetration of character and motive. A penetration that leaves his younger rivals standing. He disliked Freud; and with all his generosity and hospitality of mind he could hardly, being what he was, do other in his later years than repudiate what the twentieth century has made of the environment. He was a child of earth, nurtured in simpler times than ours. His later novels did impose, not always quite convincingly, a modern psychology on a less complex world. That is their fundamental weakness. By *Maiden Castle*, anyhow, he had parted company with the XX century, in which his temperament had always lived with an uneasy bravura. After the middle 1930's his imagination, when he was really writing freely and not from a kindly sense of duty of helping his fellow men to live, roved more and more unrestrainedly into past and remote worlds.

So it is not really arbitrary to see the books he published (in a delayed noontide) between 1930 and 1935 as the core of his whole vast achievement. He was, perhaps for the first time, more or less at peace within himself, and he was ripe and ready to survey his sixty years of life and study; and, free of urgent lecturing and journalism, to distil the whole of his truth into large works of fiction and into the self-portraiture which was the speciality of the clan Powys. In these years of his mature middle age, and these alone, we find the full man. Here we find that psychology which we are tempted to call something undercutting psychology itself in collaboration with an imagination which often bursts the bounds of anything which our modern experience contains.

But the worry of almost all readers is, naturally, does an *artist* survive these stresses, or does the art get lost? In the great *Autobiography* (and it has no superior in the English language) the question hardly arises; and even those who find John Cowper's novels hard-going can scarcely be excused, if they have real minds at all, from following the outwardly shapeless, inwardly utterly compelled and compulsive, revelation of his teased and tormented life.

We are concerned here with the three climactic novels *Wolf Solent*, *A Glastonbury Romance*, and *Jobber Skald*, and specifically with the third, often and not quite unaccountably regarded as slightly the least of the three. After *Wolf Solent*, and the *Romance*, whither? a contemporary must have asked. Into Wolf, the hero or rather anti-hero of what is in most respects his deepest *novel*, John Cowper has concentrated the best of himself and the almost inconceivably subtle exploration of a human being's capacity for being peculiar. And Wolf forms a consistent centre of interest (John Cowper most shamelessly self-centred in fact!) and the passionate love and close knowledge of the earth burn intensively if occasionally fitfully.

A Glastonbury Romance (that subtle silly title) was by violent contrast a flood, just as it culminated in a flood. No unifying interest here. The scope was awe-inspiring and bewildering, whatever the *Romance's* dubiousness as a novel in the sense *Wolf Solent* is a novel. *Jobber Skald* moved far further in the direction of being a novel—though not all the way—but the distracting fragmentation of interest is still there.

The real hero of *Jobber Skald* is not a man but a place. John Cowper's early possession by the spirit of Weymouth is not surprising. He did drink in (and retain) some vivid early impressions of the lovely Derbyshire country round his father's parish of Shirley; but he was still under eight when the monolithic vicar accepted a humble curacy at Dorchester and found a temporary home by the sea (to the rear of Brunswick Terrace) commanding views of both West Bay and Portland Harbour.

One must remember that in these Weymouth days his boyish misery had not yet been precipitated by guilt obsessions and by the school life for which he was so unfitted: "an ecstasy came to me, morning after morning, as I saw the sun glittering on the sea."[1] He recalled vividly, too, the greenish tint in the

Eastern sky at daybreak. That more than normal awareness, that being more than normally alive, began to show itself in this ancient yet exciting world. As one looks over "the Isle" one experiences the primitive surging-up in the midst of what is heavy with tradition. It is the brooding presence of this unique peninsula, climbing rock-like out of the sea which is what remains—and all that remains—of Hardy's disappointing last story *The Well Beloved*.

Jobber Skald (or *Weymouth Sands*) is the most "poetic" and to some the most *enjoyable* of John Cowper's novels, though still dubiously a novel. It is largely, perhaps not intentionally, a drenched offering to Poseidon from one hitherto envisaged as kneeling and tapping his head on the earth (quite literally and appropriately) in homage to Demeter.

There had been of course *Rodmoor* (never published in Great Britain) where the scene was transferred—as it was early in the *Romance*—from the west to East Anglia. Nobody who has read in *Rodmoor* the description of a dead sea, the very salt still deathliness of its death, could ever forget it. And the sea, once bright and sparkling as in John Cowper's Weymouth childhood, in the end claims the chief personae as its prey. But from *Rodmoor* until the more buoyant phase of *Jobber Skald*, "nature" had been terrestrial rather than oceanic or astral or even zoological to John Cowper. The elemental involves all these values, and John Cowper is nothing if not elemental. He had learned very early, from Hardy especially, to see all human feelings, gestures, actions, against the natural, the animate or inanimate world, that is so much wider than the social. He saw that White of Selborne or W. H. Hudson was not "nature" so creatively as Homer and Scott.

Jobber Skald is not only a defiance of the social novel but a step forward from its two formidable predecessors in effecting a marriage of the land and the sea. In a sense of course that *is* Portland: without the geographical and geological uniqueness there could hardly have been such a Weymouth and nowhere else could John Cowper have so mingled sand and öolite and ozone and the tang of seaweed.

> between St. Alban's Head, the White Nose, the Nothe, Chesil Bridge, the Breakwater, the town Bridge, the White Horse, Hardy's Monument, King George's statue, St. John's Spire, the Jubilee Clock, and this perpetual crying of sea-gulls and advancing and retreating of sea-tides, there might have arisen in their large confederacy, a brooding Patience, resembling that of an Organic Being; a patience that approached, if it never quite could attain, the faint, dim, embryonic half-consciousness that brooded in the sea-weeds, the sea-shells, the sea-anemones, the star-fish and jelly-fish, that lay submerged along those beaches and among those rock pools. (190)[2]

It is amazingly yet perhaps significantly an exile who recalls these things. It would be a bold man who could feel sure, exactly, when and where one so quizzical and mischievous as John Cowper actually wrote anything, but it does seem fairly authentic that *Jobber Skald* was composed in the hinterland of New York State after *Wolf Solent* and the *Romance* and *Autobiography*, and just before his (poetically, overdue) return to the legend-haunted Britain of his childish memories and Cymrian imaginings. Perhaps one should recall that the dull—American title of *Weymouth Sands* was suppressed in the English edition and the title *Jobber Skald*, with its quaint suggestion of Icelandic saga, was substituted because the author, always rather childishly afraid of the Law, had run into difficulties with the self-fancied original of Philip Crow in the *Romance*. The very precise place-names were disguised (quite ineffectively) in *Jobber Skald* and have now been restored, to little profit, in the re-issue as *Weymouth Sands*. It is with essences, not with particularities, that the majestic sweep of John Cowper's major novels is involved, happily though he may have toyed with his memories of the particular.

In *Jobber Skald*, more than ever before, John Cowper indulged his passion for the childish and the fetichistic. Some of his not unreasonable critics found the book inextricably compounded of the awe-inspiring and the ludicrous. Major poetry mingled with improbable enormities, the whole touched with a psychological cunning that could not be ignored and was yet outrageously unorthodox! *Jobber Skald* being more epic poem than drama, does incur some standard charges against John Cowper as an artist. That he is really talking to himself, for example; and that his characters have no life unless they are either women or John Cowpers. And one always has the feeling that he is perilously on the edge of the grotesque.

In Powys's essentially poetic novels one has always to reckon with a certain imbalance between humourless intensity and the wry, ironic awareness (often amounting to self-mockery) that permeates the *Autobiography* and his letters. Any conception of him which ignores this element of the side glance would be incomplete. A great novel of the elemental may be, like *Wuthering Heights*, virtually humourless, or it may, like most of Hardy's, be offset with superb comic relief: *Jobber Skald* comes somewhere between, since amid all the high seriousness such characters as Sylvanus Cobbold and Gaul have a deliberate absurdity. The humour is inherent rather than explicit. "He's not humorous in ordinary life," says the Jobber of Cobbold, "And yet he's very original. You feel it, you know, though it's hard to say *how* you feel it." Much of this can be said of the author too.

Neither Weymouth as seen in the novel nor those who people Weymouth can be set quite in perspective without this side glance.

> though the Spire was half-a-century older than the Statue, there was an historic link between them. Both represented the inmost platonic essence of the Victorian era; for what the Spire had gained in its long experience of the Queen's subjects, as people went Sunday by Sunday to worship the Queen's God, the Statue made up for by being the living image of the Queen Herself. Thus while the elderly Spire respected the brand-new Statue, the Statue looked up to the Spire with solemn confederacy. (64)

> Being a philosopher, rather than a neophyte in sanctity,
> Mr. Gaul did not feel it at all incumbent upon him to
> refrain from contemplating Perdita's legs. (162)

Rustic talkers in Hardyesque vein, though more dubiously
stylised than Hardy's, from a more slanted creator, afford a
comic outlet that has more than comic implications. Magnus's
"Wiltshire landlady" brings into consciousness not only
Sarah Gamp but the lasting legend and superstition and
earthiness of the England in which John Cowper's work has
its life.

> "There's summat on, my charmer," she said, using an
> expression of endearment that she had picked up in a
> Canon's family in Salisbury Close, "there's summat on
> that's as serious as King's Evidence . . . those two, glaring
> and staring, and nudging in whispers, like a couple of
> executioners! And don't let's forget to bear in mind how
> you saw that Gipsy from Lodmoor pass this door so
> early this morning, muttering funny-like to herself and
> dragging a heavy load, nor how that picture of your
> blessed Dad fell from its nail. The Lord be up to summat,
> my charmer; he be up to summat. But 'tis His Doing and
> So Be Still, as the canon's wife used to say to Maria the
> cook when he killed a mole on his lawn." (539)

Powys saw infinite humour in things, but most of all in himself;
and this quality is never more pronounced than when he has
one eye on the stars, as in *Jobber Skald*.

The repetitions and the blurring of male character are
certainly weaknesses in the book. The whole issue of too
subjective and too sentimental character drawing has one
must admit, been evaded or simply not perceived by the
enthusiasts among his champions (who have much to answer
for!). Mr. Roland Mathias, one of the coolest and most penetrating of John Cowper's critics, has happily differentiated
between the "intuitives" who furnish the real psychological
tension of the novels and the external figures who merely
"sinuate the plot".[3] The intuitives, whatever their age, status,

or even sex, partake inescapably of the mind of their author. They rarely if ever act as persons rather than minds, or respond to normal social pressures. Magnus Muir and Gaul in *Jobber Skald*, rather elaborate projections of the author, can hardly be said to do anything. Their significance is as sounding boards.

Mr. Mathias has perhaps illustrated John Cowper's elemental rather than social motivation even more directly when he describes the main characters as "not products of society but foci of intellectual, genealogical, geological and vegetable pressures". In effect, it is not their surface behaviour which matters at all.

It is fairly clear that John Cowper, if ever anyone did, understood his own nature and limits very well. There is almost "a touch of caricature" (of contempt he was incapable) in the portraiture of himself and of the vicar of Montacute in Magnus Muir the Latin tutor and his dead father, replete with huge fetichistic walking-stick and dominating presence. Like his author, Magnus has a deep strain of masochism in his character: like John Cowper he is seized with a "swift funk" if he gets a glimpse of himself in a mirror.[4] Like Wolf, or Dud of *Maiden Castle*, he is inevitably betrayed—though far more callously—by the familiar working-class lovely. But the unobtrusive scholarly Magnus is by no means the only or most challenging projection of John Cowper in the book. Young Mr. Gaul, who lives on a tiny private income and is evolving a vast work on world philosophy, has no role in the action and can hardly be said to step outside his author's shoes. He does however embody, in the midst of a conception of life straining hard at the infinite, John Cowper's occasional yearning to contain himself in the finite. He does, as his author creating on a larger scale could not, strive to come to terms with life. He is thus a forceful contrast to Sylvanus Cobbold, "a mystic", one of John Cowper's several fey self-projections who belong to the regions of poetry rather than prose, and to the Island rather than to what is still recognisable of Victorian Weymouth. (*Jobber Skald* was originally assigned to the period 190–, which presented certain anachronisms—perhaps adopted deliberately for disguise—but this note was abandoned on the adoption of the original *Weymouth Sands* American text on the 1963 edition.)

Sylvanus is a sort of holy ranter, with a dangerous attraction for young girls and the gift of drawing crowds, who does not substantially enter the book until social plausibility begins to give way wholly to elemental imagination. He finishes, defiantly, in a mental home. He shows, as do several of the intuitives in the book, John Cowper's increasing withdrawal from the modern world, which was to become a pronounced aversion from *Maiden Castle* on. John Cowper's people are fundamentally solitaries. The "intuitives", at least, go their own way, are concerned with their own idiosyncrasies, reflections of their creator's interest in introspection, psychology, rather than doing. This lack of involvement with others is more notable in the men than in the women. The feminine characters in *Jobber Skald* are more alive and formative of the action than the men or boys. The Jobber, however, the amphibious, classless giant, is like Bloody Johnny Geard of the *Romance* only slightly a projection. He is indispensably part of the book, of the sea and the Island and love; but not convincing in his social behaviour. He is hardly XX century. He is pledged to murder Dog Cattistock with a large Chesil pebble which he carries round ostentatiously in his pocket. His purpose he parades for the benefit of all and sundry. His language, like that of several other widely differing characters, is too naive *and* too educated; and reflects his author's indifferences as to who thinks what, revealing rather startlingly the differences between psychology where it is inspired and where it is not. The Jobber, too, is talking to himself—except where he is briefly but unforgettably making love.

This imperfection in male characterisation, except in subjective "intuitives" is of considerable significance in understanding John Cowper. Deeply concerned with evil, he draws (as Wilson Knight has observed) evil instincts rather than

evil characters. So, here Dog Cattistock and the vivisectionist—
horror of horrors to John Cowper—have their very human
side and human pathos.

Into feminine instincts John Cowper's penetration is ad-
mittedly extraordinary. Here his psychological super-awareness
achieves miraculous revelations. If the "non-intuitive" women,
the sinister Mrs. Cobbold and the irrelevant Ruth Lader, fail,
the real daughters of nature, Marret, Gypsy-May, Tissty and
Tossty, and above all Perdita Wane—all those in fact who find
their real or spiritual home in the Island or Lodmoor—are
unforgettable as the sea and the öolite and the storms are
unforgettable. "Love still hath something of the sea" wrote
Sedley and it is from the sea that Perdita, a conventional
shabby-genteel virgin of twentyfive, is washed-up to Weymouth
and the Jobber to become perhaps the most penetratingly
realised lover in literature. It is not her behaviour that is
convincing so much as her author's utter realism in showing
her emotions. It is her going to the Jobber's native home on the
"Isle of Slingers", where he sits beside her in bewildered
awareness, that opens in her all the heaven and hell of possess-
iveness.

> "Our love is no ordinary love" she thought. "We could
> quarrel fiercely, we could separate in blind anger, but
> nothing could ever really divide us, now we've once met."
> Her thoughts sank deeper and deeper down into the
> nature of this eternalized moment, into the heart of the
> experience through which she was passing. The hardness
> of the wall, as with her body thus immobile she pressed
> the stones with her fingers, gave her the feeling that her
> soul was sinking into this vast promontory of öolite as
> into the shaft of a bottomless quarry.
>
> "I'm glad I came straight to his home," she thought.
> "It's funny how I didn't really admire him or respect him
> or even altogether *like* him!"
>
> She gripped the stone with her fingers so hard that
> the knuckles went white. That bony structure of her face

showed itself in her death-stillness, as if it were her very
skull seen through the transparency of her soft, weak,
drooping fluctuating lineaments. Her intellect seemed
clearer than it had ever been in her life before, and she
derived a savage pleasure from tearing away every shred
of sentiment, every tag of reverence from what she felt
for this man.

"It's as if something of him were inside me and something
of me were inside him. It's as if there were no need for
him to take me, any more than he has taken me already!
It's as if when I hurt him I hurt myself and when he
hurts me he hurts himself."

Her fixed gaze, with its new "skull-look" transforming
her sorrowful features, seemed to penetrate the very
roots of that stone-crop at her feet and plunge into the
substratum of this stupendous sea-rock, into the foundation of it, into what lay fathom-deep below the sea-surface.

"I'm sure I don't know whether people would call what
we feel for each other 'being in love', or whether it's even
passion. I think if he *does* take me to-night he'll do it
clumsily, awkwardly, brutally, *and I shall be the same*. He
doesn't seem to want to kiss me very much, and I don't
want to kiss him very much. It's as if we were both digging
into each other's soul to find a self that was put there
before we were born." (345)

The young lady, in fact, drenched with spray, goes over
entirely to the primitive, to the man who embodies it; and the
tension of their poetry is enhanced by the fact that she remains
perceptibly a lady. Here, constrained by the *genius loci*, John
Cowper is consummately the artist he so often fails to be when
he abandons himself to wilful introversion.

As the novel, concentrating alternately on Sylvanus and the
Jobber, draws more and more poetically to its complicated
conclusion, it is clear that the Island must frame the climax.
Here the love of Perdita and the Jobber is consummated, if not
yet to final happiness: here is the home of Sylvanus. The

Sea-Serpent, an inn of *Wuthering Heights* other-worldliness, is the symbol of elemental forces, the winds and the tides breaking against the extreme western shore of Portland. Portland with its "terraces of old walls and grey roofs," with a "gigantic rope of transparent stones, agates and cornelians" (348) binding it to the mainland.

The sublimation of humanity by response to these forces is the ultimate message of the novel. "Nature," human and inhuman, is to John Cowper the ultimate solution. How the wind blows!

> Yes, the wind seemed to set itself to force her to listen to it and to enter into its non-human passions. It forced her to follow its wild path over the whistling wave-crests and amid the flying surf. It forced her to follow it, as driving the scudding spray before it, it shrieked round those jagged rocks, while beneath it, below the sea-floor level, deep-gurgling rock-chasms drew the waves in and spewed them out. The wind made (her) follow it when it left the turbulence of the rocks, and began whirling up the face of the cliff. Up the face of the cliff it twisted like the sea-serpent. It whirled up through dead tufts of bent-grass and through the wind-blighted elders and ashes and stunted gorse. It whirled up over patches of samphire, and over patches of grey rock-lichen, and over whistling stalks of sea-lavender and over chittering seed-pods of sea-thrift. And as it rose higher, it wheeled and eddied and coiled . . . (268)

Never surely, did the Ordnance Survey Map, that prosaic but desirable companion for the reader, point the way to a richer background. Weymouth as seen to the north from Portland is unforgettably realised; and the Island itself sloping down from Easton to the Bill and, westward, to the Head is intensely of this earth and at the same time a poet's dream. The people have "the very stamp and seal and unmistakable look of that ancient, mysterious, short-statured, dark population that the Celts dispossessed, ere they were dispossessed them-

selves by the invading Saxons." (269) The Bill itself marks for
Perdita and the Jobber the marriage of land and water that
parallels the marriage of contrasts in themselves.

> The Jobber and Perdita made their way out, till they
> reached the very end of this sea-jutting platform of solid
> rock. Here they found themselves standing side by side
> upon what resembled some dancing-floor of the sea-
> nymphs, so smooth it was, or the level tomb-stone of some
> ancient sea-god. It was a floor upon which a herd of seals
> might have lain down to sleep, shepherded by Proteus. It
> was dark brown in colour, spotted with some variety of
> yellowish sea-lichen, and in particular places its surface
> was roughened by living shell-fish that clung tenaciously
> to it and by minute fossils whose indwelling entitites had
> perished millions of years ago. Under it the dark-green
> water swirled and foamed and gurgled, and beyond it,
> below the tossed-up surf—for the waters of Portland Bill
> were disturbed by other agencies than the day's weather—
> there were endless whirlpools and revolving maelstroms
> of green water. It was one of those spots where Nature
> arrives at an extremity of contrast that suggests a sublime
> intention, for while there was gathered-up in that rocky
> floor, which itself was about twenty feet long and about
> half that distance wide, the very absolute of immobility,
> there was flung abroad in those breaking waters the
> corresponding absolute of never-ceasing movement. Stand-
> ing upon this platform a person felt himself held by
> gravitation to the very bed-rock of our planet's substance,
> whereas in that rushing whirl of waters he was aware of
> gaping holes out of which jets of the aboriginal chaos kept
> bubbling up. (348)

The power of precise observation of natural things which
had been very early fostered in a precocious and over-subtle
child by a simple and almost childlike father, fortifies all the
novels but none so strongly as *Jobber Skald* where the visible
world impresses itself on the mind even more strongly than
John Cowper's exploratory inwardness. And underneath it

all there pulses a life larger than life itself "between St. Alban's Head, the White Nose, the Nothe, Chesil Beach, the Break-water, the Town Bridge, the White Horse, Hardy's Monument, King George's statue, St. John's Spire, the Jubilee Clock" in and around a Weymouth that, after all, never was on sea or land.

NOTES

[1] *Autobiography* (1934), 1967, p. 29.
[2] Numerals in parentheses throughout refer to pages in *Weymouth Sands* (1934), 1963.
[3] Roland Mathias, *Dock Leaves*, Spring 1956, pp. 21–26.
[4] *Letters of John Cowper Powys to Louis Wilkinson*, 1958, p. 332.

XII

THE PATTERN OF HOMECOMING

Gwyneth F. Miles

For a wanderer like John Cowper Powys the experience of homecoming must have been both significant and familiar. As a schoolboy and later as an itinerant lecturer Powys made a great many journeys to and away from his home and his family. The importance of this home to his creative work is indicated by the settings of his first novels, all written in America but set in the English counties where he grew up. In the Introduction to the 1961 edition, he describes *Wolf Solent* as "a Book of Nostalgia, written in a foreign country with the pen of a traveller and the ink-blood of his home." Upon returning to Britain Powys asserted his long-felt sense of racial and spiritual affinity with the Welsh, and considered his move to North Wales a true and final homecoming. It is not surprising, then, to find recurring in Powys's fiction a pattern of journeys homeward, both actual and spiritual.

In many of the novels such a journey serves as a starting point, the initial action from which the subsequent action results. *Rodmoor, Ducdame, Wolf Solent, A Glastonbury Romance, Maiden Castle* and *Owen Glendower* all have as their initial crisis the return of a protagonist to a place with which he has family ties. Powys has a remarkable sense of place, and in all of these novels the locale of the homecoming is a powerful presence and influence upon the action.

Homecoming is often identified in the protagonist's mind with a search for his father: in almost every one of these novels he has been more intimate with his mother than his father, but senses a stronger identification of the latter with the physical landscape of his home, a landscape from which his mother has remained detached. The quest for the father turns inevitably into a quest for the self, and in these novels the protagonist's homecoming results in a series of confrontations and discoveries which alter his conception of himself and his "life-illusion". The experience may destroy him, as it does Adrian Sorio in *Rodmoor*, or partially recreate him as in *Wolf Solent* and *Maiden Castle*.

Some of the later novels suggest a more subtle kind of homecoming beyond the familial and personal in the quest of certain mystical characters for spiritual contact with older races and civilizations with which they identify themselves. Even these transcendental journeys, however, are linked with physical places—Mr. Evans' Glastonbury, Uryen Quirm's Mai-Dun and Owen Glendower's Mathrafal. The search for origins, the turn backwards and inwards, the plumbing of psychological and spiritual depths are the qualities of Powys's fiction represented in the recurrent image of homecoming. While the pattern can be found in much of Powys's fiction, this essay will concentrate upon three major novels in which "homecoming" is central to both action and theme. These are *Wolf Solent* (1929), *Maiden Castle* (1937) and *Owen Glendower* (1942).[2]

Powys the wanderer turned in his imagination to the Dorset of his childhood, and *Wolf Solent* opens as its protagonist journeys back to the Dorset town where he grew up and now seeks to reroot himself. Wolf returns to Ramsgard (Sherborne) from a teaching post in London which he had lost as a result of an outburst reminiscent of Powys's own "malice-dance" at Sherborne School.[1] His flight to Ramsgard should not be dismissed as escapism, although it does involve a return to the country and to a superficially less demanding way of life. For while Wolf is escaping from the social and material demands of London, he is also conscious of escaping from an insensitive, brutal and trivial world to a place where he will have greater freedom to know and be himself. There is no suggestion of the security of the womb in Ramsgard and Blacksod; rather, they force Wolf to confront, as he had never done before, the basic forces of life and of his own personality. His homecoming challenges, and eventually destroys, that "mythology" which Wolf had considered "the secret substratum of his whole life" (15; 7). He finds himself undergoing a painful process of rebirth: he is forced out of the security of his former life with his mother into a new world where he must stand alone.

One aspect of Wolf's homecoming that recurs in others of Powys's novels is the identification of the "home" with the father, in opposition to the influence of the mother. In *Wolf Solent* the conflict between the spirits of his mother and father exists not only in Wolf's consciousness but in reality as well— years before, Mrs. Solent had taken her son to London, leaving her husband to complete his self-degradation in Ramsgard. Wolf's return to his father's town is in part a rebellious gesture of interest in and sympathy for his ambiguous begetter. The spirit of the elder Solent is a powerful presence in the novel, identified always with the scenery and atmosphere of Dorset.

> The green, heavily-grassed meadows through which the train moved now, the slow, brown, alder-shaded streams, the tall hedge-rows, the pollarded elms—all these things made Solent realize how completely he had passed from the sphere of his mother's energetic ambitions into the more relaxed world, rich and soft and vaporous as the airs that hung over these mossy ditches, that had been the native land of the man in the Ramsgard cemetery. (14; 6)

Upon his arrival in Ramsgard Wolf feels "free of his mother," and "bound up in some strange affiliation with that skeleton in the cemetery" (29; 20). His father's spirit encourages him to seize his opportunities with Gerda; it advocates liberty, pleasure and the cult of sensation in opposition to Mrs. Solent's more conventional ambitions. Thus Wolf's homecoming is to a world where the individual, interior life assumes a much greater significance, where the nature of his job and his personal relationships are bounded much more by individual vagaries than by the regulations of society.

What effect this homecoming will have upon the vagaries of his own soul, his private "mythology", concerns Wolf from the outset. For a time, sensing that the land is "whispering . . . some inexplicable prophetic greeting to its returned native-born" (35; 26), Wolf hopes that "this wonderful country must surely deepen, intensify, enrich his furtive inner life, rather than threaten or destroy it" (35; 27). But nonetheless he does feel threatened.

> Would he be crafty enough to keep that secretive life-
> illusion out of the reach of danger? Would his inner world
> of hushed Cimmerian ecstasies remain uninvaded by these
> Otters and Urquharts? (29; 20)

It does not, and herein lies the essential matter of the novel.
The landscape and the emotional intimacy of his relationships
in Dorset manage to attack the sanctities of his inner life as no
physical or personal contact in London had done. Unlike
Adrian in *Rodmoor*, however, Wolf Solent is not himself
destroyed by the collapse of his life-illusion. Filled with a new
compassion for "all the nameless little desolations around
him" (642; 613), Wolf resolves to "have the courage of (his)
cowardice" to accept both the beauty and the ugliness of
reality, and realizes "I can plough on and I can forget" (641;
611). He returns at the end of the novel to his own house,
admitting his wife's adultery and his own personal and social
failures. This is a homecoming fit to be compared, in its sense
of the pathos and courage of an individual's acceptance of life
as it is, with the homecoming of Leopold Bloom.

In *Maiden Castle* the pattern of homecoming again provides
a starting point and a central theme for the novel. We encounter
at once the now familiar figure of the unsuccessful literary
man, Dud No-man, returning to a Dorset town with which he
has family connections, and there discovering new facets of his
identity. A further development of the homecoming pattern,
however, appears in the figure of his father, Uryen. He too is
engaged in a search for his past, for his "home," but his conception of past and home is more mystical and remote than
that of Wolf or Dud. It has, nonetheless, a "local habitation"
in the prehistoric earthwork of Mai-Dun or Maiden Castle,
near Dorchester, where Uryen seeks communion with the
primitive gods once worshipped there. Dud himself is interested
in an earthwork, Maumbury Rings, where the heroine of his
novel was executed in the eighteenth century. The differences
between the size of these earthworks, and the antiquity of the
events which interest Dud and Uryen, respectively, are an
indication of the differences between father and son. Home-

coming to Dud is a complex psychological experience, but it lacks the metaphysical dimension of Uryen's search for his past.

Dud's experience is the more familiar and comprehensible one, and it is the focus of the novel. *Maiden Castle* begins the day after Dud's arrival in Dorchester, and his homecoming there is the impulse behind the novel's subsequent action. Although Dorchester was not his boyhood home, the graves of his family are there, his father lives there, and his coming to live in the town provokes as great a disturbance in his inner life as Wolf's return did in his. Dud bears considerable resemblance to Wolf Solent in his ungainliness, his unsuccessful literary labours and his misalliance with an attractive, unintellectual girl. And, again like Wolf, he proves to have an inner resilience due in part to his cult of sensation which enables him to survive the trials of his homecoming.

Dud's interest in Dorchester is partly historical; he recognizes in the aura of the town a "magical power" which enables him to tap "levels in his consciousness that he had not known he possessed" (100; 112). But the effect of Dorchester upon Dud goes beyond the stirring of his historical imagination. It stirs his emotional life as nothing seems to have done before. On his second day in Dorchester, Dud recognizes that "his coming to this town coincided with the lifting of a great sluice-dam in his emotional fate" (61; 73). His earlier life seems to have been spent in scholarly detachment from personal relationships: "nothing but his imagination had been *really* real to him before he came to Dorchester" (250; 263). Even his love life was carried on with the spirit of his dead wife, rather than with a real woman. When he visits his dead in Dorchester cemetery he releases them and himself from their morbid attachment. Immediately after this visit he becomes involved with Nancy, Wizzie, Thuella, Jenny and his own father. These encounters with real persons, unlike his dalliance with his submissive "Mona-wraith," disturb the complacency of his self-contained, self-centred world. Like Wolf's, Dud's homecoming is not an escape from but an engagement with the realities of life and other people:

> he thought how, if he were writing a story about himself, he would make All Souls' Day, this last autumn, appear like a new birth, the birth of a middle-aged man over forty into normal human life. (249; 261)

Part of the disturbance produced in Dud by his new life in Dorchester comes from the unexpected discovery of his father there. Unlike Wolf, for whom Ramsgard was inextricably identified with his aead father, Dud had known nothing at all about his father and was not consciously coming to him in coming to Dorchester. There is a suggestion, however, that Uryen's psychic power may have brought his son to the town (221; 233). Certainly, it is Dud's awakened curiosity about his begetter which causes him to cry out in the graveyard, attracting the attention of Nancy Quirm and thus setting in motion the train of complex relationships which make up the novel. Dud is at first repulsed by Uryen, and shirks identifying him as his father. He even declares that "after all, fathers are nothing! It's who your *mother* is that matters" (161–162; 173). This un-Powysian remark is merely an attempt at evasion and self-defence, a futile attempt since Dud must indeed come to terms with his ambiguous parent. Uryen's gesture of giving him the other bed-post is an overtly symbolic act, restoring to the son the other half of his inheritance. Just what sort of inheritance Uryen can give Dud is questionable. He cannot really even give him a name, for "Quirm" is as much an assumed name as the "Smith" which Dud had discarded. (Dud's babyish first name and his chosen surname "No-man" indicate the sense of inadequacy and impotence engendered by the absence of his real father.) Ironically, it emerges that "Uryen" was to have been Dud's own name, and his hostility to it indicates his inability to follow his father into the occult mysteries of which Uryen would have made him heir.

Uryen Quirm is a much more complex father than the sensual, life-loving William Solent. He himself forms part of

225

the pattern of homecoming in that he too is engaged in a search for his origins. But while Wolf and Dud are interested in their immediate begetters and the locale of their recent family history, Uryen seeks much further back, to the ancient civilization which he believes had built Stonehenge and Mai-Dun, "a civilization possessed of secrets of life that Aryan science has destroyed" (242; 254). The locality of Maiden Castle, both as actual place and as symbol, is necessary to his attempts to realize his full nature as Uryen, the god who bears the pain of man's efforts to "break through" from the natural world into the spiritual dimension (235, ff; 247, ff.). It is at Maiden Castle that Uryen worships and receives communications from the supernatural powers. In a sense, his whole personality is represented in that immense, mysterious earthwork. He believes it to be a stronghold of the ancient peoples now represented by the Welsh of whom he is one, and who alone among the races have retained "the old magic of the mind" (240; 252).

The sceptical Dud is unable to follow his father into these occult realms of metaphysical speculation and mystic identification with the ancient gods. Son and father both seek their identity, but while Dorchester brings the former into contact with the real world, with vivid, painful human relationships, the latter is led by Maiden Castle away from the sort of human involvement which is the salvation of his son to probe unfathomed depths of spiritual experience. It is a great strength of Powys's major fiction that it can portray two such different means of coming to terms with life, and can allow the value of both. Dud eventually acknowledges the validity of his father's search, but recognizes that the dimensions of experience which Uryen opens up are impossible for Dud himself to explore. He must remain Dud No-man, for he is no Uryen. "It was no good. He could *not* live, as" . . . Uryen had done, "in a wild search for the life behind life" (484; 496). At the end of the novel Dud, accepting his suffering and his limitations, faces existence with the same kind of courage that Wolf Solent shows. Both have "come home", and in so doing have been reborn into a new knowledge of themselves and other people. This rebirth involves suffering and the destruction of their former security, but inasmuch as this security was based upon illusions its loss becomes a creative process,

The pattern of homecoming in *Owen Glendower* is found in the two central characters, Rhisiart and Owen himself. But as Rhisiart, like Dud and Wolf, returns primarily to the local habitations of his immediate ancestors, so Owen resembles Uryen in his absorption in the more distant past. Rhisiart's homecoming is to Dinas Bran, the castle of his ancestors; Owen seeks, in Wales and in his own soul, the sacred places of the most ancient peoples. He comes home, in a spiritual sense, to Mathrafal, Tywyn and Mynydd-y-Gaer. Both Rhisiart and Owen experience in their return to their origins a stirring of the depths of their life-illusions, and both recognize a fatality in these places which claims them and marks their destinies.

Rhisiart's arrival in Wales, and his sensations upon encountering a new land and new people, occupy almost the first half of *Owen Glendower*. Although raised outside Wales, Rhisiart has a profound sense of being a Welshman, but his relationship to the native Welsh is fraught with complexities. Some of the tensions he experiences upon coming to the land of his fathers were no doubt experienced by Powys himself when, with his Welsh name and love of Welsh history and legend, he went to live in Corwen. Until Chapter V Rhisiart's interest in Wales is focused on the castle of Dinas Bran, which fascinates him both because of the legends surrounding it and because a recent ancestor of his had betrayed it to the English. It is with a romantic and vaguely defined intention of atoning for this family treachery that Rhisiart comes to Wales. Dinas Bran is the central symbol of his life-illusion, the "mystic terminus of every vista of his imagination" (9). How his youthful idealism and self-conceit are altered by this homecoming is a central theme of *Owen Glendower*.

Tension is generated in the opening pages of the novel by Rhisiart's apprehension that the reality of Dinas Bran may prove less than the ideal image on which his imagination had been nourished. That it does not may be in part due to the obvious limitations of that imagination, and in part the accident of season and light which cast a glamour over the hill fortress. The boy's awed recognition that Dinas Bran was "not less, *it was more*, than the picture he had in his mind" (12) enables him to fuse for a moment the ideal and the actual, and to find his sense of his own significance confirmed in the magnificence of his chosen symbol. Thus is introduced another major theme of the novel, the tension between the seen and the unseen, the material and the spiritual. This theme is developed later, and more dramatically, in the figure of Owen Glendower himself. But for the moment of Rhisiart's vision the tension is resolved, and the possibility of such a resolution, however momentary, illuminates the spiritual struggles of the rest of the novel. The castle becomes an archetype "of all the refuges and all the sanctuaries of the spirit, untouched by time" (12). This is the illumination which his homecoming has granted him, and which never entirely leaves him during his subsequent trials and sufferings.

Dinas Bran serves as the scene for a number of tests of Rhisiart's character, including his attempts to rescue Mad Huw and Simon and to resist the lures of Lowri and the Tower ladies. Closer acquaintance with the castle and its denizens makes Rhisiart realize the impossibility of his dreams of liberating it himself, and the reality becomes once more separate from his ideal.

> The imaginary one lifted itself clean out of this draughty mad-house of broken stones . . . and limned itself on those flying cloud-wracks of the mind's horizon that no madness could touch and no burning blacken. (261)

In the meantime Rhisiart has discovered a new ideal in the person of Owen Glendower who, upon the day Rhisiart met him, "took his place, easily, naturally and with a fatal inevitableness, on the ramparts of Dinas Bran and gathered into himself their mystic enchantment". (122) After coming home to Wales

Rhisiart replaces his attachment to an idealized place with a commitment to a real, and often very demanding, person. In this sense his homecoming resembles that of Dud, who also is attracted by a place but finds himself inadvertently drawn into the lives of its inhabitants. Owen, in part a father figure to Rhisiart, embodies that same spiritual power and occult knowledge which Dud comes to recognize in Uryen, and, like Dud, Rhisiart is brought by him to acknowledge dimensions in life beyond his own understanding.

> And he felt that no success or prosperity, no crashing disaster or devastating ruin, would henceforth ever make him forget he was a Welshman, or that he knew with Welsh knowledge that the things which are seen are un-essential compared with the things that are unseen. (934)

The importance of the unseen is never doubted by Owen himself. In seeking his origins and his spiritual home he is moved by no simple desire for personal and family glory such as inspired Rhisiart to seek Dinas Bran. His search extends into the prehistoric past of Wales, where he believes there existed a civilization with an understanding of life deeper than that of his own age, and his desire is to master that secret wisdom and keep it alive in modern Wales. The search is carried out through his study of ancient manuscripts, through necromancy and through submission to the undefined supernatural forces which take possession of him. Although this search is on a spiritual level, there are certain physical locations with which it is identified and which represent for Glendower's solitary spirit a kind of home. These are the ancient sacred places of the Welsh people—Mathrafal, Tywyn and Mynydd-y-Gaer. Other sacred places such as the mound at Glyndyfrdwy, Dinas Bran and Harlech serve him as temporary homes, and give significance to present actions by linking them with those of the past.

A central episode in this novel is Owen's journey to Mathrafal and his visionary experience there. He undertakes this journey immediately after his coronation, when he has symbolically shattered his crystal ball. Henceforth his spiritual exploration will be into the past, his back toward the future. The idea of sinking—downwards and backwards—into the past, into introspection and a self-sufficient passivity, is preferred to occult attempts to know and to influence the future, attempts he associates with political and temporal, rather than spiritual, power. At the moment of revelation in Mathrafal Owen cries *"The Past is the Eternal!"* (415), and in a sense his subsequent actions may be seen as an effort to make himself part of the past, to establish his spiritual and symbolic significance for eternity, rather than to grasp at success in the immediate future.

Owen's real homecoming is to Mynydd-y-Gaer, the hill fortress near Corwen where Powys has him spend his last years. This prehistoric labyrinth is as appropriate a symbol for Owen's understanding of life as that other hill fortress on the Dee, Dinas Bran, was for the romantic idealism and erotic complexities of Rhisiart's nature. The secret passages of Mynydd-y-Gaer correspond to the deep parts of the soul into which Owen would penetrate. At Mynydd-y-Gaer Owen has returned to the sacred place of the most ancient inhabitants of Wales, and in so doing has cast off all forms of power but the spiritual. Spiritual triumph in the midst of political defeat is Glendower's vision of his own destiny, and that of his nation. This is the secret revealed to him by his study of the origins of his people.

> . . . why shouldn't the whole race of Welshmen increase its power by sinking inwards, rather than by winning external victories? . . . What I'm doing now . . . is what all Welshmen can do who've got the least drop of . . . the ancient people's blood in their veins; sink, that's to say, into the 'Secret Passage' of our race. (914–915)

In choosing to "come home" at last to Mynydd-y-Gaer Owen makes complete his assertion of affinity with the ancient people, and with what he believes to be their secrets of life.

Both Rhisiart and Owen find their return to their origins the means of liberating themselves, through gaining perspective on the present and its concerns. They draw from their roots in the past the courage to maintain their independence, to assert *themselves* against the demands of the present. Owen's cry, "The Past is the Eternal!" gives a good indication of why the pattern of homecoming is so important in Powys's fiction. Homecoming is a gesture of turning in upon oneself and one's past, of "sinking inwards" and seeking the sources of one's being. The affinities with psychoanalysis are clear, although Powys never ties himself down to any system. What effect the experience of homecoming will have is determined by each individual nature. Adrian Sorio is destroyed by it. Wolf is stripped of his illusions and purged. Dud is forced by it into a new awareness of other people and of his own limitations. The young Rhisiart also grows in self-knowledge, and learns the value of areas of life outside his own comprehension. The most complex form of the pattern is in the magic figures, Owen and Uryen, who seek a spiritual home in "the life behind life." Their search ends in death, but in these death scenes Powys manages to suggest a final, apocalyptic homecoming of the human spirit, as it is received into that further dimension which the great magician-heroes have sought so long.

NOTES

[1] *Autobiography* (1934), 1967, p. 126.
[2] Subsequent numerals in parentheses refer to pages in the following editions of these three novels as they come into discussion:
Wolf Solent, 1929; 1961.
Maiden Castle, 1937; 1966.
Owen Glendower, 1942.

XIII

THE SACRIFICIAL PRINCE:
A Study of *Owen Glendower*

Roland Mathias

"*Owen Glendower*", wrote Professor G. Wilson Knight in 1964, "might be called Powys's greatest *artistic* achievement; a maximum of its contents in human insight, historical learning and intuition, archaeological exactitude, theological disquisition, social understanding . . . all can be fully received without reference to Powys's other works, though the relation is there. In it he allows full scope to idealisms, Christian and bisexual, that do not again recur".[1] Much of this is as it may be. If the implication is that *Owen Glendower* is artistic *because* it is intellectually and metaphysically autonomous rather than yet another comment upon ideas already expounded in earlier books, I would not seek to quarrel with such a judgment. My purpose does no more than begin with this point. I am interested, in passing, in discovering whether a well-defined subject from Welsh history is the basis of this artistic autonomy and, much more fundamentally, in trying to determine whether John Cowper Powys's distinctive metaphysic can be said to grow out of this subject or whether it has been imposed upon it. Is it in any way possible to ascertain whether *Wales* contributed to the "achievement" in a sense other than the choice of subject, and the demands on the author that must necessarily arise from that, would inevitably dictate?

It may be helpful, perhaps, to clear the ground with a generalisation or two. The theme of the rebellion of Owain Glyndwr provides JCP with characters set, many of them, in a ready-prepared context of status and action and it is this context, in not a few instances, which enables such characters to escape from the symbol-fixations with which he initially burdens them. Time, too, is an aide in this. The sixteen or more years covered by the novel are infinitely more important than the 938 pages (not many more than usual, after all) in strengthening both the narrative and the *development* of individuals. To read *Owen Glendower* carefully is to notice the way in which ideas are set in motion, sometimes through straightforward exposition, sometimes through character-symbol identification, only to be cast off one by one as the pressure of the historical setting compels. It would not be too

234

much to say that the survival of characters possessed of feelings, failings and actions within a credible context is due both to the time-scale and to the unalterable outline of the historical subject-matter. Another subject from Welsh history, utilised in *Porius*, is less compelling and less successful. The enormous cuts in the original manuscript apart, the matter of history is here very thin, the time-span is, incredibly, that of one week, and the totally improbable 'room' for the protagonists of myth removes the novel from the area of credibility. Such a judgment is not intended to outlaw myth, or even fantasy, as a vehicle for moral and metaphysical ideas. But JCP, though rarely doctrinaire, was undoubtedly a preacher and his ultimate intention was 'serious'. It was to present a vision of Truth. For his writing, then, the credibility test, applied not to details but to the whole intention, is entirely relevant.

I ought to make plain here, too, that it is no part of my thesis to set myth and history in opposition to each other. Those who do so set them are often, in my opinion, guilty of wilfully romantic thinking. Myth is either history imperfectly remembered as a result of oral transmission or history deliberately used and shaped, either by some dominant element in society at the time of the shaping or by popular imagination (assisted by the craft of individuals) released by some great disaster or some happening inexplicable in terms of the common knowledge of the time. The form taken by myth was often one intended to promote the health or unity of a primitive society, and those who romantically advocate a return to myth are doing no more than saying that some useful lessons or releases or pressures known to primitive man, particularly in the fields of imaginative or religious experience, have been forgotten and ought to be made available once more. There is no intention, then, to castigate John Cowper Powys for being 'mythic' in his emphases, provided that in so being he can make the connection with a contemporary credibility (both that of the reader and that of the society depicted, which are, of course, inter-related). I am concerned rather to show, in my consideration of *Owen Glendower*, that he deliberately disregarded the body of political myth which was germane to the heart of his subject in favour of ill-connected and sometimes irrelevant strands of myth which were actually inimical to the main theme. That he did this in the cause of his own 'vision of truth' is sufficiently obvious.

In choosing to write about Owain Glyndwr JCP chose a subject overtly political in its emphases. It is concerned with national unity in the face of outside oppression, with warfare, with tribal and family relations, with known events, with qualities, ethnic and social, which are attributable to the Welsh in the light of those groupings and those events. There is, except by twisting history's arm, no real room for mythic interpretations which had no validity at the time and it is noticeable that *Owen Glendower*, which begins in the Powysian all-shaping manner, is limited in the end to one basic antithesis powerful enough to destroy Owen himself as a character and denude the political scene of credibility. That other characters can still flourish their freedom is a measure of the enormous scope of the book and of JCP's imaginative powers when they are freed from didactic intention. It is this contrast of vision with non-vision that links *Owen Glendower* with JCP's other novels, a link far more significant than the autonomous comprehensibility of ideas which Professor Knight postulates as setting the book apart.

A consideration of the first half of *Owen Glendower* may illustrate the point I made earlier about the gradual shedding of ideas and symbols as time-scale and subject-frame begin to press their demands. The opening has, for Powys initiates, so familiar a tone as to offer a depressant against the buoyancy. Rhisiart ab Owen, for much of the narrative "our friend" and observer's eye, is seen entering the Dee valley en route from Oxford, where he has been a student, intending to see the Dinas Bran of his ancestors and possibly to offer his services to Owen as secretary or scribe. The reasons for this (since Owen was not then in revolt) are as arbitrary as those for Wolf Solent's departure from London for Ramsgard. Both Rhisiart and Wolf return to the land of their fathers without their mothers' approval. Both have a shameful ancestral secret— Wolf that of his father's disgrace, Rhisiart the treachery of a more distant ancestor in handing over his province to the English (though JCP cannot for some time make up his mind what the treachery is to be: its first statement is vague; on page 226 the story is launched and withdrawn: on page 341, when the reason at last is given, what we see is one of history's first victories over the obfuscations, the hints of peculiarity, of which JCP is so fond). That something so straightforward as treachery was not originally intended may be deduced from the uncertainty surrounding Rhisiart's reasons for coming: he is not simply and comprehensively patriotic like his room-mate Morris Stove: his primary intention is to see Dinas Bran and exorcise from it the nameless guilt of his ancestor: only second-arily and rather casually does he consider the possibility of commending himself to his distant and reputedly unlikeable cousin Glendourdy. It is, indeed, the almost-usual JCP opening, equivocal and voluble, creating the suspicion that the author has no clear idea of the way in which he is going to use his observer-figure and that he is prepared to let the writing decide.

Two points may be made immediately. The first is that Dinas Bran, as the focus of ancestor-mystery, proves to be relatively unimportant. The second is that the animal and vegetable levels of sensibility, so intermingled with the human in other Powys novels, are rapidly squeezed out. That these unusual factors are the direct response of JCP to Wales, in soil as in spirit, I have no reasonable doubt.

The second point is the simpler and may be taken first. Within a page or two of our meeting him, Rhisiart is hiding in the copse to let Walter Brut and Crach Ffinnant go by: cater-pillars, moths, grubs, butterflies and "armadas of drifting midges" settle on him and his old horse Griffin. He is about to identify with a currant-moth, but his human speculations prove too strong. And so it is to be, with a few significant exceptions, throughout the book. There is "the anxiety of a Worcestershire gnat to taste Welsh blood" (819)[2] and a certain

amount of Griffin-identification, but no more than many
animal-lovers might manage. The Forests of Tywyn provide
a mute philosophical background for the renunciation-scene of
Rhisiart and Catherine, Owen's daughter, in a chapter that
may induce in Powys-enthusiasts some slight surprise. For
the negativity, the inaction, which characterises both the
Forests and their pre-Brythonic inmates is a direct reflection
of and adjunct to the human dilemma. In other words, JCP
is seeing and feeling his characters as people rather than
bundles of representative or symbolic emotions: they have
independent life. And if the inaction they choose is a reflection
of his own philosophy or one aspect of it, this does not alter the
fact that the treatment of man and vegetable here is unitary,
with human emotion the pervasive factor. There is a sense in
which this scene in monochrome, sad and unstimulating though
it is, may be regarded as the most disciplined and convincing
in the book. JCP's other levels of consciousness, while marvellously evocative for a man *on his own*—providing unrivalled
distillations of natural scene and atmosphere—are often a
liability in the treatment of human inter-action. They stress
always the discrepant, the individual: they fail to express or
explain agreement, community of purpose, social understanding. The Forests of Tywyn, as a chapter, is the first fruit of
JCP's narrative pressure and his acceptance of a vast, pre-
ordained human subject. It may also be, as I shall argue later,
that Wales provided him with a relatively thin diet of 'atmospheric' food.

Certainly amongst the few natural *effects* he employs one or
two are unprofitable, even misconceived. The Goosander, who
gives his title to a chapter, proffers a purely visual image which
repetition does not develop. With his "round, mild, greedy-idiot
eye" (645) and his race-memories going back to Caer Sidi and
Carbonek, he puts his head on one side to see Owen, "a grey
forked beard and a forehead circled with gold", peering out of
an arrow-slit in the walls of Harlech Castle, drawn, like the
fish and the seaweed, to the moon, "the great Whore of Eternity".
But with all his "race-memories of sea-castles and sea-kings"

he has no feeling of having seen such as Owen before. Instead he has an "indescribable feeling" and the whiteness of the scene produces "a beauty so extreme that it resembled the passing from love to death". This extremity of beauty has no significance that I can discern at that point in Owen's history. Nor is there any metaphysical breakthrough which this image provides. That as a single (not a repeated) visual image it has its own satisfactions need not be in doubt, but the chapter-heading suggests much more. In the preparation of the image, too, JCP picks up and throws down again another, much more applicable in human terms:

> . . . he had a strange feeling, as he stretched his head through this stone slit in the great wall and listened to the breaking of the waves, that all these blackened towns and ruined villages were the result of an enchantment, like that flung by the magicians upon the persecuted Pryderi; and that if only the clue-word, the exorcising word, could be uttered on such a night as this, all the waste-lands of ashes and blood would grow fresh and green again. (644)

Here, in the tale of *Manawydan fab Llyr*, is a symbolism which could have been extended to cover Owen's rebellion in its entirety, even if the appearances would have had to be handled in reverse—a symbolism, moreover, which would have connected Owen in the most effective sense with the land and its people. By means of Pryderi's tree (in the chapter entitled The Forests of Tywyn) JCP in some sort couples in the same branch of the *Mabinogi* but without explanation (Lu saves her author the trouble by breaking off on page 581) and Owen's play-acting in it, through which he punishes himself for Catherine's marriage to Mortimer, makes no obvious symbolic contact with the Pryderi-Manawydan story. To pursue this argument further, however, would involve one in wondering why JCP didn't write the book quite differently. The Pryderi parallel would, it is plain, have meant a further strictness, the exclusion of many floating ideas. Better, no doubt, to throw off an unproductive image like that of the goosander and remain free to keep divergent thoughts in the arena. But it is not unfair to record some confusion in the Pryderi symbolism.

The first of my two points has wandered a little from levels animal and vegetable. My basic suggestion is that the invocation of these is rare and not very productive (witness, again, the owl before Bryn Glas). In the second place, Dinas Bran as a focus of myth and history is less than potent and only intermittently observed (it must be remembered, however, that Rhisiart, unlike Wolf Solent, is not ultimately the focal character, his early status as observer notwithstanding). At the first sight of it, Rhisiart insists that it is *more, not less* than he imagined. But JCP's subsequent work on it is sporadic. "Tis our wold Corfe, looks "ee', declares Jimmy Mummer about to die (375), trying to import some of the Dorset magic. But in the main it reveals itself, despite its ruinous walls, as a feminine stronghold, in which Ffraid and Tegolin stand for Bran and Lowri and Efa (niece (284) or daughter (299) of Rhys ap Tudor?) for Derfel. Possibility the Bran association is confused, on this site, with that of the Mithraic raven: possibly it is a weak association in any case (I find it relatively impotent, too, at Harlech, where Bran-pictures are frequent). It is significant, that Owen, to whom the Bran-mask is intended ultimately to adhere, enters the castle on one occasion only, to carry out in person a rash and unnecessary exploit which accords not at all with his supposed metaphysical development. The confusion grows worse when we learn that Adda ap Leurig, the seneschal of Dinas Bran, has in his keeping the sword of Eliseg (which is associated with Derfel, the "saint" of the superstitious and carnal) and that this, when united with the belt of Eliseg (last seen in Owen's household around the neck of his son Griffith), "will reach across all Wales". Perhaps Adda's keeping of the sword inside Dinas Bran is the fifteenth century version of the treachery of Griffith ap Madoc (if so, it is a treachery aided and abetted by Owen). Perhaps, in his wishing both Welshmen and Englishmen to live peaceably side by side, he is renouncing Derfel for Bran, seeking a bridge to save not one people but two. For this he is more sacrifically treated than ever Owen is.

I record my personal conviction either that these symbols are seriously confused or that, as soon as mentioned, they mean nothing: as essences of the past they are lost among the contradictory voices of the present. In the end the only clear impression is of Rhisiart's initial happiness in the castle (when his "insect" is trying itself out), then his restlessness under the feminine *tynged* (particularly that of Luned) and ultimately his readiness for total identification with Owen when he sucks blood out of the wound made by the Dorset arrow.

There is, indeed, good reason for supposing that Dinas Bran provided JCP with few emanations. He appears to see it and see from it with the commoner landscape eye that many of us possess. At first sight, it is true, Rhisiart is aware not so much of battlements and bastions as

> . . . an impregnable mountain called up out of that deep valley by some supernatural mandate . . . its foundations . . . sunk in that mysterious underworld of beyond-reality whence rise the eternal archetypes of all the refuges and all the sanctuaries of the spirit, untouched by time, inviolable ramparts not built by hands! (12)

But this is couched in one of JCP's normal, if extravagant, formulas. It amounts to saying, not feeling. And it is very much later, when Rhisiart is watching the girls dancing, that the next 'placing' comes.

> He was tall enough to see through a gap in the battlements the whole plain of Maelor spread out before him.
>
> And as he gazed he was aware that a peculiar and emerald-coloured light had obliterated all impertinent and teasing details, leaving intact only the universal aspects of the world—the earth, the air, and the water. Yes, stretched out before him in that curious Homeric light . . . Maelor melted into Bromfield and Bromfield melted into the pastures of Shropshire. The light was indeed so green that it was as if a fiery sun had changed into a huge translucent emerald. The rich aftermath of meadow grass broke the distance into a vast chess-board of the Immortals,

and so enchanted in its windless calm did the scene look
that the smoke that rose from the plain and kept forming
itself into filmy wreaths took the shape for him of god-like
Beings moving across an emerald stage. (324)

This is Maelor seen, truly, on a given day and at the same time
a vision of unity soon to be disrupted by the black billowing
clouds of Owen's rebellion. It is Adda ap Leurig's irrecoverable
world, Welsh and English side by side. Despite the Homeric
light and the god-like Beings, it is a purely human scene,
political and social in its implications. Rhisiart, in seeing it, is
involved mentally with the mass action that is to come.

And this is virtually all of Dinas Bran as a castle and a
mountain. At the very end Meredith ap Owen, coming down
at dawn from his father's funeral pyre, sees it once more:

> . . . there was the eastern sky beyond Dinas Bran growing
> already golden! He couldn't distinguish the castle itself
> yet. But it had always been like that. Rising as it did at
> the valley's entrance, that ramparted hill-top *ought* to
> have been seen from many a hill above Corwen. But it
> rarely was! Indeed he himself had seen it only once from
> here. And yet it was there all the time. But the puzzle was
> to disentangle it from the Eglwyseg Rocks that rose
> behind it. Bran the Blessed! How characteristic of that
> *Deus Semi-Mortuus* that his dwelling should be visible and
> yet invisible—a true *open secret* of "the Glen of the
> Divine Water!" (935)

This is the Dinas Bran that any traveller might see and not see,
a matter of geographical observation, and the Bran-attachment
is perceptively made. But it is as distant from Denis Burnell's
ruinous but extensive castle as from the 'presence' that JCP, in
Dorset form, might be expected to create. Perhaps the weakness
in the end is attributable to JCP's own perversity in seeking to
evoke in Bran a *Deus Semi-Mortuus*, whose power lay in his
ability to give his followers peace after victory and oblivion
after loss (as did the Head of Bran when his commands were
strictly followed), as the putative motivator of an Owen who

spends all but the last chapter ostensibly engaged in warfare. It is also a weakness that the Bran-figure of the book, Broch o' Meifod, has no connection with Burnell's castle.

Can it be said that Welsh landscape elsewhere charges the narrative with additional depths of consciousness? There are the Forests of Tywyn which, their human sorrows apart, have a Pryderi-tree of uncertain implication and supposed emanations (which remain at the level of statement) of the pre-Brythonic people exemplified previously at Meifod by Morg ferch Lug, Broch's wife. There is Harlech, much more centrally placed in the Mabinogion story, where

> Bran the Blessed comes wading up with the tide . . .
> carrying on his back the ghosts of half a dozen bards.
> (643)

This is confusion indeed, unless time the telescoper is given no check. There is the ride to Mathrafal, which might be over any moorland anywhere towards a site with walls visible above ground and passages under it. Mathrafal is a name much invoked, but only at the end does it appear clearly as anything other than the ancient home of the Princes of Powys. Haverfordwest from Tom's *bwthyn*, again, is without even the merest topographical qualities. My point is not merely that some of the description has a perfunctory quality but that, where there are *emanations*, their scale and what they evoke are minimal in comparison with those found in JCP's Dorset novels. Nor need this surprise us. The theme of *Owen Glendower* limits severely the scope for an individual consciousness of the complexity that JCP loved to develop. Even more, I would suggest, the landscape of Wales and its myth-impregnation (despite the claims made by and for Owen Evans in *A Glastonbury Romance*) did not afford JCP the degree of sustenance which he had readily obtained from the chalklands of his childhood. This, again, need not be matter for surprise. Anyone of sensitivity who has contemplated those south lands in silence and alone, noting their swelling feminine breasts and the dramatic bareness which seems to whisper continually of the Bronze Age Celts or pre-Celts who once were there and now are not, might—according to background and disposition —either share JCP's sense of deprivation in Wales or breathe a sigh of relief. The chalk is an empty arena in which the first achievement of man in his emergence from the savage has audible echoes. They are there, whispering around overt memorials like Stonehenge, the Cerne Giant or the White Horse, and there, even more, in the mute unapologetic pride of the Earth-Mother. The contrast with Wales is as much a matter of history as of land-contours. The Wiltshire Downs— and, indeed, much of what was later called Wessex—provided the setting for a proud civilisation soon after 2000 B.C., when the area of Wales (the Preseli hills and a coastal fringe perhaps excepted) was poor and backward. Even if that area became celticised by, say, 200 B.C., it was probably not till the coming of Cunedda (the brief glories of Cradoc Freichfras apart) that any comparable pomp and hierarchy established itself west of Severn. When it did, it was always under pressure both from Gwyddel and Angle. The rough, masculine nature of the Welsh terrain sharpens the issue further. It speaks of defence, not an opulence of power. The Iron Age A Celtic 'provincials' who mingled with their unidentifiable predecessors in this unpromising region were in the end Welsh and separate because their mountains fought for them, kept others out.

JCP's dilemma, then, was that he came to Wales already armed with the myths of power and the Celtic heritage that went back across Europe to an original *Gwlad yr Haf* in Ceylon or Southern India. But Wales itself, with which he sought to identify both because of blood and because it was the largest surviving unit of that heritage, was geographically the home of few of those myths and derived what it had from Irish sources with which he was less acquainted. When he chose to disregard the specific myths of leadership which the history of Celtic defeat had engendered, he was left with the random bag and the confusion I have already indicated.

His response, indeed, was to set a few historic and mythic hares running and stand back to see how long they could go before the coursers of narrative ran them down. There is, first, the supposed influence of "Saint" Derfel, powerful with the men of Gwynedd and epitomised in the one-eyed, birthmarked person of Crach Ffinnant. The Derfel theme, based on Derfel Gadarn, the image at Llandderfel Church, and the relic of the wooden horse there, seems in part intended to highlight the impulsiveness and irrationality of Rhys Gethin. It is also useful in introducing an argument about the Church. But with Rhys Gethin dead, it becomes redundant and Owen, in fashion uncharacteristic and thematically uncontrolled, has Davy Gam murder Crach Ffinnant as he is in the act of raping Efa.

Next there is the running of a pseudo-historic hare, anti-clericalism among the bards. That this is very partially correct is perhaps no great matter. Dafydd ap Gwilym, like Iolo Goch, to whom JCP ascribes a very particular dislike of the Church, in fact had a quarrel with the Grey Friars, Mad Huw's order, Iolo, who in history was not known to be disloyal to the Crown of England, is in *Owen Glendower* given the privilege on his death-bed of calling for rebellion, but the bards are denied any monopoly of patriotism since John ap Hywel and Rheinalt, one the Abbot of Llantarnam, the other a monk of Valle Crucis, are the first to swear the oath of fealty to Owen. This issue is further blocked when several passages are given to Owen's preference for the poetic forms of antiquity, as practised by Iolo, over the tricky 'modern' style of Griffith Llwyd. It transpires later that neither Iolo nor Griffith Llwyd are bards of the sort whom JCP would like to see in his narrative. At the making of the Tripartite Indenture, Rhisiart, after seeing his vision of the dead Hotspur, feels that all present are "timeless . . . puppets in a masque". There is, he senses, "some hidden reality" of which we see only "shadows on the wall of a cave", as Plato did. This reality

> had more to do with bards than with priests; but not with bards like Hopkin or the Scab, or even old Iolo—not with *cywydd*-makers at all; but bards more like Merlin and Taliesin, if *they* could ever come again. (660)

But they couldn't. Not in this story, anyway. So the bards, except insofar as Hopkin ap Thomas provides a theme (that of the Maid in Armour) to break through Owen's passivity, also come to their inevitable end.

Both the Derfelites and the bards have their symbolic part. It is inevitable that the Church should be similarly rigged. The interview with Abbot Cust at Valle Crucis provides the opportunity. The Church, says Walter Brut the Lollard, makes saints out of devils, consecrates superstitions. Ah, argues the Abbot, but Wales may yet be saved by its legends: the Church "has always been tender to the instincts of awe and worship . . ." (243). In other words, the reader is asked to see it as almost powerless and irrelevant as a separate force. It is not so much Christian as a compendium of the folk-feelings of the Welsh, suitably blessed and consecrated. "Not in our superstitions but in our *language*", cries Walter Brut, "is the salvation of our race". There must be a return to the rigours of St. David and the purity of the original Celtic Church. Thus the Lollard, correctly recorded. JCP really did read his Brut.

But any value this exchange may have, most of all in attaching labels to forces in the Wales of *Owen Glendower*, is dissipated almost at once by the scatter of directions which the Churchmen take. Of the Valle Crucis Cistercians Rheinalt virtually abrogates his priestly functions, becoming Tegolin's "good begetter" and the foil for the sadistic excesses of his ex-love, Lowri: Pascentius, that "Monking monk from a monkery of mummers" (576), in his first role of the learned and inflexible conservative, has something to say both about the schismatic Pope and about Lollardry, but is soon botanised and humanised into a figure capable of offering revelation of a sort about Rhisiart and Broch, but one which has rapidly thereafter to be discarded. John ap Hywel, Llantarnam's Abbot, has a rough, bucolic manner of speaking and is affectionately excused from anything more intellectual than practical patriotism and warfare. Griffith Young, for no discernible reason described as "a statesman" as early as page 108, settles down in the strictly political capacity, full of words and calculation, for which JCP has destined him. Mad Huw, the wandering friar with Richard II as his bonnet-bee, is less any kind of Churchman than an exposition of the nature of unselfish love. The bisexual characteristics observed in him by Professor G. Wilson Knight[3] seem to me unimportant: Mad Huw's would have been a Christlike figure if the punch had not been intentionally pulled. Once Richard II "was expelled Brother Huw could hardly be regarded as mad at all" (683).

Walter Brut the Lollard has the longest run of all, though it is by no means clear from the narrative why Owen should ever have been impressed by his arguments as of real assistance to the cause. At a later stage (643) Owen feels that there is something about the Lollard's doctrines "to which his Welshmen responded like wild geese to the waters of Llyn Tegid", but this is otherwise unsupported. It looks like an author's note: 'Delete Derfelites: continue Lollards'. Brut's role—and it is fully and affectionately drawn—is that of evangelical, principled, rational man, still interpreting the Scriptures but possibly seen at the beginning of the road to a *modern* and empirical fragmentation. His inability to cope with the carnal (in the person of Alice) helps him in the end to escape from the limited scope of the doctrinaire evangelist: his day-to-day gallantry in prison is his individually. Learned, radical man, generalised, has no right to it.

The religious speakers, then, scatter into personal or marginal roles. And this is not to be complained of on historical grounds, for the interests of the various Orders and of the Church itself did not constitute, nor could constitute, a single voice. But it should not be forgotten that it is the shape of the book's subject—Owen's rebellion—that brings the coursing to an end. Even Walter must die before Owen. The fate of Wales must, in the last analysis, be treated either as a collective fate or personified in that of Owen himself. There cannot, in the end, be other and dissonant voices.

That is why the only enduring dialogue is the one between Owen and Broch, albeit a dialogue of remarkably little speech. It is difficult to understand how Professor Wilson Knight can call Broch "a peripheral figure"[1]: he is physically the personification of Bran ("Mother of God! . . . he *does* look like Bran", thinks Rhisiart (633)) and embodies the death-ideal, the sacrifice for his people, which Owen intermittently embraces. There are signs that Rhys Gethin was intended to play a subordinate third part in the argument, but his early death does no more than remove what is essentially a duplication (Owen being as open to Derfel and life-love as he, though less rash in action). If perhaps we attach to Rhys, in the end, the first of the aphorisms which JCP produces for the Brythonic stereotype—

> We pure-blooded Brythons . . . are good at a pinch, but we can't *keep it up*

–it does no more than underline his supernumerary quality as a symbol, for the stereotype is intended fundamentally for Owen himself.

It would be well, therefore, to examine in some detail how the Owen-Broch argument develops. The scene is set before Owen himself appears and the first statement of the Owenite stance is given to Rhisiart, in whose actions and those of others at the Tassel we see the thesis of inaction within the typhoon of action, the individualising of the action which results and its essentially supra-rational basis. From a distance all is activity. Tegolin can be heard shrieking. Some crowd action is taking place, and fast. But when Rhisiart and Walter and Crach arrive the scene immediately becomes static. Even John ap Hywel, the symbol of straightforward, blunt action, is lost in the pervasive sense of waiting. Ultimately Rhisiart,". . . in another dimension altogether", in a "deep time-vacuum" (45) draws his crusader's sword and moves a pace or two forward. It is not so much this action which is comic or ridiculous: it might equally have been produced by a romantic lack of proportion. What is so far from convincing is the deliberate halting of all other action, the stilling of so many wills and intentions so that one, and that an important one, may be overborne by destiny. This individualising in the midst of conflict is not made more impressive by a ridiculous drawing-room speech by Meredith ap Owen directed exclusively to Rhisiart. The preamble to JCP's thesis reads far from well.

Owen, when he does appear, is the very symbol of inaction. His eyes are "of a flickering sea-colour, sometimes grey and sometimes green, yet always with an underglow of light in them that had the effect of an *interior* distance" (120). In another place they are "sea-green, mutable, equivocal". His voice is low for a prince, he is subject to "attacks" of interiorisation or exteriorisation—withdrawal, either way—and he has "an infinitely, pathetic look, as if the figure thus adorned and tended had been prepared or had prepared himself for some mysterious sacrificial rite" (122). There is, however, another aspect of Owen which, even in JCP's terms, proves more viable and realistic. His nose is of the type called Roman, he wears a purple mantle clasped by a massive gold brooch, round his head is a twisted gold thread, and his beard is forked and very carefully trimmed. This is the delineation of the Celtic stereotype as found in classical writers. One quotation from Strabo must suffice for example: the Celts, he writes

> wear ornaments of gold, torques on their necks, and bracelets on their arms and wrists, while people of high rank wear dyed garments besprinkled with gold. It is this vanity which makes them unbearable in victory and so completely downcast in defeat.

Professor Wilson Knight makes much play with *gold* as Owen's colour[3] and associates it with the sun, the principle of "upstanding action"[4], which appears a contradiction of the Powysian thesis about Owen. Gold, in the ornaments of the La Tène civilisation, represented the Celtic love of beauty. It emphasised too, the short-term bravery, the volatility which was the weakness of a sensuous nature. This is not far from the reflex quality of the action JCP attributes to Owen, and Owen's gold represents, in all probability, a serious attempt to associate the known qualities of the Celtic stereotype with the course laid down for this sacrificial prince.

The *attacks* or withdrawals are merely the machinery which screens inaction. The sacrifice for which Owen is preparing his body is a sacrifice *for Wales* in the manner of Bran the Blessed who lay down so that his army could cross the dangerous river over his body. "*A vo pen bit pont*", as Rhisiart's nurse Modry put it—"He who is the head, *he* will be the bridge" (258). Sacrificial inaction can only be made plausible in a future battle leader by the supposition that fate, the unseen direction of events, will 'elect' him as Prince and carry the sacrifice to a conclusion by some sort of corporate will. Unfortunately that corporate will is almost totally lacking in JCP's narrative: the characters he collects to 'hoist' Owen have no collective force or credibility. The truth is that JCP objects to and refuses to use any kind of corporate mentality or feeling as a force to be measured against the individualism of his characters, and the army that passes over the bridge appears to consist of one rank of diverse and relatively unmotivated intellectuals, rarely in step and supported only by pages. If this is an exaggeration (as indeed it is), it is nevertheless obvious that the part of Bran-the-Bridge is not a true allegory. Sacrificial action is not to be confused with sacrificial inaction. Owen decked for sacrifice has more in common with the Head of Bran, allegiance to which was a kind of inexorable fate. And that Head was concerned with *peace*, with comfort for the survivors after the fighting was over, not with the active conduct of war.

JCP's thesis of inaction compels him to conceal the means by which decisions are reached. Owen is allowed what may be called reflex actions—the return of the ring to Griffith Young, for instance, which presumably implies an abjuration of the calculations of politics—but takes real decisions offstage. The council of war in Owen's chamber at Glyndyfrdwy listens to excellent expositions of the views of Griffith Young and Walter Brut, but no discussion follows: absolutely nothing is decided. Yet the following morning orders have been given and dispositions made. This pattern repeats itself at Dinas Bran, Where Owen's shooting of Jimmy Mummer is a reflex action, though his reasons for involving himself personally in the rescue of Rhisiart and Walter, at that stage unimportant individuals, and the means by which that decision has been reached, do not sufficiently appear.

Rhisiart's sucking of the blood from Owen's wound not merely binds him in loyalty: he becomes part of Owen—the active part. This is perhaps to be coupled with Owen's breaking of his crystal ball, by which he abjures the practice of the priests and druids of "*meddling with the future*". He prays thereafter for the "absolute darkness of your impenetrable purpose" (393) to a fate which has already given him Rhisiart as a leg-man. On the unlikely ride to Mathrafal (how decided upon?) he several times makes observations like "You're a perfect wonder, lad" which seem to have little or no foundation in any action of Rhisiart's. At Maen-y-Meifod Rhisiart is immediately ready to move against Morg, to go out to the water-wheel ahead of Owen. This chapter ("Mathrafal")— though the intention languishes thereafter—allots to Rhisiart even that reactive or reflex part of action which Owen was formerly allowed. Owen himself becomes like "an old massive spar of ship's timber" he sees in the mill-race. It "*has* to float . . . It can't jump" (434). And he, in the guise of *deus ex machina*, rescues from the dam another piece of wood, rotten, with a living plant growing on it. The symbolism is heavy hereabouts.

Broch, who enters the narrative at this point, can be seen as the exponent of a divergent philosophy only because Owen does not know that his wife Morg is one of the "old people", the hidden aboriginal inhabitants of the land. There are two pointers to his existence as a symbol: first, that Owen comes in person to ask his help (a procedure contrary to all likelihood, both because of the timing and because Broch is worth little as a military counsellor) and second, that Broch is Owen's greatest friend, appropriately in Owen's destiny-governed mood. Ignorance of Morg's identity is an unlikely adjunct to this. It affords the opportunity to distinguish Owen's Brythonic inheritance (of which fatalism was much less a part) from the everlasting endurance handed on by the aborigines. Broch, although physically like Bran, is increasingly identified with his wife's people (Owen sees him (472) as "the corpse-god of those old mound-people"). There is no explanation of how the Celtic Bran can be so identified. Although Broch has little to say of any value about the conduct of the rebellion, he emerges as the spokesman for a philosophy that is both old and so new that it has not yet come to pass. He tells Owen that the comet that so startles him in the mountains of Snowdon comes "from outside both the *Primum Mobile* and the Empyrean . . . From a new-born Spirit in unknown spheres it is pushing upon our old degenerate world" (472). That this Spirit, while capable of a manifestation like the comet, is also pluralistic, the voice of all the lonelinesses that the love of Christ will never, can never, reach, has already been made plain. Another "and a different Revelation" is promised (456). Later Broch offers a little insight into his old/new stance:

> I don't regard death as an evil. But I regard pain as a monstrous and unnecessary evil . . . Death is the basis of my religion. (539)

To this Pascentius, from within the circle of his unitary belief, replies with some force that

> If death hadn't been the worst, the Son of God would'nt have died. (*ibid.*)

The application of a concept like "evil" when there is no assigned responsibility, no single First Cause even, is as unclear as the relevance of the separate sensibilities of fish, birds, rocks and stones to an argument over human attitudes to a single *destiny* powerful enough to decide the future of Wales (and with it that of both Owen and Broch and many more). Broch complains of Owen that

> What I can't get him to understand . . . is that *this earth* is no more than a distorted mirage of the reality. (610)

But if that reality is pluralistic, then Owen's overriding destiny is a sham from the beginning and what will be said later about human participation in it puts the whole theme out of court.

Not for the first time, JCP may be convicted of working in his own philosophy at the cost of the *required* structure of the narrative.

If the voice of the old/new Spirit be ignored, the problem then is to distinguish the attitude of Broch from Owen's own "monstrous fatalism" within the concept of destiny. It is true that he has almost nothing to say of any practical value and that he is seen to absent himself both from Owen's triumphs and from "parliament-time" (675). Per contra, he is present at the *willed* departure of the Maid and earlier—of all the individuals who might counsel Owen—had been the one to insist that the Welsh must have a battle plan at Bryn Glas. Both these actions are highly discrepant.

Owen, meanwhile, is also being less than consistent. In the chapter entitled "The Comet" he becomes so detached from any recognisable point of view (except that he loves his daughter Catherine) that he is no longer believable as a person, let alone a leader. Here again there are signs that Rhisiart—interrogating the comet—is his active part. But in killing Hywel Sele of Nannau he is again allowed reflex action, masked perhaps in the 'natural' compulsion which creates the body-in-the-tree symbol, one that he himself imitates in the Pryderi-Tree in Tywyn Forest. Later, however, there is some undoubted double-talk. Owen as *drych-dyn*, the mirror-man ("Light the candle and you'll see how dark it is"), sees Catherine and Rhisiart as the best weapons he has. They are "my grand tribute to destiny" (453). The word "best" indicates an exercise of judgment, and when the Mortimer marriage comes into Owen's head, are we prepared to accept that such a political expedient is pressed on him solely by fate? If there is no exercise of judgment or movement of will involved, why is his putting of the Maid in armour a matter of will? Because lust is involved in it? It is an odd definition of "destiny" which makes lust a matter of will and a political marriage inevitable. The truth seems to be that lust is one of the only two *evils* marked in JCP's armoury because it could continue to exist in a pluralistic world—one loneliness having its way with another. But that such a value could be attached to Owen's conduct under another dispensation is very dubious indeed.

The true intention with which JCP entered the episode of the Mortimer marriage emerges on page 484, when Catherine tells Tegolin:

> Father . . . doesn't count. Because, while he knows everything, he *never* interferes.

But the total impracticability of such non-interference from one in Owen's position is already sufficiently manifest, and becomes more so, despite the excision from the narrative of the non-instinctive. Owen is not shown taking part in the *planned* ruse to capture the Greys, even though the plan was not his. Rhys Gethin and he have an understanding over the Maelienydd scheme—one involving political calculations about the Mortimers—though such a scheme is supposedly foreign to both their natures. But the understanding does not extend to anything more than getting the expedition on its way. Strategy is totally absent and tactics are ultimately dependent on treachery and Henry Don. No wonder that Don should remark that "Owen's isn't the air of a dare-devil patriot or a ruthless statesman" (541). It is so mutable as to become no air at all.

The "vast results" following from the victory at Bryn Glas "gave him the feeling that there were forces on his side, obscure, unfathomable, tremendous" (561). During his stay at Tywyn Owen's detachment begins to "create a temper essentially dangerous to human happiness". At this time he prefers *the two twilights* of Ceredigion to either sun or stars, "life-lover though he was" (564). He wants to assure Catherine that if she would lie down on the altar of the gods, as he is doing, he would love her even more. "Life, not death, was what his own heart wanted" . . . (573) These contradictions remain at the level of assertion, the second more credible than the first. At the same time the contrast between Owen's passivity and his rejected role as a wizard or druid is pointed by the expectation attributed to Catherine that "the wizard father would find a

way to give her her Love as he was giving Wales its freedom"
(586). Finding this expectation hollow, Catherine also chooses
to do *nothing* and disregards Rhisiart's harebrained plans to
elope. Nature itself aids this alignment.

> The Forests of Tywyn had yielded, the mist had its will of
> them . . . the correspondency between the element within
> them and the element without them was complete.

The disciplined and consistent writing of much of this chapter
all but overcomes the reader's disbelief in Owen's attitude, the
more since in it there is implicit, for once, a tragedy of individual
human dimensions.

When the scene moves to Harlech, where Bran's influence
should have been strongest, the spell is broken. In part this is
intentional. The mysterious young archdeacon, Father Ignotus,
is no more than the presiding mask of evil, and with the signing
of the Tripartite Indenture, by which Owen is to receive a part
of England and Northumberland and Mortimer the other
parts, the war becomes nominally one of aggression as well as
defence. Yet the evil is a mark in the margin, so to speak:
Owen arranges the signing on impulse (after hearing Gilles'
complaint against Rhisiart)—an unconvincing formula, but
one used several times before—and there is no indication of
the way in which a moral label may now logically be attached
to the continuing process of destiny. It is indeed only when the
ludicrous Hopkin ap Thomas (who in history was not a bard
but a gentleman learned in the work of the bards) produces
his prophecies, "from the crowning of a Welsh prince in London
to the anointing of a great King by a girl in armour", that the
mark of evil becomes more emphatic. It is not, however, set
against vaulting ambition but against Owen's lust for Tegolin
(the symbol of chastity throughout) and the ecstasies he has
about undoing her armour. This choice is clear and distinctive
all the more because JCP has already determined that this
episode shall mark a revival of *will* in Owen and a breach in
his fatalism. It is scarcely necessary to underline again the
oddness of the categorisation of the Mortimer marriage as

submission to destiny, of the murder of Crach Ffinnant as the result of his wizard-hold (elsewhere denied him) over David Gam, and of lust for Tegolin as an exercise of will.

The pronouncement which supports the last is as dark and gnomic as anything of which Hopkin was capable:

> Perhaps it might be said that he was too much in love with life, as a thing of more than one level, ever to succeed in the manner in which his royal enemy succeeded. He took life too seriously to take success seriously. (651)

To take success seriously, it is true, would mean the sacrifice of his own life: though how, in failing to do this consistently, he can love life in a manner totally different from that of "his royal enemy" (of whose life-style we get the merest glimpse in Worcester gaol) is very far from clear. Can it really be called "taking life seriously" when, after months, years, of passivity, his "insect" wants a bite? In another place we are told that Gilles" "torture-insect" is too "purely evil not to be as weak in the presence of a great life-lover [Owen] as it had been in the presence of a great death-lover [Broch]" (652). My reaction is increasingly to doubt whether *life-lover*, *death-lover* are categories that have any logical or consistent meaning in the context of the novel, however many times they may be repeated.

After Woodbury Hill, in which part of the narrative the French (not for the first time) wear the mantle of evil—an evil which, be it noted, has its origin not with the Maid in Armour but in the earlier Tripartite Indenture and the Treaty with France—the narrative by-passes Owen and rattles on with a consequential glee. Much the most imaginative and symbol-free writing describes Walter and Rhisiart in captivity. Once again the background is suffused with the human emotion of the central protagonists. Owen, meanwhile, has had his love of ceremonies (part of the Celtic stereotype) underlined in his dealings both with Gilles and the Maid, though JCP seems to have no idea of the fashion in which ceremonial and impulse would conflict. Did he really think that any but simple ceremonies could be improvised? I imagine what Pascentius and his choir would really have sounded like on the occasion of the Maid's send-off if Owen's decision had been as described. It scarcely bears thinking of!

When we see Owen next he is in his last hiding-place under the Gaer-mound. Even here he wants to make a ceremony of his rejection of the new King's pardon, and this provides the last knot of narrative and the occasion of Owen's death. Broch has assumed his alternative identity as Cawr-y-Gaer, the giant of the prehistoric mound-people, who made three undiscoverable hiding-places, under the Mound at Glyndyfrdwy at Mynydd-y-Gaer and at Mathrafal. In his Brythonic identity Owen still trims his locks: his blood inheritance from the prehistoric "Lords of Annwn", however, which in his last pronouncement he declares, opens his mind to the significance of the legend of Twrch Trwyth: he *knows* that the land of Wales is the preserve of the *mythology of escape*.

> This is the secret of the land. This is the secret of the people of the land. Other races love and hate, conquer and are conquered. This race avoids and evades, pursues and is pursued. Its soul is forever making a double flight. It flees into a circuitous *Inward*. It retreats into a circuitous *Outward*. (889)

> You cannot force it to love you or hate you. You can only watch it escaping from you. Alone among nations it builds no monuments to its princes, no tombs to its prophets. Its past is its future, for it lives by memories and in advance it recedes. The greatest of its heroes have no graves, for they will come again. Indeed, they have not died; they have only disappeared. They have only ceased for a while from hunting and being hunted; ceased for a while from their "longing" that the world which *is* should be transformed into Annwn—the world which *is not*—and yet was and shall be! (890)

The excuse for this amalgam of imaginative truth and distortion is the fact that of the hundreds of Welshmen who know where Owen is hidden not one has betrayed him. "They cannot *catch our souls!"* It is not that the myth here propounded has no validity. Defeat, especially constant defeat, creates its own kind of mythology: the Celts were adept at glorying in the last victory, however long ago, at looking for and prophesying the return of Arthur, of a variously-identified Owain (before the time of Owain Glyndwr), at choosing their dream even in the face of reality. Ernest Renan thought the Celt had "the invincible need of illusion" and Henri Martin that he was "always ready to react against the despotism of fact". That JCP's *mythology of escape* bears some relationship to a part of the Celtic stereotype need not be doubted. If it has been edged toward the portrait of Owen—the portrait of inaction under the whim of destiny—much further than Roman writers and Giraldus would have accepted, if the relationship with Annwn is fanciful, what is far more striking is the omission of what the book all along has omitted, the simple, personal loyalty of the Welsh to Owen and to the idea of an independent Principality. And not merely their loyalty, their organisation and the history and nature of their political beliefs. *Owen Glendower* has many incidental splendours, but one ingredient missing is that of political credibility. Historically Owain Glyndwr and his cause created the first wave of widespread nationalism in Wales: militarily, the means by which he kept his forces in the field for almost fifteen years, with never a rift or a rebellion against his leadership despite the terrifying devastation of Wales, continues to puzzle historians: recent opinion underlines the loyalty and solidarity of the cousinhood of squires, some of them related to Owain, some of them not, who supported him through thick and thin in a manner impossible in the days of Llewelyn Olaf. If I single out the lack of political and military credibility, then, I am not referring to details, many of which are both colourful and correct. It is characteristic, in this context, that JCP mentions the replacement of the single lion of Powys on Owen's standard by the four lions rampant of Gwynedd, though the implications pass without comment. Again, if Davy Gam becomes Owen's slave and the account of his ransom a dramatic fiction, this in itself affects the novel's structure not at all. The variation of the details is relatively unimportant. What *is* important is that the core of the book should be seen to express, credibly, the kind of metaphysical, even sociological, truth that JCP seeks to convey through it. And this is where the failure can be pinned down. Where are the references to Adda Fras, Y Bergam and other fourteenth century bards in the incessant prophetic tradition, crying always for the Owain that is to come, for the prince who will deliver Wales? And where, even more, are those linked, determined squires whose intent it is that Owen shall fulfil those prophecies? With the exceptions of Rhys Gethin, and others like Henry Don and John ap Hywel who are rapidly despatched to the periphery, Owen appears to be served by an assemblage of theological and intellectual curiosities—Broch, Pascentius, Rheinalt, Rhisiart and Walter Brut, not to mention many others who could have been of no possible assistance. We are even asked to believe at one point that Rhisiart alone in Harlech Castle appreciated the possibility of an English attack. This omission of the supporting cast is entirely in accord with JCP's practice elsewhere (one may refer, for example, to the supposedly representative *society* in Mother Legge's inner room in *A Glastonbury Romance*). He does not take society and its pressures into account: he has little conception of a man who is less an individual than a pressurised component. Correspondingly, he has no appreciation of a group, a patriotic unity for a common purpose. Or rather, it is outside his metaphysic.

"I know those Tudors—they'll rush for pardon to the King" (664) says Owen despondently at one point. And why should they not? In the book's terms he does not appear to know why he is rebelling, offers no focus whatsoever for patriotic feeling, and as a rebel leader is inactive except for such reflex violence as his author allows him. That these deficiencies arise directly from the nature of JCP's thought is evident. They are not accidental, the results of insufficient research. Nor are they misunderstandings. They are imposed on the material, in a sense much more serious than the fabrication of characters or the alteration of the roles of some genuinely historical figures.

It is impossible to accept Professor Wilson Knight's verdict that "it is unlikely that we shall find anywhere a work in which so close a regard to historical exactitude is accompanied by so profound a metaphysic".[6] The historical exactitude lies in the promulgation of *some* contemporary ideas, in the brilliance of the visual imagination, in the extraordinary range of sensibility. The metaphysic is JCP's metaphysic.

For all their lack of success since the days of the Celtic Confederation (*c.* 500 B.C.), the Celts have always been intensely political—interested, that is, in the wielders of political power. There is a sense in which their culture is about politics. JCP himself recorded (in *The Welsh Review*, June 1939) his initial misunderstanding of this. While appreciating that "an aged ex-postman . . . speaking of Glyndwr as an Irishman of today might speak of De Valera" could refer to his going "to Dolgelley along the crest of the Berwyns", he also interprets in his own fashion the story told him by another ancient inhabitant. This old man held forth at length about a battle between "two generals", at the end of which one killed the other in single combat and buried him in a grave which was still visible. JCP tumbled to it that this was the story of Gwydion and Pryderi, lapsed from gods to heroes and from heroes to generals. It is impossible now to assess the likelihood of his identification. It *is* possible to observe, however, that JCP himself had no conception that Gwydion and Pryderi, if such they were, might have been historical characters, disguised by centuries of oral myth-making. Nor did he take to heart that, as almost always, these two were concerned with battle and the realities of power.

Daniel Defoe, not at all interested in antiquities (as he duly records), passed through Maelienydd soon after 1720 and felt compelled to set down that

> The stories of Vortigern, and Roger of Mortimer, are in every old woman's mouth here.

Such stories were inescapably political. The name of Vortigern spelt the great treachery that brought the Celts down (monkish tales, no doubt, and especially favoured in a region with which Vortigern is traditionally associated). The name of Roger of Mortimer spells out the only occasion when a lord of the area, albeit a Norman, was briefly heir to the English throne. A tribal emphasis, subsequently entangled in the feudal, and reaching out only vaguely to the wider patriotism. But political, desperately concerned with leadership, all these stories were. And the bards of Owain's day, in their prophetic poems, had the same concern. It is a pity that John Cowper Powys, for all his gifts, should have decided to tackle a subject so intrinsically concerned with the nature and the making of a *Prince*, and yet to circumvent history, against all credibility, with a formula of his own. He might have done better with the cliché of Shakespeare's wizard. The "exteriorising" of Owen's soul—a term not without promise – is never politically fulfilled.

NOTES

[1] *The Saturnian Quest*, p. 71.

[2] Numerals in parentheses throughout refer to pages in *Owen Glendower*, 1942.

[3] *A Review of English Literature*, IV, 1 (January 1963), p. 47.

[4] "Owen himself moves stealthily like 'a great golden cat' (p. 655). Gold is his colour: beard, armour, accoutrements, robes, circlet, all are golden. In his 'fantastically gorgeous attire' he appears like a 'golden image' (p. 511). He responds, brilliantly, to the sun (p. 769)." *Ibid.*, p. 45.

[5] "Harlech presents a *blending of sun and sea*, which means a blending of the principles of upstanding action and elemental endurance, of Owen and Broch, the union twice compacted in our sight of Broch as a creature of *gleaming* sea-shells and gulls' feathers and with limbs dripping from the waters the while his bald head is 'aureoled by sun-sparkles' (pp. 633–774)". *Ibid.*, p. 51.

[6] *Ibid.*, p. 41.

XIV

THE ANARCHY OF THE IMAGINATION

John A. Brebner

I

Porius: a romance of the Dark Ages, the tenth of John
Cowper Powys's novels, was first published in 1951. It appeared
ten years after *Owen Glendower* and, like its predecessor,
explores the past.[1] The setting is again Glyndyfrdwy, "where
Deva spreads her wizard stream;" but the terrain is scarcely
recognizable. The year is 499 A.D. and virgin forests still
cover the Dee valley. Although based on a few scraps of
documented history, the story is largely conjectural, dealing
as it does with Arthur's attempt to unify the quarrelling tribes
of Edeyrnion against Saxon invaders. Powys convincingly
assembles his cast from fact, legend, myth and imagination.
King Arthur is conceived as a perceptive military strategist
with an engaging if slightly whimsical personality. He and his
"silly courtiers" camp near the newly named village of Corwen
in North Wales. Myrddin Wyllt and the enchantress Nineue
figure importantly in the tale as does the Emperor's traitorous
nephew Medrawd. Prince Galahaut is briefly but intriguingly
portrayed as a self-pitying youth; while the poet Taliessin is
depicted as a boy-prodigy working absent mindedly in his
Patron's kitchen. Some native tribes trace their ancestry to
Greek or African sources (Arthur himself is said to have had a
Roman father and an African mother), still others claim to
descend from the survivors of Lost Atlantis. Porius, the book's
title-character, shares in this mixed inheritance. Besides being
the son of the reigning Brython Prince, he has the blood of the
Romans, the forest-people, and the Cewri in his veins.

Although he does not dominate the narrative, his role in
the novel is central. His decision to fight with Arthur places
him in disfavour with many of his people who fear, in a pact
with the Emperor, the loss of their already vanishing tribal
identities. He is further alienated by his sceptical attitudes to
the religious beliefs of both Pagans and Christians. Schooled
in the teachings of Pelagius, he has gone on to develop a
personal interpretation of life which in its vital humanism
contrasts sharply with the narrow fanaticism of local Christianity as well as with the austere Mithraic practices of his

foster-brother Rhun. He is convinced that the human imagination must defy "not only the Bull and the Slayer of the Bull, but the Crucified and the slayer of the Crucified, yea! and all the God-Bearers and all the God-Slayers from the beginning of the world unto this hour! The human imagination must never be robbed of its power *to tell itself other stories*, and thus to create a different future." (44)[2] His story telling faculty is neither naive nor evasive; it performs "miracles" of self-discovery and self-preservation. He knows "Pelagius is right. Man's imagination and not God's will is what creates."

Porius is about the imagination, what it creates, and the meaning of its creations. Its themes are astoundingly contemporary considering the remoteness of its overt subject. In an age when the cry for relevance in literature is frequently raised, this novel speaks with more than immediate emphasis. Its accents are prophetic. The conflicts depicted during this one week in October 499 touch on essential human activity—masculine-feminine attraction in both its sexual and non-sexual extremes; the uneasy relationship between literature and politics, especially in the forms of contemplative study and aggressive fighting; the effects of revolutionary change on a disappearing race and on the birth-pangs of a new nation; the effort required for personal survival in a limiting atrophied society. Powys predicts the succession of Pisces by Aquarius, and introduces the portentous sorcery of Myrddin Wyllt who is "the latest incarnation of the god of the Golden Age." Cronos (Myrddin) is a principle of creative continuity. Speaking to Neb ap Digon, his *gwas* or servant-boy, he enunicates the novel's fundamental statement of passive revolution.

> "Nobody in the world, nobody beyond the world, can be trusted with power, unless perhaps it be our mother the earth; but I doubt whether even she can. The Golden Age can never come again till governments and rulers and kings and emperors and priests and druids and gods and devils learn to un-make themselves as I did, and leave men and women to themselves! And don't *you* be

deceived, little one, by this new religion's [Christianity's] talk of 'love'. I tell you wherever there is what they call 'love' there is hatred too and a lust for obedience! What the world wants is more common-sense, more kindness, more indulgence, more leaving people alone. But let them talk! This new Three-in-One with its prisons and its love and its lies will only last two thousand years. The thunderer I begot—and I'd have swallowed him if his mother hadn't given me a stone instead—lasted for ten thousand years. But none of them last for ever. That's the hope of the world. The earth lasts and man lasts, and the animals and birds and fishes last, but gods and governments perish! (276–277)

The context here does not admit of petty ecological arguments; Powys is writing in terms of millennia, not of decades. He opposes the notions of spiritual trinity by the assertion of elemental powers—those of earth, air, fire, and water. As Gogfran Derwydd, Druid of the Forest people, states, the real issue of the struggle between the contending forces lies in its religious significance. The confrontation is dramatic and, conclusive. Both Druid and Christian priests die. The former after being impaled by a spear, seems to achieve a moment of transcendent awareness denied to the latter who suffers a convulsive stroke following an impassioned speech—this, presumably, because the Derwydd's trinitarian beliefs, antedating Christianity by centuries, embrace physical knowledge excluded from the priest's narrow doctrine. At the moment of crisis, Myrddin hides his head in the earth, his passive resistance drawing on the elemental strength of his conviction. When he rises, he speaks, his head "swaying a little from side to side as it uttered its mandates, as if it were the head of an inanimate automaton or at least of a *deus mortuus*, or a 'corpse-god', risen from its tomb, but towering now by reason of its height over them all." (489) The word he utters is *Cymry;*

> . . . and no sooner had it been flung out upon the air by Myrddin Wyllt's enormous head—that darkly looming head with its great flapping animal-like ears that was

swaying now from side to side, above spearmen and archers, above horses and riders, as if it were the decapitated head of Bendigeitvran, the head of the never-dying yet eternally dead being whose destined nature it was to be the ghastly but imperishable medium between the buried past and the new born future—than it was caught up in a thundering shout from thousands of ecstatic throats—Cymry! Cymry! Cymry! Cymry! (490)

As always, Powys's logic is imaginative rather than intellectual. He sets the scene for the conflict between Myrddin and the priests of the triad to coincide with the Feast of the Sowing. At this festival, ancient "orgiastic mysteries" are celebrated to the accompaniment of the Fisher-King's chant. The main ceremonial act consists of plunging "a huge seven-times-elongated African spear . . . carved in certain respects to convey the impression of a collossal and hideous phallus" into Saint Julian's Fount. On this occasion, the sexual ritual is surrounded by the bloodshed and screams of battle. Myrddin's mental energy penetrates the confusion and causes a psychic change which withers the frame of the ranting priest and impels the soldiers to peace. Slaughter and generation are reconciled by an act of the imagination.

If we recall the imaginative ordering of experience revealed to Sam Dekker in *A Glastonbury Romance* and the mystic elementalism of Sylvanus Cobbold in *Weymouth Sands*, we discover that the national unity symbolized by the word "Cymry" is an extension of this "caput-anus" attitude to life. Powys has broadened his conception of personal salvation. It is now apparent that imaginative creation involves society as well as the individual. The secret lies in Myrddin's dual personality as magician and god. He is not only an old man reincarnated through the ages, he is also Cronos embodying the future. Powys is suggesting that men living in time can shape the direction of events by dissolving the contrarieties of life into the harmony of imaginative acceptance.

The process of integrating human consciousness with the inscrutible workings of time is emphasized in the characters of Porius and Taliessin. The former indulges in an activity he refers to as "cavoseniargizing":

> He used the word as one of his precious sensation-symbols and to serve as a description of those recurrent moments in his life when the gulf between the animal consciousness of his body . . . and the consciousness of his restless soul was temporarily bridged; so that his soul found itself able to follow every curve and ripple of his bodily sensations *and yet remain suspended above them.* (83)

Porius's cavoseniargizing uses the immediate matter of experience in its interpretive process, thereby humanizing it. It is rooted in the present, not in the past. It is devoid "of all religious mysticism and . . . of all spiritual illusions." Its subject includes "inanimate elements and inanimate objects"; especially those composed of earth, air, fire, and water.

Porius is a man of action: his virility is obvious on and off the battlefield. He thinks as little of deflowering two women —one his wife and the other a giantess—on his wedding day as he does of facing an armed man empty-handed. Because of his intensely physical preoccupations, his cavoseniargizing is a self-reflecting transcendence, providing only short respite from bodily necessity. A more permanent way of overcoming time is through art, particularly poetry. Taliessin's method of versification rejects temporal restrictions. Myrddin Wyllt, an obviously competent judge, thinks that it is

> . . . the enjoyment of a particular essence, an essence to be found not only in things and persons but in historical and mythological events, and that this essence could best be reached by so close and intimate an identification of the poet with the thing alluded to, or with the event described, that it was as if he stripped himself to the skin but retained his bodily senses as he plunged into the thing's essential being and became a conscious part of it, carrying the impressionability of his human senses into

something which to the uninitiated might be merely a drop
of lifeless water, or a piece of inanimate wood, or some
formal grouping of traditional symbols grown fabulous
and dim in the remote past. (414–415)

Although Taliessin's poetry receives its impetus from the same
source as Porius's cavoseniargizing, namely individual sensations, it achieves an altogether different completeness in its
final depersonalized objectivity. Powys traces this quality to
"the boy-bard's absolute immunity to all the human emotions
where sex plays a dominant part." This asexuality characterizes
the poet himself who "seemed to have no sex either. He resembled not so much an hermaphroditic idol come to conscious
life with the vivid intensity of both its sexes, as an elemental
creature entirely devoid of all sex instincts and of both sex
organs."

Both Porius and Taliessin represent extremes of behaviour;
both play essential roles in their society; both use the same
mental powers—the one to accept the principles of personal
physical action, the other to understand the harmony of
universal being. Together, they attest to the current of imaginative energy which winds like a river of life through the maze of
human endeavour.

There are others, however, who would dam up the life-stream:
Medrawd seeks to thwart Arthur's plans for a better society by
subverting his uncle's allies; Nineue would imprison Myrddin
and his magic for selfish ends. Although possessed of a few
redeeming qualities—Porius makes allowances for him and
assists him to evade capture—Medrawd gains little of the
reader's sympathy. He is the direct literary descendent of
William Hastings in the early *Ducdame*, but is much more
insidious. Whereas the Parson, until mad, contented himself
with writing about his nihilistic attitudes, Medrawd puts them
into practice. He tries to seduce Euronwy, Porius's mother; he
later succeeds in debauching Teleri, a half-mad servant; and is
eventually caught "scrabbling in the grave of a dead whore,
and wreaking his passion upon her corpse." His necrophilia is

only one aspect—perhaps the least odious—of his personality. As a traitor to the Emperor's cause, he instigates dissent among the soldiers and contention among the tribal leaders. He states his motives and aims clearly in conversation with Porius:

> "In life there's more pain than pleasure, more ugliness than beauty, more lies than truth, more misery than happiness, more cruelty than pity, more illusion than reality. So I have condemned life to die, and I have appointed war its executioner. The twin children of life, Hate-Love and Love-Hate, I have likewise condemned to death with war as their executioner. I am come that the world should have death; and I am strong because death is more powerful than life, higher than life, larger than life, older than life, and deeper than life. It existed before life appeared and it will exist after life has disappeared." (570)

Nineue is less interested in universal problems. She stands behind the action of the novel where, Delilah-like, she practises tricks of sexual domination. She is reported to have "more power than any woman in this Island," for she controls Myrddin who, in turn, controls Arthur. Her dark beauty combines with "a sort of immaterial emanation" as the expression of her "inmost identity." Porius suspects her of knowing a method of cavoseniargizing; and the general public considers her an enchantress. Myrddin is totally infatuated with her. He eventually succumbs to the pressure of her entreaties and reveals the location of "the stone on top of Wyddfa under which he's going to disappear" to await the Age of Aquarius. This he calls his Road to Annwn. Once there "she'll know where to find him when she wants to be loved; . . . she'll fasten the stone down so that no one but she can lift it. And then she'll have him really to herself. She'll go to him whenever she wants his love; and she alone in all the world will know where he is and he'll never be able to come out." (593–594)

Imaginative energy is not so easily stopped up. Myrddin's apparent disappearance under the stone is only a ruse to deceive

Nineue. He plans, with help from Porius, to escape from y Wyddfa (or *gwyddfa*, translated significantly as "tomb") and to go "to an island in the Sea where he'll be served and tended by the fifty beautiful daughters of the Old Man of the Sea, very young and very lovely young girls, *who never grow up . . .*"

The book culminates with the joint struggles of the magician and the soldier. When Porius arrives at the peak of y Wyddfa, Nineue has already placed the stone over Myrddin. The enchantress seems filled with supernatural power as the setting sun falls upon her, "turning her body to magnetic gold." Porius feels "his lust gathering within him like uprushing lava." He touches her. "Her whole figure had become transmuted into glowing gold. And . . . she now deliberately, heedless of the icy air about her, exposed one of her breasts. And lo! the sight of it froze his desire at the source." Porius is attracted "to fully and largely developed breasts only when their nipples were abnormally small;" it is Nineue's misfortune to have "an unusually large nipple in the midst of an unusually small breast." These details may seem silly and arbitrary, but they are extremely purposive. Erotic desire is forced to depend on circumstance or personality; its power can be completely reduced by the slightest chance influence. In her final bid to insure Myrddin's captivity, Nineue offers Porius a temporal age of sexual gold in place of the magician's permanent Saturnalia of the imagination. Her defeat is graceful. "For instead of being angry or showing the least [sense (a typographical error occurs in the text)] of affront in the presence of the worst insult which femininity can suffer, this extraordinary woman smiled at him more indulgently than he had ever seen her smile, and . . . she drew forth from between her unequalled thighs a small, hard heavy, pear-shaped lump of iron-ore and handed it to him." It represents a pledge of understanding. It is a thunderbolt that had been in Myrddin's body since, as Cronos, he was struck down. " 'You can give it back to him now,' " Nineue tells Porius. " 'He has escaped from the wheel that turns.' "

271

While Porius wrestles with the stone covering Myrddin, Nineue rides away. The retreating "metallic strokes" of her horse's hoofs remind him of "some mineral space-clock, matching the motion of time's water-clock." The sound blends with his reflections on cosmic change and on his sensation of being at "a centre-point in the midst of appearing and disappearing universes." As he looks down upon the prone figure of the magician, his thoughts remind us again of the vast scale on which Powys has conceived this novel:

> He felt as if he stood on an earth-crust that covered a cosmogonic cavern wherein the bones and ashes and the mouldering dust of gods and men and beasts and birds and fishes and reptiles had been gathered into a multi-tudinous congregated compost, out of which by the creative energy of Time new life could be eternally spawned; spawned, it might be for the use of other universes, when this one had been dissolved. (678)

It is not surprising that Porius in the company of Cronos should feel himself, in Eliot's phrase, "At the still point of the turning world." His experience is raised to revelation when Myrddin, after emerging from the hole, offers him "an extremely greasy leather bottle" which contains a "Saturnian nepenthe." Under its influence

> ... he fancied he could catch moving up to that mountain-top a vast, indescribable, multitudinous murmur, groping up, fumbling up, like a mist among mists, from all the forests and valleys of Ynys Prydein, the response of innumerable weak and terrified and unbeautiful and unconsidered and unprotected creatures, for whom this first-born and first-betrayed of the wily earth, this ancient accomplice of Time ... was still plotting a second Age of Gold. (681)

Before falling asleep, he accepts the terrible loneliness of each individual in a "chance-ruled chaos of souls," but considers this better than existence in "a world of blind authority, a world ruled by one Caesar, or one God." He wakes the following day to find Myrddin gone and himself magically transported to Harlech. There, reflecting on what has gone before, he decides: "There are many gods; and I have served a great one."

Porius is a profoundly religious novel. It strives to discover some code of behaviour, however tenuous, which will give meaning to human action. Its bizarre explorations reveal unexpected wealth. In a confused world of disintegrating values runs a thread of purpose—the imagination, creating a future which can be shared on an individual basis. Society, as the sum of its parts, will necessarily benefit from this concentration of positive mental energy. It will also change radically.

Powys is aware—no one is more, perhaps—that men and women have physical as well as cerebral needs, that they must live in close proximity to each other, that there must be some underlying ethical bond to prevent discord. Nevertheless, he is a convinced anarchist who believes that compassion—not love, for that leads to possession and domination—results from an imaginative grasp of each person's essential loneliness and that the kindest attitude to our fellow man is one of noninterference. He is equally aware that our lives are subject to spatial and temporal contingencies which are materially unalterable. Our struggle against these natural restrictions is expressed in aggressive war and organized religion, not to mention minor disputes such as domestic conflict or social ambition. We cannot choose to reject or evade unwanted experience; we must learn to live with it, even accept it. Some form of commitment is now required. In Powys's earlier novels, characters like Wolf Solent and Dud No-man achieve personal compromises with circumstance, but always in exclusive terms. For Porius, decision constitutes involvement. From the novel's inception, he knows that "he had to take, for the first time in his life, full, absolute, solitary personal responsibility for a choice of action that would affect, and affect catastrophically, every person connected with him." (3) In none of Powys's novels are people more concerned with each other than here. Cavoseniargizing, or some similar feat of mental gymnastics, would formerly have been the high point of self-knowledge—Johnny Geard of the *Romance* and

Owen Glendower are notable in this regard. *Porius* presupposes self-knowledge, or some approach to it, in its concentration on the violence and tension behind human relationships. Never before has Powys been as free with open discussions of sexuality, politics, militarism, and revolution. The book's emphasis on a matriarchal society seems to forecast such recent develop- as the Women's Liberation Front, while its concern with the anarchy of the imagination anticipates and transcends the contemporary fixation on personal freedom advocated popularly by the like of Charles A. Reich in *The Greening of America* and Jerry Rubin in *Do It!*

There are of course points of contention about this novel; but the context is so large, the range of speculation so far-reaching that minor discrepancies are dwarfed. To allow anachronisms—Arthur's eyes are as gay as those of "a boy steering a canoe"—to destroy the whole is like condemning Stonehenge for a chip in one of its columns. Techniques are often impressionistic rather than photographic (Powys describes his method, in a note on the story's background, as "*representative* rather than historical"); dialogue is fluent and colloquial; invention is fertile and extravagant. These factors contribute to a relaxed immediacy of tone which translates the remoteness of the subject matter and the density of the thematic movement into an urgently needed critique of our modern age. Humour plays an important part in establishing rapport between the reader and someone removed from him by roughly 1500 years. Life is injected, for example, into Porius's father as he urges his son to touch the broken tip of his sword: " 'It must have hit a rock,' " he says. " 'Feel it, for Christ's sake, boy!' " Lot-el-Azziz, the Jewish doctor, conducts an anachronistic ante-natal examination with a quaint show of delicacy. These and other touches ground the novel in an unequivocally human setting.

Porius is in many ways Powys's most comprehensive and successful statement of his life-vision. It surpasses all of his earlier fiction in the daring breadth of its scope. Man is seen in cosmic terms—not simply in relation to the cosmos as was the case in the *Romance*—struggling personally with the abstracts of time and space. On the periphery of this world, we sense the lurking shadows of Blake's Four Zoas. The concept of a single authoritarian god is rejected, although not denied, in favour of a pluralistic set of divinities who take their being in the mind of man. The body, its passions, and reasoning faculties are harmonized by the imposition of an imaginative unity which, in turn, incorporates planetary and cosmic forces into a total synthesis. Again, like Blake, Powys sees all these levels in constant flux and in a continually shifting perspective. There is no ultimate resolution, nor can there ever be.

II

Powys's argument in his last four novels is a definite extension of his belief in the anarchy of the imagination as developed in *Porius*. In the "Prefatory Note" to *The Inmates* (1952) he writes:

> I want to show that between all manner of quite different types of patients in a mental institution there is . . . sufficient mental agreement to constitute what I would like to have the courage to call the "Philosophy of the Demented". In other words, though these unfortunates differ greatly in their aberrations from one another, they really do possess, if we drain off or skim off those details of their manias which are obviously peculiar to the individual, certain dominant attitudes to life, to nature and to the cosmos, which, though contrary to all the accepted notions of the conventional minds who make up the world's judgement, have a deep abiding philosophical truth. But this "truth", this Philosophy of the Demented, is naturally under the ban of our authorities in Church and State. And being condemned at the top level it is very noticeable that it is anathema to the underlings, whose personal power and glory depend, of course, as they mount up, on the conventional ideas they have at last, after many rungs of the careerist-ladder, come to embody and represent. (vii)

As specific views are aired throughout the novel, a general framework of reference is established. Individuality is to be both cherished and protected at all costs; freedom must be achieved on either the mental or physical level, preferably both; suffering and pain of all sorts should be mitigated or, where possible, abolished. We are reminded that "Every living soul has one right that none can give or take away, one right in the infinite chaos of the innumerable warring worlds among which we are born, one right and one necessity, and that is the right to be free and alone in our thoughts." (273)

These contentions confirm a growing trend in Powys's later fiction. Myrddin Wyllt and Taliessin spoke about a similar ideology and acted in accordance with it, Owen Glendower used it as his life-spring into eternity, Uryen Quirm of *Maiden Castle*, Sylvanus Cobbold of *Weymouth Sands*, and Johnny Geard of the *Romance* made themselves its priests; nonetheless, it has never been expressed in such extreme terms. In their anarchistic formulation, these ideas lead to ultimate dissent from and total subversion of contemporary social values. *The Inmates* asserts the wisdom of insanity. The words of no less a revolutionary figure than Mao Tse-Tung have disturbing relevance to our discussion:

> A revolution is not a dinner party, or writing an essay, or painting a picture, or doing embroidery; it cannot be so refined, so leisurely and gentle, so temperate, kind, courteous, restrained and magnanimous. A revolution is an insurrection, an act of violence by which one class overthrows another.[3]

And there is plenty of violence in the last chapters of this novel. The sadistic Gewlie is destroyed or, more accurately, disintegrated by the mental powers of Morsimmon Esty, a Thibetan mystic; Dr. Echetus, the institution's head, is shot by a misguided but likeable Communist; a woman falls on "a twisted, sharp-edged six-foot iron stanchion" which breaks her back and crushes her skull. The impetus behind these events is personal at its source but widespread in its effects:

276

> . . . men are men, women are women, and their association
> together through many years has the power of heaping
> up, day by day, and from thousands upon thousands of
> microscopic details, such smouldering stock-piles of
> explosive and even annihilating resentment that once
> released it seems to tap some Satanic crater that can draw
> upon the central lava of world-destruction! (310)

The images of nuclear armageddon fit the context. Supra-
physical powers are epitomized in Morsimmon Esty's magic.
Before it, Gewlie undergoes "almost chemical dissolution," as
if the Thibetan "had found a crack in the heart of life" and
"thrust an atom-bomb into it." (278) It later reduces Dr.
Echetus's body to dust through the operation of "some
devolutionary cosmic ray that has the power of magnetising
people back from human to animal . . . and so on down the
scale to bodiless gasses and even, perhaps, to atoms and
mesons." (279) This force lifts the Doctor's death "out of the
sphere of the criminal and tragic into the sphere of the fantastic
and miraculous." (309) The final limits of revolutionary
doctrine have been reached: murder is condoned as an imaginative necessity. Magic, a key-word throughout *The Inmates*,
sublimates the unnatural into the acceptable as man's thought
triumphs over matter.

By piercing through the book's jumble of psychological
analysis, philosophical debate, social comment, and political
criticism, we discover the tale's overpowering rationale, which
I shall call the truth of fantasy. Powys exposes, albeit in chaotic
fashion, the moribund condition of our apathetically ordered
world. The limitations we impose on ourselves are, he reveals,
of our own making. By assenting to the uniformity of conven-
tion, we destroy the unique possibilities of individual, creative
living. We vacillate between extremes of *"ennui"* and *"angst"*,
unable to retain the "Ideal Now." (182) Only by a freely
willed integration of our imagination with the myriad lives
around us can we fulfil our personalities. Powys foresees the
need for a radical adjustment of each man's personal attitudes
to the challenge of multiversal phenomena, for a philosophical

change which, although generated and sustained imaginatively, must have an impact on physical behaviour. Thought, the magic-catalyst, produces revolution, and revolution breeds anarchy, and anarchy brings freedom.

A liberated consciousness clearly springs from the creative imagination. Powys makes this abundantly clear in all his fiction. (That the novels themselves are, so to speak, existential proof of imaginative powers is obvious enough to be overlooked.) But what of the operation of this faculty? What are its essential properties? How does it complete its function? The answer, I think, lies in the concept "parthenogenesis." Described as "the Self-Birth of Psyche" in *A Glastonbury Romance*, it is a prominent term in the majority of the novels, but especially in the last ones. In these, inspiration drawing on sexual and imaginative co-ordinates—an essentially parthenogenetic process—is expressed through generative symbolism. A precise instance is given in *Atlantis* (1954). When Zeuks, the son of Arcadian Pan, who has propounded his philosophy of *Prokleesis* (defiance or challenge) as "the best clue to life we can have", presides at the death of Ajax, he enacts a ritual of self-revelation. Placing the dead man's head between the knees of a statue of Hector, he thrusts his own head between Ajax's thighs. "Thus were the three figures united, one a corpse, one a work of art, and one a living creature; and this uniting of life with death, and of life and death with a graven image of human imagination had a curious and singular effect." (283) Zeuks questions his idea of *Prokleesis*, rejects it, and replaces it by "*Lanthanomai*, or 'I forget', followed by the still simpler word, *Terpomai* or 'I enjoy.' " Death, art, and life fuse into an imaginative and sexual illumination. The discovery is accompanied by "the bitter smell" of genitals and "the salt, sharp taste" of sweaty hairs. By rooting itself in concrete earthiness, his imagination breaks through cerebral obfuscation to the clarity of vision:

> "It is ," he told himself, ". . . as if I had been given by the gods the power to suck and draw and drain from the lapsing semen of this dead body such magnetic force into

the peristaltic channel of my spirit that a fresh and a new insight into the whole of life radiates through me." (285)

This image of necrophiliastic fellatio bridges the gap between life and death to affirm the continuity of the human spirit. There is no trace of the morbidity so characteristic of Dud No-man in *Maiden Castle* nor of Medrawd's almost vampirish predilections in *Porius*.

Although the moment of parthenogenetic revelation is positive in its effect, the sex-imagination relationship in itself is scarcely a panacea. It can be perverted as may happen in unwarranted scientific experimentation. This, we learn, caused the destruction of Atlantis. Its ruler discovered "the secret of some new magnetic stone that can influence unborn embryos" and which "may have the power of making the embryo bi-sexual." The gods (Powys thinks of them in the Greek sense as being personifications of natural forces) keep "sex, and birth, the issue of sex, completely under their control" and thereby rule us. Man's biogenetic science—the "Embryo Stone"—threatens to subvert the natural order. The Ruler of Atlantis is himself, or herself, the monstrous androgynous product of rational experimentation. As such, this creature is bereft of all human qualities; it speaks in the "mechanical, automatic, and metallic voice" of science. When finally confronted, it enunciates the law of Atlantis with computeristic inhumanity:

> "This law will be absolutely and entirely scientific. As it is born of science, so it will grow, century by century and aeon by aeon, more purely scientific. Its one and sole purpose will be science for the sake of science. It will care nothing about such trifling, frivolous, unimportant matters as faith, hope and charity. It will care nothing about the happiness of people, or the comfort of people, or the education of people, still less, if that be possible, about the virtue or the righteousness or the compassion or the pity or the sympathy of people. (451)

These extremes of imaginative creation are given explicit formulation in *The Brazen Head* (1956). In this novel, partheno-genesis receives its fullest documentation, and the forces of good and evil are exactly balanced. Although Roger Bacon's "mechanical Head capable of uttering oracles" is introduced as one of his "world-changing inventions," it is nowhere described as scientific; rather, it is referred to as an act of worship, as one of his "magical creations." It is vitalized by "the inspiration of Virginity." Bacon induces a Jewish servant-girl, Ghosta (her name reverberates), to straddle the Head while he repeats "the sounds of an ancient invocation." During this ritual, the girl experiences "a weird erotic ecstasy;" she retains her maidenhead while "drawing from the inmost depths of [herself] a dew-drop of living creation." Thus, the Head is activated by the vicarious sexual union of the Friar and the girl—definite parthenogenetic creation; it becomes a cerebral force, given "that unique power of revelation, of illumination, of ultimate vision, that virgins alone possess!" As the psychic child of human forces, the Brazen Head has a dualistic nature, containing an "imprisoned demonic power" as well as oracular benevolence. Bacon believes it is "a rival creation to Adam and Eve." Such a position does indeed constitute a new revelation.

As the symbol of a wholly human apocalypse, the Head is exceptionally fitting. It is the "child of the *essence* as well as of *the being*" of Bacon's soul, "a man-created machine" brought to life by the parthenogenetic union of man and woman; its power flows from the elemental energy of brute matter; yet it functions on a totally cerebral plane to communicate earth wisdom to man. Here we again catch a hint of that prophetic voice—never quiet in Powys's later fiction—which, in *Atlantis*, foresaw the dangers of biogenetic permutation; now it suggests man's development of computer-techniques, especially in the field of cybernetics.

Although possessing the dual nature of its origins, the Head is intended to be a positive, constructive power rather than a harmful one—its oracles are to be "very helpful" at both the personal and national level. The oracle, properly embodied in a head, is equated with the rational soul of man. But man has another side—his physical, animal nature. That force, if not directed upward—sublimated to the mental plane—may be directed downwards towards a negative, destructive pole.

Such a negative perversion is allowed for in Peter Peregrinus, a "great student of magnetism." The lodestone he has "newly invented" permits him to manipulate "his own sexual force . . . for the domination of the souls and will of other entities." He is uncertain of its absolute effect but is sure that with it he could destroy so much of the present order that he could create a different one. In this he is like Roger Bacon: both seek a "new revelation." Unlike the Friar, however, who is working on a humanist level, Peter thinks of himself as Antichrist: his doctrine smacks of Atlantean perversity:

> "What I would do then," he told himself, "the moment I had got the world entirely under my control, would be to build up an absolutely different kind of world altogether. . . . and what I would aim at in *my* world, . . . in my super-scientific world, would be to create a new race of beings altogether, creatures as superior to what mankind is now as man is superior to beasts, birds and fishes! (243)

Both Peter Peregrinus and Roger Bacon are playing God; the former's attempt is nevertheless much more dangerous than the latter's. The one would destroy humanity—both its qualities and defects—to substitute a non-human structure, while the other merely wishes to assist man within his natural framework. Ironically, the two are using the same human power to arrive at opposing goals. Bacon himself admits that without Peter's "inspiration" he could never have invented his Brazen Head; and elsewhere the Friar's "authentic inventive genius" is contrasted with Peregrinus's "extremely exalted imagination."

Since the lodestone is shown in operation a number of times while the Head is not, we might infer that its powers are the stronger. It is only in the final confrontation of the lodestone with the Brazen Head that the relation between the two is defined and finally resolved. At the book's conclusion the two forces clash: the Head utters its sole—incomplete—oracle; the stone transmutes itself, its inventor, and his sex-companion into a "single fiery ball" which falls upon the Head. Both are annihilated: their powers are equal.

Our knowledge that Peter's magnet draws "like to like" points to the exact meaning of these events. The Head and lodestone are similar in having powers beyond those "in harmony with Nature;" they have no place in this world; consequently they neutralize each other. We are left with an affirmation of certain basic life-values advocated in most of Powys's writing. The words are Roger Bacon's (he has by this time grown indifferent to his creation): " 'As long as we are considerate to other people,' he said, 'and as kind and sympathetic towards them as our circumstances permit, we have all got to live to ourselves, for ourselves, in ourselves and by ourselves.' " (340–341)

The achievement of *The Brazen Head, Atlantis, The Inmates* and *Porius* relies on imaginative authenticity. In the Powysian context, imagination can transform all activity, including the sexual urge, into unlimited, universal energy with creative or destructive powers. This premise underlies Powys's most radical statement about our sexual and imaginative identities. In *All or Nothing* (1960), his last published novel, he counterbalances his attitudes toward heterosexual relationships with an assertion of phallic power. The Cerne Giant—a favourite figure in so many novels—states:

> "In the matter of sex, . . . what in the English language is called masturbation—that is to say, the excited emission of semen by the use of our imagination—is a much more important and creative act than ordinary and natural fornication . . ." (192)

It is worth noting that copulation and reproduction are understood as fundamentally *physical* acts; consequently masturbation, a primarily *imaginative* force is "much more important and creative". Choice rests of course with the individual.

The novel's concluding paragraph—a fitting valediction—contains the seed of Powys's life-vision:

> "But remember . . . that All is not Nothing, neither is Nothing All, but both of them have one home-star, where they can sink to eternal quiescence, or mount to everlasting activity, and that home-star, my children, is the heart in every one of us." (219)

NOTES

1   For a discussion of the historic and mythic perspective of *Owen Glendower*, see my article "Owen Glendower: The Pursuit of the Fourth Dimension," *The Anglo-Welsh Review*, XVII, 42 (February 1970), pp. 207–216.

2   Numerals in parentheses refer to the pages of the novel under discussion.

3   Mao Tse-Tung, *Quotations from Chairman Mao Tse-Tung*, 2nd ed., Forward by Lin Piao, Peking, 1967, pp. 11–12.

XV

JOHN COWPER POWYS AND HIS PUBLISHERS

Malcolm Elwin

Jonathan Cape introduced me to the work of John Cowper Powys. It was he who published the first English edition of *Wolf Solent* in 1929. He also published my first four books, and after the press reception of my biography of Charles Reade I was considered an author of sufficient importance to be invited occasionally to lunch at the restaurant in Charlotte Street where Cape and his partners entertained their chief reader, Edward Garnett, on his weekly visit to London.

Cape was expounding his habitual theme that some books published for prestige had to be paid for by popular sellers of inferior merit. "Look at *Wolf Solent*," he said: "a long book, expensive to produce, and we shall be lucky if it pays its expenses. Yet a novel of genius, isn't it?" He smiled at Garnett; he had an enigmatic smile, his eyes remaining glassy while his dentures flashed. Old Garnett merely nodded his large head, and peering through his thick spectacles, questioned me about the curious behaviour of Thackeray's granddaughter.

It was characteristic of Cape that he didn't give me a copy of *Wolf Solent;* I had to buy it. Having read it, I tried in vain to find copies of Powys's three previous novels, *Wood and Stone*, *Rodmoor*, and *Ducdame*. When the Bodley Head announced *A Glastonbury Romance* in the spring of 1933, I ordered my copy before publication, and on my next visit to Cape asked him how the Bodley Head came to publish the book. Leaning back in his chair, he said with his glassy smile, "We rejected it."

"Good God," I protested, "it's probably the greatest novel yet written this century."

"You may be right," he said. "But we just decided it was too long to be a commercial proposition. You writers never appreciate what it costs to produce a long book . . ."

I was then living at North Stoke in Oxfordshire and about the time when the Bodley Head published *Jobber Skald* in 1935, Allen Lane, his brothers, a sister and his parents became my neighbours at Berins Hill. Nephew and successor of the firm's founder, Allen Lane was always courteous, but smooth, shrewd, and discreet—made for material success. One of his brothers, killed in the war, was more expansive.

He told me that Powys had received nothing from their edition of *A Glastonbury Romance* because somebody in Somerset had insisted that he was caricatured as Philip Crow and threatened an action for damages till the lawyers agreed that he should accept Powys's royalties in lieu of damages. So when they received Powys's next novel, published in America as *Weymouth Sands*, they had to insist on changing the title to *Jobber Skald* and on altering the names of persons and places so that nobody in Weymouth might claim to be libelled.

Such legal iniquity seems to me as appalling now as it did then, yet the law remains unaltered. I know the name of the person who claimed to be caricatured as Philip Crow, but must not publish it lest he should be still alive and might sue me for repeating the alleged libel. Powys's close friend Louis Wilkinson suffered in the same way with one of his novels; a Scotsman insisted that his daughter was slandered because her name was the same as that of a character in the novel, and though the action of the novel took place in London and the Scottish lady had never trespassed beyond the border of her native land, the publisher settled out of court by paying Louis's royalties to the plaintiff. It is indeed always the author and seldom the publisher who suffers in such cases, as the publisher settles for such a sum as may be earned in royalties and deducts the amount of the payment from the author's royalty statement.

Powys's next novel, *Maiden Castle*, was begun on 28th January 1935 at Dorchester in lodgings exactly the same as those attributed to Dud No-man in the novel. Just a year later, when he had been six months settled at Corwen in North Wales, he wrote to his brother Llewelyn on 17th January 1936, "I hope I'm on my last 100 pages of Mss, long-hand, of my Dorchester Book, a book far more deeply and obstinately and indurately made up of me wone antick notions and chin-

digging obstinacies . . . than any other. But this is in a measure
. . . due to Fear of Censureship, not wanting Lane to shirk
calling it by its local realistic names, or to get the Lawyer to
change the names and insert things at his legal (but not very
literary) pleasure to put people on the wrong scent!" Three
months later, on 9th April 1936, he told Llewelyn, "Lane has
given my *Maiden Castle*, my Dorchester book, into the hands
of his lawyer to look out for what he calls (and suspects the
danger of) Obscene Libel, tho' what this means baffles me. But
I *think* it is the Moral Censor for Obscene Books he fears this
time; *not* Ordinary Libel against persons, but Obscene Libel
against God knows what." Not surprisingly he felt it necessary
to entrust his business to a literary agent, happily choosing
Laurence Pollinger, who had fostered the interests of D. H.
Lawrence so well and whom he soon described to Llewelyn as
"of inestimable value to me in standing up to the publishers
for money."

Though immediately accepted by Simon & Schuster in
America, *Maiden Castle* was eventually published in England
by Cassell after having been rejected, not only by the Bodley
Head, but also by Chapman & Hall—curiously, as this firm
published in that summer of 1936 *Welsh Ambassadors*, Louis
Wilkinson's book about the Powys brothers. Its successor,
Morwyn; or The Vengeance of God, was the least successful of
all Powys's books—rejected by Simon & Schuster, his loyal
American publishers since *Wolf Solent*, while the English
edition by Cassell was remaindered at 3*s.* 6*d.*

To appease his publishers on both sides of the Atlantic,
Powys had to lay aside his *Owen Glendower* (the first chapter
of which was written by August 1937) to compile the book of
essays called by Simon & Schuster *Enjoyment of Literature*
and by Cassell *The Pleasures of Literature*. Clifton Fadiman
had been replaced as Simon & Schuster's reader by a younger
man, who objected "that St. Paul is *not* one of the pleasures of
reading," so Powys had to defer his novel again while he
wrote the essays on Milton and Goethe to replace St. Paul in
the American edition. "I am half way thro' my *Owain Glyn-*

dwyr," he told Llewelyn on 22nd November 1938, but the novel was only finished a few weeks after Llewelyn's death on 2nd December 1939. Though published in two volumes by Simon & Schuster in 1940, *Owen Glendower* was rejected by eight London publishers before its acceptance by the Bodley Head, which was no longer directed by those who had feared "obscene libel" in *Maiden Castle*.

The failure of a firm so celebrated as John Lane The Bodley Head caused a sensation in the publishing world, especially as Allen Lane had recently achieved a brilliantly successful innovation by publishing paperbacks. By one of those convenient curiosities of commercial law Penguin Books turned out to be a separate concern from the Bodley Head, and while Allen Lane increasingly prospered as a paperback publisher, the authors published by the Bodley Head were the losers by its bankruptcy. Three other publishers combined to keep alive the Bodley Head imprint, appointing C. J. Greenwood as manager.

It was Greenwood who published *Owen Glendower* in a stout volume of 952 pages—a bold venture in 1941 when wartime paper-rationing encouraged most publishers to concentrate on short books. Greenwood had published Llewelyn Powys's *Love and Death* in the year he died; he published the volume of Llewelyn's *Letters*, edited by Louis Wilkinson, which led me into correspondence with Llewelyn's widow, Alyse Gregory, and into undertaking my *Life of Llewelyn Powys*, for which Greenwood gave me a contract.

Writing this biography brought an intensive correspondence with John Cowper Powys, who decided that I was "providential" after Louis Wilkinson had reported favourably on me, and wrote to me on 24th August 1944, "Yes, *ask me anything*, only remember that my memory needs *something else than dates* to go upon." Sometimes no more than a name was needed to evoke a spate of reminiscences. Often his letters ran to twenty pages or more in length and came as frequently as twice a week. As he had more than once mentioned that he was working on "my long Romance of only eight days in the year 499 A.D.", I expressed concern lest my questions about Llewelyn were taking up too much of his time. He replied that he had other diversions, as he had to write other books for money while his novel awaited completion.

"Yes," he wrote in 4th March 1945, "my *Rabelais* (from *my* point of view) *IS* finished, but whether it is finished from the point of view of the Publisher, i.e. Bodley Head, is another & a very different Proposition! They have given it to their special *expert* 'Reader' (expert on 16th century France and French) to decide whether it is *finished* or rather whether it isn't *prolonged* beyond its appointed adequate & dedicated finale! I have been Revising my much smaller & shorter book on *Dostoievsky*, the best part of which is a summing up at the end on the connection real & imaginary between D[ostoievsky] & the present World-Crisis!"

More than two years elapsed after that letter before Greenwood published *Dostoievsky* in April 1947. Another year followed before *Rabelais* appeared under the same imprint in May 1948. Accustomed to the pre-war efficiency by which a book was usually published six months after delivery of typescript, Powys was so irritated by these protracted delays that he thought (18th August 1949) of asking his agent to insert a clause in his contracts insisting that a book "must be published in a year from the date of receiving it or I have the right to send it elsewhere." Yet in this same letter he confessed a fear lest the Bodley Head might find *Porius* "*too long to publish*", as in fact happened.

Perhaps Greenwood could not be blamed. Paper-rationing was still in force, and the system worked unfairly against the smaller publishers, as the allocation was according to the amount of paper consumed by a publisher in the last complete year before the war. Macmillans, for instance, were able to acquire several valuable new authors because just before the war they had the good luck of frequently reprinting that bulky bestseller, *Gone With the Wind*. When my *Life of Llewelyn*

Powys sold out within six weeks of publication in December 1946, Greenwood wrote that he would be reprinting "as soon as conditions allow," but more than two years elapsed before paper was found for the reprint.

Meanwhile, as general editor of Macdonald's new series of Classics, I had invited Powys to write an introduction to Sterne's *Sentimental Journey*. Characteristically he asked pemission of both his agent and his publisher before accepting the commission, writing on 2nd July 1947, "My dear Malcolm, I've had both Mr. Pollinger's & Mr. Greenwood's friendly benediction on our Preface for Mr. MacDonald's new *Sentimental Journey* under your Editorship." On 2nd October following he sent me the typescript of the introduction, explaining that his Dorchester typist had "found from her exact numbering that it contained 6463 words," which "excessive number I have reduced to 5400." But instead of being deleted, his cuts were left within square brackets "*for your own private eye as a biographer* interested in Sterne as a thrilling figure," and he added, "if you prefer to delete any other passages by all means do so, or if you prefer to delete *other* passages and *restore* some of what *I* have deleted, do so by all manner of means, for as you know I'm not (as Hardy says in a moral— or erotic I think it was—connection) *in a literary sense I am* not a particular man!"

In fact I accepted only one of his proposed cuts and the published introduction is over 6,000 words. The joint-managing director of Macdonalds was then Eric Harvey, who appointed me "literary adviser" to the firm and planned with me a series of Classics one morning on the beach at Buck Mills in North Devon. When he read the introduction, he was so impressed that he proposed to double the agreed fee and asked me to suggest that Powys should write a further introduction to Sterne's *Tristram Shandy*. "I'll get to work on this exciting task at once," Powys wrote to me on 20th October 1947 "and this, most gratifying appreciation of our *Journey* preface makes your own good 'Mediumship' (of which you speak so lightly)

a thing most lucky and *most noteworthy* for me." As appears
from his published *Letters to Louis Wilkinson*, he had received
a grant from the Royal Literary Fund, and £200 for his Sterne
introductions came opportunely.

Having finished his long introduction to *Tristram Shandy*
he returned—as he told Louis Wilkinson on 18th March
1948—"to my 'Dark Ages' *two* last chapters." When, no less
than seventeen months later, on 18th August 1949 he told
Louis that he was "*revising* & correcting the typed-script of
my completed 'Porius', a Romance of the Dark Ages in 33
long-hand chapters," his *revising* meant that he was cutting
the length, as scholars will discover who consult the original
manuscript of the novel, now at the University of Texas. Even
with the cuts, "My huge 'Romance of the Dark Ages' did *not*
find favour in America," he informed Louis on 5th December
1949.

Curiously, publication of *Porius* was delayed by Louis's
breaking his leg in April 1950, as this accident postponed his
proposed visit to me from April till September. For I felt
diffident about writing to Powys to ask why *Porius* was so long
delayed lest he should feel embarrassment in having to tell me
that it had been rejected. I had to wait till I could explain my
diffidence to Louis, who exclaimed in his emphatic manner,
"Oh, it's been rejected I don't know how many times—so
many times that I believe Pollinger has stopped sending it
out. It's too long, of course, too *long*, like all Jack Powys's
novels." At my request Louis then wrote to suggest that
Powys should ask Laurence Pollinger to send the typescript
to Macdonalds, who would send it to me for advice.

I still have a copy of my report on *Porius*—more than
5,000 words, including a chapter-by-chapter synopsis and
concluding:

"This gigantic book of 999 pages in type script is equally
gigantic in conception and achievement. The historical and
legendary background reveals profound scholarship, the
characters and situations are endowed with dramatic vitality,

and the book can be read as an historical romance by a skilled craftsman. While the story reveals all the romantic imagination of Scott, it is also such a satirical allegory as Swift might have conceived. Redwood Anderson wrote of Powys's previous novel, *Owen Glendower*, as "an authentic fragment—though but a single and broken sentence—of the history of the World-Spirit itself"—a description that seems even more appropriate to *Porius*. Without any doubt this is a work of great genius . . . the crowning achievement of a veteran novelist who has already written at least one novel, *A Glastonbury Romance*, which ranks among the outstanding works of this century."

As I seldom expressed enthusiasm about novels sent for my opinion, even Eric Harvey's colleague, the late Murray Thompson, was impressed and felt he ought to make an attempt to read a book that excited such reaction. *Porius* was accepted for publication by Macdonalds within a few days of receiving the typescript—some time before my wife and I drove up to Corwen, stopping at the roadside to watch the full October moon rising above Bala Lake.

Next morning as "I climbed the hill to Powys's cottage above the little town of Corwen, I felt like a pilgrim bent on consulting the wisdom of a hermit seer in his mountain retreat. No pilgrim ever met with richer reward. With perceptions and enthusiasm not indeed dimmed by time, but enhanced by time's experience, he impresses with a sense of goodness as apparent as his genius. *And surely the combination of goodness and genius makes the man who is truly great among his fellows?*"

This I wrote in that excellent magazine "Everybody's", of which Kenneth Hopkins was then assistant editor, at the time of the publication of *Porius* in August 1951. I wrote much the same to Eric Harvey, who was usually shy of meeting his authors but was soon persuaded to make a similar pilgrimage to Corwen. As a result, Powys never had to worry again about the publication of his books in England, and has any writer remained so prolific throughout the eighth decade of his life? Each book was read by both Eric Harvey and myself in typescript, and I also read them all in proof to save the strain on the author's one remaining eye—for he lost the sight of one eye (or "nearly so", as he would put it) in 1948.

Porius was followed by *The Inmates* (1952), *In Spite Of* (1953), *Atlantis* (1954), the new editions of *A Glastonbury Romance* and *Visions and Revisions* (1955), *The Brazen Head* (1956) and also *Lucifer: A Poem* (which was originally entitled *The Death of God*), *Up and Out* (1957), *Homer and the Aether* (1959), *All or Nothing* (1960), the new edition of *Wolf Solent* (1961) and the first real version of *Weymouth Sands* in England (1963). After Powys's death in 1963 *Maiden Castle* appeared with my introduction in 1966 and the *Autobiography*, with an introduction by J. B. Priestley and a note by R. L. Blackmore, in 1967. *Owen Glendower* was planned, and the list would have continued if Macdonalds had not been swallowed up in a "merger"·

After Eric Harvey left the board of directors, the dismissal of his colleague and former production-manager, Walter Parrish, soon followed. A medley of accountants and business "executives" with no practical experience of publishing, moved in—"big thinkers," prepared to lose hundreds of thousands of pounds on encyclopaedias and cookery books, but without interest in investing a mere £5,000 in publishing a work of genius. They have not lasted long; even they have had to learn—as Leonard Woolf pointed out in *The Journey Not the Arrival Matters*—that books cannot be packaged like soap, for the good reason that "every cake of soap is exactly the same, but unfortunately for the publisher every book in his list is unlike every other." Perhaps it is just as well that John Cowper Powys did not survive to see his centenary.

XVI
ATHENE PROVIDES

Jonah Jones

My youth was truly coloured by the Powys family. I had not met any of them, but I knew them intimately, it seemed, from reading them widely. Each one in his different way, John, Theodore, Llewelyn and Littleton (who mirrored them all and contracted that most wondrous of marriages with Elizabeth Myers in his last years), they all made a kind of physical impact. Photographs of their vast, curly British skulls bear this out. Big, bony, strong-bred, patrician, behind them all one imagines a noble line of ancestors, all larger than life. Certainly one felt at least the presence of father and mother at Montacute, either as begetters and guardians of the unique Powysian family spirit, or as something to flee from and defy, albeit to love always. John's autobiography surely bears the greatest portrait of a father in English literature.

When John came, miraculously it seemed, to live at Corwen only 30 miles away, it was as though a sun had wandered into our orbit, yet shyness, and of course respect for another artist's time, kept me away. When he came even nearer, to Blaenau Ffestiniog, Raymond Garlick insisted that we should meet. Of course, it was on the cards that a portrait bust would ensue. John had some vague story of Theodore Dreiser stalking off through the streets of New York with the only portrait bust in existence: has anybody heard any more of it?

On the way up the narrow flight of stairs, I was always struck by a photograph of the handsomest brother of all, Willie, whom I had not known about, and who did not write but simply farmed in Kenya. John spoke of him with great tenderness.

What a sitting, when it finally came about! Ludicrous! By now, of course, John was old and rather weak, but mentally very lively indeed. Full of years, he rested his long limbs on a sofa across the upper window of his tiny quarryman's cottage. His head lay back on the cushion, the silver locks curling in Powysian splendour over the vast cranium. The brow was Socratic, deeply furrowed but untroubled. The eyes were deep-set, piercing yet benign, and also, I remember, strangely

296

odd, one different from the other. It was with the nose, hawk-like, the nostrils wide-winged, that the Powysian spirit began. Then the great wide upper lip, cruel, ready to boom, That was John. The mouth was built for rhetoric, his greatest love, and as I worked, or tried to, the great head moved about ceaselessly as he poured forth line after line from *The Prelude* or from Tennyson's *Morte d'Arthur*. He made the latter live in a way I had not thought possible. His voice, his whole rhetorical manner, was electrifying, spell-binding. He always addressed you in a great cataract of speech, as though drunk with the sheer beauty of words. The whole effect of the head was of a falcon, of Horus the hawk-god, belying the angelic tenderness of the John who prayed daily for the deliverance of animals from the agonies of vivisection.

I never really got a sitting. I struggled up the stairs with stand, bust-peg and clay, committing a sort of sacrilege in that booklined room. He quaffed his raw egg, picked up an ancient Greek Drachma, looked eye-to-eye at the owl effigy of Athene thereon and prayed in wondrous Greek for the gods to look with favour on our joint project. And that was it. He sat fairly still, even stiff, for a minute and I opened up the sort of desultory, relaxed talk that often passes between sitter and sculptor. An artist does not want a posed sitter. And so John opened out, at once, and never stopped. My hands worked distractedly. His fluttered like birds, expressing most of all pleasure, sheer pleasure in life. He was up and down, a gangling impossible model. I could only pummel clay about. Yet I left it at that, cast it and took the thing lovingly to the foundry and it has always been my favourite bust.

XVII

POWYS IN GWYNEDD: the last years

Raymond Garlick

I first met John Cowper Powys when he was a few months short of eighty. In the spring of 1951 he had become a subscriber to the magazine now called *The Anglo-Welsh Review*, which I was editing from Pembrokeshire. Happening to be in north Wales in the summer of 1952, my wife and I went one day to Corwen and called at 7 Cae Coed. It was a brief but memorable meeting—and a hospitable one: I remember that the coffee-cups stood on a silver salver that had belonged to William Cowper.

In the summer of 1954 my family and I settled in Blaenau Ffestiniog, that dramatic and unforgettable mountain town whose human warmth is in inverse ratio to its winter temperatures and icy rainstorms. In the middle of one of these towards the end of that year, I was astonished to come upon John Cowper Powys and Miss Phyllis Playter in the main street of Blaenau—and even more surprised and delighted to learn that they too were to join those few for whom Blaenau was somewhere sought out, found, chosen as a home. He had always wanted to settle there, attracted by its remoteness, but had been deflected to Corwen on the advice, I believe, of James Hanley. But now, after all, the largest completely Welsh township in Gwynedd was to be the scene of the last seven years of the life of this descendant of the ancient princely house of Powys.

By May 1955 the little house at 1 Waterloo was ready for them. Over the next five and a half years there was close contact between the two households. For parts of 1956 and 1957 I kept a journal, from which the following are extracts:—

Tuesday 3/*i*/56: Phyllis still suffering from a racking cough. J.C.P. naturally worried. He spoke of the encounter between Ajax and Sarpedon in the Iliad, when Ajax hurled a huge boulder—for which the Greek word (μάρμᾰρος) means something glittering, with jagged edges: reminded him of our rocks hereabouts. Phyllis spoke in warm praise of R. S. Thomas's poems, which I had got Smith's to send down to them before Christmas. They spoke of Gilbert Murray's 90th birthday broadcast yesterday, and of an impressive reading of a poem called "Almanac" by John Redwood-Anderson which preceded it in the wireless programme.

Sunday 8/i/56: Phyllis mentioned her great concern lest they should run out of ink and be left "without a drop in the house": J.C.P. says he can't write in pencil—the thoughts don't come. Upstairs to see him, wearing scarlet mittens and sitting between two electric fires and one coal fire, writing madly. He told me that the source of his *Porius* was the *Brut Dingestow* (Henry Lewis, Caerdydd 1942) and showed me a copy. I asked him if he could read this old Welsh text and he said that, with a dictionary, he found it much easier than Chaucer. He spoke of his discovery (as a result of having forgotten the significance of the Epiphany) that "We have seen his star in the east" (Matthew II, 2) is, in the Greek, εἴδομεν γὰρ αὐτοῦ τον ἀστέρα ἐν τῇ ἀνατολῇ and that Anatole France's Xtian name therefore meant "the east." Spoke of his worship of Rabelais, of how R. was one of the first proof-readers: he bought a book on Gargantua at Lyons fair one year and the next his own book was on sale there. There were no bookshops at the time, hence books were sold on booths at fairs. J.C.P. felt that Rabelaisian humour was richer, deeper, more human than that of Aristophanes.

Friday 13/i/56: Phyllis's cough still bad; she is not sleeping and looks very ill and exhausted. J.C.P. says rightly that he is much tougher: this is because he is nourished—raw eggs, milk etc.—while Phyllis eats hardly at all.

Tuesday 17/i/56: Elin and Iestyn had called to see how Phyllis did: a little better. Iestyn and J.C.P. played wildly as usual, throwing a wastepaper-basket about apparently.

Sunday 22/i/56: Phyllis much improved. Iestyn, as usual, at once removed and distributed his outer garments: J.C.P. put on his red and white stocking cap which, on his white curls, looked very piratical. Later he bound round this, turban-like, Iestyn's plaid scarf and announced that he was Genghis Khan. Phyllis was surrounded by darning impedimenta—a warm winter-afternoon scene—and amid this was what looked like a dark brown button, $1\frac{1}{2}''$ in diameter. She said it was a kind of horse-chestnut—called in the States a "buck-eye"—which her grandmother had used when darning socks. J.C.P. delighted with the name, which he appeared not to have heard before, and delighted to learn something new. I was interested in this desire, and that it should be possible to fulfil from the limited material surroundings of everyday life after so many years' familiarity with them: his ability to derive pleasure and interest from the simplest sources.

Sunday 29/*i*/56: J.C.P. and I agreed on an affection for Captain Marryat's *Children of the New Forest*. He quoted with approval Louis Wilkinson's reference to the "barbaric naivety" of the Powyses: applied it to his father, who excelled at mathematics at the university, his other great interest being nature-study—particularly birds'-eggs: said his mother was the intellectual and literary partner of that marriage. He spoke of a former correspondent, a Mr. White of White Hall, somewhere in Ireland—a friend of Casement. Said he had just reached the end of the twelfth book of the Iliad in the Loeb edition: praised this—the Greek of Homer faced by plain English prose: said verse translations—Murray etc.—meddled with the original.

Sunday 5/*ii*/56: J.C.P. and Phyllis both well and very warm and comfortable. J.C.P. wearing six waistcoats (one leather, he boasted) and looking forward to the seventh which Iestyn proclaimed to be nearly finished. He showed us a beautiful travelling clock which had belonged to his brother Littleton. Iestyn played with the Greek coin showing the head of Athene: J.C.P. said that he had read of such a coin fetching £27,000: Phyllis dubious.

Sunday 12/*ii*/56: We all visited J.C.P. and Phyllis this afternoon, and presented the peacock-blue waistcoat with bronze buttons: J.C.P. insisted on donning it at once—his ninth waistcoat-layer. Spoke of a newly-completed 200-page story—"blasphemous but not obscene"—which concludes with God and the Devil committing suicide. They had bought a box of coloured blocks for Iestyn to play with when he goes there—which he proceeded to do with great pleasure.

Thursday 23/*ii*/56: Elin and Iestyn had been down to 1 Waterloo this afternoon: Phyllis out and J.C.P. already getting a trifle worried about her whereabouts. He and Iestyn apparently shouted "Baa, baa, black sheep" at each other and showed each other, boastfully, their warm underpants—J.C.P. rolling up his trouser-leg for the purpose. Elin brought back a copy of *The Welsh Republican* among other things.

Sunday 18/*iii*/56: Went out walking on the Manod—saw J.C.P. out on his customary route-march.

Saturday 24/*iii*/56: Iestyn and I went to see J.C.P.: Jean Ware, the journalist, was there.

Saturday 14/*iv*/56: We all went to see J.C.P. They expect Jacquetta Hawkes on the 25th. J. B. Priestley was to have come too, but has to go to Canada. J.C.P. very distinguished in a cherry-coloured corduroy jacket. He spoke of his hatreds —Robert Graves and Bernard Shaw: explained that his loves and hates are rooted in physical reactions—faces, hands. Showed us a fine photograph of Pius XII—who he says is the most beautiful living person. J.C.P. has written a letter on vivisection to *The Observer*. He showed us Lawrence Irving's book about his grandfather and described Irving's Hamlet— the door opening, one foot put forward: Hamlet's foot, not Irving's. J.C.P's theory of Shakespeare is that it is the actor who matters.

Wednesday 18/*iv*/56: J.C.P. much taken with the word "impetigo", which he wrote down in the front of his Bible.

Friday 27/*iv*/56: He spoke of Milton's gentleness towards the younger Dryden: of the night watchmen crying through the streets of London "John Dryden, the great poet, is dying in his lodgings in Soho". I asked him about his alleged remark that if he met Browning he would take pleasure in knocking him down. He said he would never have used the latter words: might have said he would "go for" him—he would like to have gone for Shaw. Not particularly irritated by Browning. He spoke of E. E. Cummings: Phyllis said his room at 4 Patchin Place was full of ashes from the grate, which he never carried out: he always had several bouquets of flowers from the florist's, in vases. At Phyllis's prompting, J.C.P. recited with gusto the first poem he had ever written (at his prep. school)—about two grisly spectres meeting in Corfe Castle. Mentioned a prize poem about Corinth, into which his form-master had inserted two stanzas about St. Paul and love, thereby much annoying him. They spoke with enthusiasm of Jacquetta Hawkes, who visited them last Tuesday. She was born a Hopkins, of the family of G. M. Hopkins. They had just received from Alyse Gregory the rough typescript of Llewelyn Powys's diary, beginning just before he went to lecture in America: I read the first few entries—he did not much want to go there. They had a copy of a new book by one Phillip Callow, of Coventry: a really proletarian writer, they said.

Saturday 27/*x*/56: Evening with Mr. Powys, who gave me one of the superb copies of *Lucifer*, in which he wrote some typically kind words. Phyllis described how Mr. Sims had called to ask if they had any MS for sale. They welcomed the opportunity and in the course of a hunt for some discovered this long poem at the bottom of a trunk. J.C.P. had forgotten all about it—it was written in 1905. He again chanted the fine Swinburne poem which I have never been able to trace—"Back to Lesbos": a vision of Aphrodite in her dove-drawn car which comes to the poet when he lies unable to sleep. We talked of words we had created as children. He mentioned the Sherborne prep. tabu word "Fenn" (forbid, opt out) and said he thought such words had a long and disreputable history. He spoke, of his invention, as a boy, of the "Volentia" army—to which he conscripted all his brothers.

Sunday 11/*xi*/56: We all walked over the mountain to J.C.P.'s. The waterfall like a great, many-fingered hand, throbbing with innumerable veins of white water. J.C.P. spoke of his current work—a "paraphrase" of Homer: he was engaged on p. 243

of his MS as we interrupted him. He talked of Zeus's exclamation to Poseidon – 'Ὦ ποποῖ – and of the word πέπον; of Helenos (son of Priam)'s telepathy and consequent forewarning of Hector.

Thursday 27/xii/56: Mr Powys and Phyllis well. On Christmas Eve a child was born in the terrace adjoining them. J.C.P. said he saw a white seagull again—his harbinger of birth. He re-iterated his belief that all the best writers are French but with German names (apropos the author of *Double Exposure*, which we all admire). ✗

Sunday 6/i/57: We went down to Ty Powys. J.C.P. in fine form—pleased, among other things, to discover from a book-review in *The Observer* that Columbus was half-Jewish. Told him I was re-reading Scott's *Redgauntlet* and he spoke warmly of the gentleness and simplicity of Sir Walter. Although he had not read the novels since boyhood, he quoted incidents from them and Scott's poems with pleasure and excitement. He was annoyed by an immense American "bible" of literature garnished with vacuous comments by critics down the ages. As we walked home, an immense Sinai-like deep purple cloud covered the two peaks of the Moelwyn: the rest of the sky very clear and still.

Tuesday 29/i/57: J.C.P. spoke of his mother's family, the Moilliets. His maternal grandmother lived in Weymouth, her husband having been purser (bursar?) of Corpus and having secured for himself the fattest College living.

Sunday 10/ii/57: Elin and Iestyn to Ty Powys this afternoon. J.C.P. had got something into his eye some days ago, but this had now passed: suffering a little from lumbago.

Saturday 16/ii/57: J.C.P. in good spirits, suffering much less pain. He spoke warmly (re a book of Thomas Gilby, O.P. that he is reading, on St. Thomas Aquinas's Aesthetics) of Albertus Magnus and Aquinas. Said he was sorry to see that Edith Sitwell had dismissed Lady Mary Wortley Montagu as "a pretentious macaw". This led to talk of Pope and he said what a difficulty his deformity must have laid in the path of his desire to be a great man. I told him of the moving decision, after an irascible meeting, of Pope and Swift not to meet again since their friendship would founder. He said that today two such great figures would not harness their spite, but would set out to wound each other as much as possible.

Sunday 24/*ii*/57: About 4 p.m. to Ty Powys. Saw photograph of one of Augustus John's drawings of him: face too long, eyes too deep and dark—a romantic illusion. Excellent photograph by Douglas Glass of J.C.P. leaning on the parapet, stick aloft, with the waterfall, mill, cottages and mountain-face behind him. Phyllis told us he had begun keeping his diary in 1929: volume after volume of it there on the top shelf. He told us his present lumbago makes it more painful for him to pick up worms off the road and carry them to the grass—an act of reparation for chopping up worms as a boy. Said his sister Katy was an atheist from babyhood: didn't like her father because he was a clergyman.

Sunday 3/*iii*/57: J.C.P. spoke of his strong dislike for Belloc, whom he had known. He told me again about William Barnes —"so old fashioned"—C18th coat, white stock, breeches, silver-buckled shoes: "gave us good teas". About Hardy: his sister was a Sunday School teacher at St. Peter's, Dorchester, of which Powys *père* was curate. J.C.P. said it was Hardy who educated him—"we were naive barbarians and he tamed us". Hardy's pride in his set of Britannica on his study shelves, his admiration for E. A. Poe. J.C.P. spoke also of Dreiser, E. Lee Masters, E. Arlington Robinson, E. E. Cummings (from whom they have just heard) and Fr. Tyrrel—"a very nice man". J.C.P. once wanted to be a Catholic, rang doorbell of priest's house at Eastbourne, no one answered. He spoke also of Mr. de Kantzow and J. W. Williams ("The Catholic") and the old Duke of Norfolk.

Tuesday 12/*iii*/57: Elin and Iestyn thought they saw Phyllis and J.C.P. get on the 'bus—an epoch-making event.

Saturday 16/*iii*/57: J.C.P. in high spirits, quite unaffected by the appalling weather, his lumbago not recurring. Prompted by the news that Louis Wilkinson is going out to Lisbon, J.C.P. and Phyllis decided to go out too—to Cricieth. This is where they were going when seen on the 'bus on Tuesday. J.C.P. eloquent about the beach—only 2 shells, but the most beautiful pebbles set in the sand, separately, at regular intervals. Typical of him that this is what he should notice and remark on first. They bought a guidebook to the castle.

Saturday 6/*iv*/57: In the evening I went across to see Mr. Powys: found him in bed—where he has been since Thursday.

Thursday 11/*iv*/57: Elin and Iestyn called on J.C.P. this afternoon: he had been out for a brief morning walk and is quite recovered again. Iestyn demonstrated the drawing of various letters to J.C.P. and Phyllis: he has learnt S today. Apparently he couldn't think of any words (Welsh words, of course) beginning with S, and Phyllis suggested several.

Monday 15/*iv*/57: Wilbert came, as arranged, and we planned a half-hour programme on J.C.P. for the last week in June. I took him round to 1 Waterloo afterwards, and he tried (in vain, of course) to get Mr. Powys to agree to record.

Friday 10/*v*/57: Jonah to lunch: he had spent the morning modelling a head of J.C.P. in clay—not without difficulty, because his subject naturally talked animatedly the whole time so that his expression was constantly changing.

Friday 17/*v*/57: To see J.C.P.: the first time since I got back from Rome. Great reunion. Talked of Wordsworth—"a great ox"; Nietzsche (his cousin took him to the house at Weimar to meet Frau Förster-Nietzsche just after N's death in 1900: while the women made tea, J.C.P. was allowed to browse in N's library: no German or English books—all French, mainly Pascal); Pius XII—"he is king of the world". J.C.P. laid stress upon the thickening beneath the lower lip as an indication of great sensitivity, and this indeed the pope possesses—as I see from my photograph. Retailed account of visit of a gypsy—

Juanita, and her small son Jasper—friend of Theodore, who recently visited him. J.C.P. on the affinity between second childhood (i.e. himself) and first childhood. Story of the child born in the cottage opposite his own (and called Dylan Thomas). J.C.P. had repeated "I simply must see it. I've got to see it". So the mother brought it across—aged 5 days—wrapped up in shawls. In time it extended a tiny finger, which J.C.P. took and kissed with reverence. He says he is going to write about this childhood theme when he has finished the Homer book.

Tuesday 11/*vi*/57: This evening I took Janine Debay to see J.C.P. Steered the conversation to his friend at the Sorbonne— M. Jean Valh. Janine knew him by repute—an eminent materialist philosopher, who has recently moved to the Collège de France. J.C.P. said that *Jobber Skald* is about to appear in French under the title *Les Sables du Mer* (its original title was *Weymouth Sands* but this, like *Glastonbury*, gave rise to expensive libel actions). Gabriel Marcel was instrumental in securing a publisher.

Wednesday 19/*vi*/57: J.C.P. spoke with deep affection of his son, who lies buried—his mother beside him—in Bath. Of Cowper—I had told him of the pleasure my sixth-form was getting from his poems: which overjoyed him. Phyllis got down Cowper's two volume translation of Homer—folio, bound in leather, dated 1791 or so.

Friday 5/*vii*/57: J.C.P. in good spirits, but feeling the heat—his favourite month is January. Talked about Will Durant, American author of *The Story of Philosophy*, and *The Age of Faith* (just published). He visited them in Corwen.

Monday 22/*vii*/57: J.C.P's admiration for grocers—Mr. B. who has written to me is one, and spends his profits on Powysiana. It was another grocer who introduced him to Huw Menai.

Monday 5/*viii*/57: Jonah's head of J.C.P. in the Arts and Crafts Pavilion (*i.e. at the Llangefni National Eisteddfod*) attracting much attention.

Sunday 8/*ix*/57: J.C.P. bubbling over with enthusiasm about the bit of the Iliad he has got to at the moment—praising Homer for his domestic scenes and details, which lie beyond the genius of Dante, Milton, even Shakespeare. He is living in the Iliad, which is quite as real to him as *The Observer* and *The Sunday Times* which lie beside his copy. Giles Wordsworth, a great-great-great nephew of the poet, has recently visited them: he and others on holiday at Graves's cottage in Llanbedr. Story of J.C.P. retelling the story of *Frankenstein* to Charlotte, his grandmother's parlourmaid, while rowing her in a boat: she fainted and he had to row back quickly and carry her into the house.

Sunday 10/*xi*/57: To see J.C.P.—I had not been there since before I was ill. He was bursting with enthusiasm about his Homeric recension, having reached Book 22 of the Iliad, and as full hatred for Achilles as if he were an eminent living vivisectionist or big-jaw.

At the end of 1960 my family and I left Blaenau and settled in the Netherlands. There, three months later, the last letter I was to receive from him (now in the possession of the National Library of Wales) reached me. It was dated March 5th 1961: ". . . We have both recovered from our recent attack of what they call Asian Flue although from just where in Asia it comes I have no idea. As I lie on my couch now by my window up eleven steps from Miss Playter's parlour on the ground floor where we sleep at night I can see Venus the evening star very clearly and also the light upon the telegraph post at our turn in the road. It is I think now just about half-past-five in the afternoon. On my right when I turn my head from the window to my big book-case I can see the 4 great folios of Littré's Dictionary of the French Language which made it possible for me to write my book on Rabelais a book that now rests for good and all in the room where Rabelais was born. I love what you say about Iestyn and Angharad . . . and I do pray so hard every night that both Hera and Pallas Athene, wife and daughter of Zeus the king of the gods will keep you all in the light of their countenances for many many many many years to come".

In the summer of 1962 I was in Wales and saw J.C.P. for the last time, as I was vividly aware on the occasion itself. He was no longer in his own upstairs room—with its breathtaking view across the town's chimney-pots to the soaring peak of the Moelwyn—where he had always lived, worked and slept. He was lying on the divan in the downstairs room; not so much lying, indeed, as laid out, calmly and of his own will. He was very still and composed, silvery, fragile, gothic, the long limbs and magnificent head aligned and supine as though on a catafalque. I had a clear intuition that my old friend had turned the whole of his immense inner power towards the serene conclusion of his life—that he intended to complete his ninetieth year on earth, and then pass from it: deliberately, of his own volition. We talked gently, briefly, his ineffable courtesy quite undiminished, his mind far away in time and place from that still, small room in the huge amphitheatre of the mountains. When I said goodbye and he gave me his hand—the hand that had taken that of William Barnes, born in 1801, of Yeats, of Hardy—I had, as always, that vivid sense of bridging a century and a half, of being momentarily linked to the great tradition, of shaking hands with English Literature.

Shortly afterwards I returned to the Netherlands. A month or so later came his ninetieth birthday. In 1963 I had news that he had been admitted to the little hospital at Blaenau, perched whitely on the brink of Cwm Bowydd where he had so often walked, where I had lived. He was very weak but in good spirits, and sang a good deal. There he died on 17th June 1963.

"Such, Echecrates, was the end of our friend, who was, we may fairly say, of all those whom we knew in our time, the bravest and also the wisest and most upright man."

XVIII

JOHN COWPER POWYS (1872-1963)

Robert Nye

JOHN COWPER POWYS (1872–1963)

Knowing the horror of the house
more intimately than its mere ghosts,
you practised to unstitch
the mirror from its silver
and write down your name without wondering who.
O Prospero, no elegy for you.
You have been sent to Naples, that is all,
and this bare island is the barer for it.

SOME EARLY LETTERS FROM J. C. POWYS TO T. F. POWYS

Envelope addressed to: Master Theodore Powys, Rothesay House, Dorchester, Dorset, Datestamp: Sherborne, Dec. 9, 1883.

My dear Theodore

Yesterday there was a concert in the King's School room which I went to but Powys Mii could not as he had some copies to do it was very nice and I heard some good music, the people who played were nearly all boys but there were three masters there.

The boys played on fiddles except one who played on a flute which I liked best, two of the masters played on fiddes the other one on a thing I don't know the name of like a very big fiddle. On wednesday the school played Exiter and beat them by three touches. Lyttleton and I stayed to watch the match all the afternoon. On Tuesday It will only be a month before the hollidays it will be great fun then wont it?

On Friday we went to see them put up some banners in the Abbey. one was the Union Jack and two others, they had won some battles the Cape of Good Hope, it was very prety to see them pass.

I have sent you two birds for your scrap book. Remember to write if you want any money.

Are the Volentias[1] prospering? I hope they are.

    I am Your
        Affec brother
           John
           Cowper
           Powys

March 10th [1901]   *Southwick*

My dear old Friend
Hast thou a thought on this sweet Spring weather
Hast thou a thought for thy brother and friend
Dost thou forget how we wandered together

There where the Downs and the sea beach blend?
There by the waters of perilous Lodmore
Where a grey-ruin'd wall doth in loneliness stand
Dost thou forget how we played with our pleasure
Spirit with spirit and hand in hand?
What though the Gods that beheld our desire
Gave us *their* gifts in exchange for *our* prayer
What though if saved by the flood and the fire
So at the last the same Heaven we share.
Hath not each soul that beholds his Ideal
First to be purged by the darkness and dew
Only through doubt and the shades of the Real
Can we attain the Ideal and True.
Hold just my hand then Brother and lover
Tread we life's measure thro' weal and thro' woe
Then to the gates of Death's Night to discover
Whether Earth's flowers in Paradise grow.

---

written on this
The first day of Spring Sunday March 10th.
It all comes to the same thing at the End

Yours forever Jack

March 15th 1902 *Burpham, nr Arundel*

Gentle Theodore, I intend when my term's work is over and
Mr. de Kantzow's[2] book in the hands of the publisher to turn
my attention to the literary work of that quarter of the globe
you inhabit. The Catholic,[3] whose evenly balanced, yet searching, mind nothing common or unclean can entice, recognised
in your writing originality and character. Indeed I am almost
inclined to think he regarded the works of John Cowper as of
inferior interest to the works of Theodore Francis: such a
verdict I can understand and would believe if it were not for
that inherent trust in my own potentiality, in my own forces,
which, sans evidence and sans likelihood, supports me under
all misgivings. Such a self-confidence—dear gentle soul who

dost like Cadmus bask with thy Harmonia far, far from here, where the Adriatic breaks in a warm bay—such a self-confidence added to what you already possess, added, that is to say, to sensitiveness and tenderness and the affections of the heart and the taste for literary form which comes last but is most needful, would enable you to do almost anything. But who am I that I should prophecy unto thee? Shall his elder brother instruct Joseph? Shall Ishmael speak unto the Beloved of the Lord? Were it not that I know how much there is in common between us, were it not that I see my weaknesses in thee and thine in me, were it not that the angel of Romance hath breathed upon us both, I would hold my peace, I would keep silence. But we are of the same mother, but we are of the same blood—but we both live in this world of northern men and women like exiles from a far country; exiles are we; and it is only at rare moments —at the whisper of the rushes by the river, at the waving of the fir-tree in the wind, at the glance of a child, at the sunshine upon a stone on the edge of the hill,—that our spirits with a great outflowing of their desire, a wild out-rushing of their hope, reach even for a moment the land which is their natural inheritance.

O my Theodore! Whatever dreariness befall you, whatever quagmires and quicksands await your feet, believe me, I have known them, I, John Cowper have known them before you. Like Christ I have trodden the wine-press. Little do those who lightly accuse me of lethargy and ease know how I have trodden it. Sometimes looking anxiously into a future which for both of us is obscure I feel a longing that in one handshake which could express all, all we have enjoyed, dreamt, imagined, believed and disbelieved together—might find its expression and its speech. From the days when, in the Volentia[1] army, you followed me, from the days when we rested speaking of our impossible loves on the broken wall of Lodmoor, from the days when our sister[4] was to us more than a sister, from the days when (not without a stronger arm than our own to support us![5]) we climbed the summit of Snowdon—you and I intellectually and nervously have been akin—you have more tenderness than I; I (perchance) more force than you; but when we have gone down into the house of shadows crowned or uncrowned with deathless bay, men will say after us they were of the same race, of the same suffering, of the same joys; They have gone to the same place.

If I cannot come down and see you, as it is my fear that I cannot this Easter, some-time in the early summer in May or June when "things that love the sun are out of doors" you may expect me. Until then May must bring us news of you. Give her our love and say we anticipate with pleasure her visit to our Sussex coast and customs and crosses;

Your J.C.P.

Sunday [*30th August 1902*]

A lively and lusty Boy born at the end of Saturday afternoon now makes the house resound with his crying. He is to be called Littleton Alfred, after dear Littleton and Margaret's Father: also Alfred De Kantzow who is to be his other God-father—that is to say if he can be induced to enter a church. I have asked L.C. to the Christening and if you can come over and sit with me in the churchyard while the service goes on it perhaps will keep away evil spirits.

If there is small-pox at Studland for Heaven's sake leave the place at once! Yrs. Jack.

[*April 1910*][6].

My dear old Theodore
your dialogue[6] gave me great pleasure and I shall certainly keep care of it. I read it aloud to Lulu—who also was impressed. I understand and appreciate all of it except the part about Father Mother and Child—that is always the portion of your discourses that puzzles me—in fact I feel as though that were a sort of doctrine like the Trinity into which the natural

317

mysteries of life were being deliberately and artificially, if you follow my roundabout speech, put. When you talk of straws and sticks and rubbish I understand you well—and when you talk of ice cold caverns I know what you mean whether I've ever felt that or not—and when you talk of emptying slops and yet being a Buddha there I am entirely with you though I don't like doing it myself—for no doubt Jesus was the one in his family to dig holes in the garden. When you speak of love too I know what you are talking about whether I am capable of such feelings myself or not—but it is when you use these particular terms that I get perplexed or at any rate do not see the necessity for them. I am ready to grant that you have got some spiritual secret which I haven't got—and which I daresay the oriental mystics and more modern illuminants possess—but when you come to express it so definitely then I get the impression of something unnatural. It isn't that I feel the secret itself to be unreal but only this particular expression of it in terms of the family if I may say so. After all there are probably depths and currents in the great stream of world-life which may as well be expressed in this way as any other but what I feel is that this particular expression—or doctrine rather—tends to cramp your own power of expressing in ever new ways the inspiration or secret you feel. But I suppose it is just there that the artist or poet in you appears and turns into a sort of mythology what is really and truly only a feeling. I expect I am wrong in attacking this method: for after all, all philosophs have their own favourite tricks of speech their allegories and their symbols: but as you know I to whom any kind of mysticism is a little difficult am apt to be above all things choked off by *allegory* which always seems to me so tedious & unreal! Mysticism I should not be impertinent enough to treat in this manner because I know well the great stream of evidence in its favour. You say I call you a protestant—well I think this allegorical vein is Catholic and doctrinal or dogmatic as well as protestant—and yet I daresay I am wrong there. Individual mystics like Swedenborg and Blake though they curse the dogmas of the church are always coining their own as fast as they can spin them off! Forgive me. The truth is I am in all mystical matters a hopeless fool and a rooted materialist much though I may try not to be. If you want to influence me in the direction of the spiritual life you must be careful not to choke me off with the doctrinal part of your philosophy.

As long as you describe in plain and simple language exactly what you *feel* really and truly whether of inspired ecstasy and oneness with the hidden springs of life or of hopeless melancholy and lapsings into the caverns of gloom—I am sympathetic and ready to listen to all and perhaps even lift my materialism a little bit out of the way: but when you speak in parables all my interest dries up and I feel like a child when one sayeth "let us pray" or "it is well that we should remember" or "it is important not to forget"—etc.—

You can't say I don't love mysticism for I love all your mystical way of writing and all your writings except when you mention Father Mother or Child. Then I am as ribaldly inclined as if you had referred to the Father Son & Holy Ghost! I daresay the world *is* triplical or whatever you call it & I daresay from Horus Osiris and Isis all mythologies divide it into three—all I can say is that it doesn't present itself as Three to me or even as *One* but as MANY and always as *Many*, a mass of details a lot of impressions persons ideas events principles virtues vices etc etc all following each other in a funny sort of procession like wavering puppets which Destiny like a huge Punch & Judy man with a fantastic rather than evil voice and a stupid rather than a wicked look shishes them on from behind as if he were a child driving geese. But enough! I am the *pedant*, my boy if you're the prig so we're a fair pair! As indeed we've ever been since in very old days I led you by my pedantic and artificial follies into all sorts of cursed unnaturalnesses from which it has taken you half of your life to recover and from which perhaps *we* shall never recover! But all this is silly stuff because I suppose the real explanation of what I stumble at in your writings is simply the legitimate self-assertion of the Artist in you engaged like any old mythological poet in turning the world into parables after your own heart. Don't let my stupidity or cynicism influence you my dear. I have been spoilt I daresay by materialism and by the world and by money making etc etc and by . . . What I should like you to write are still these semi-humorous dialogues and also unrhymed unmetrical poems in the style of Walt Whitman! I believe you would do that well. I should like to do it myself, in fact its my one great ambition—but I'm too *clever* to do it and too fond of the ordinary metres and rhymes. Your genius my dear is unspoilt by cleverness and so you may thank heaven you can't spell! I have now taken cleverness as my portion and money making Mammon as my God! But believe me when I say this—all *your* feelings sensations inspirations and ideas, especially such as spring up amid your pots and pans and potatoes are of profound value and if you wrote them all down you will be a famous sage *when you're dead* but unless you drop this Holy Family business you'll stop the natural growth of your genius. Believe it—Even the Elder sometimes utters truth!

I who have probably the iciest heart of all of us have a certain dog like affection for you as I have our old Littleton although of course I can "get on" as they say more easily with the irresponsible younger ones! But after all we were young together before the Mabelulu was born! You are a funny old Conjuror my dear and so am I! Love to V. & T. & F.

Yrs. Jack.

NOTES

[1] Alfred de Kantzow   }   *Autobiography* passim.
[2] John William Williams   }   See the Index to the 1967 edition.
[3] "Volentia Army"   }

[4] Eleanor Powys, 1879–1893.

[5] Littleton's arm: *Autobiography*, 1967, pp. 189–190.

[6] Theodore's "dialogue", discussed in this letter, cannot be his *An Interpretation of Genesis*, written in 1905 and printed in 1907, because J. C. P. ends "Love to V. and T. and F.", and Francis Powys was born in November 1909. It may be one of the unpublished "Dialogues 1909" now in Mr. E. E. Bissell's collection, and, as J. C. P. "read it aloud" to Llewelyn, the letter appears to have been written from Clavadel in April 1910.

PLATE 2

About 1920?

PLATE 3

PLATE 4

1940.

PLATE 5

PLATE 6

Bust by Jonah Jones, 1957.

PLATE 7 (a)

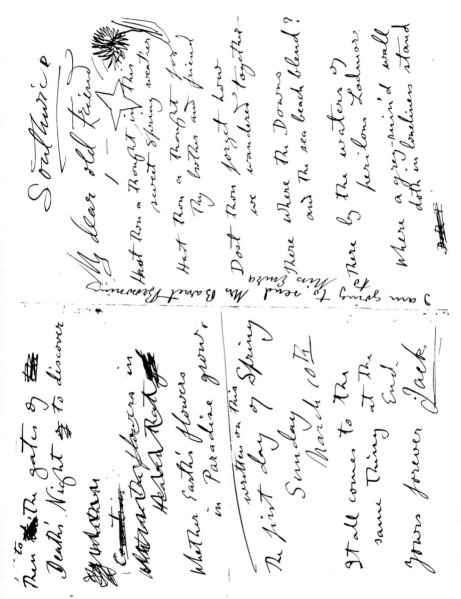

From the letter to T. F. Powys, March 10th (1901).

PLATE 7 (b)

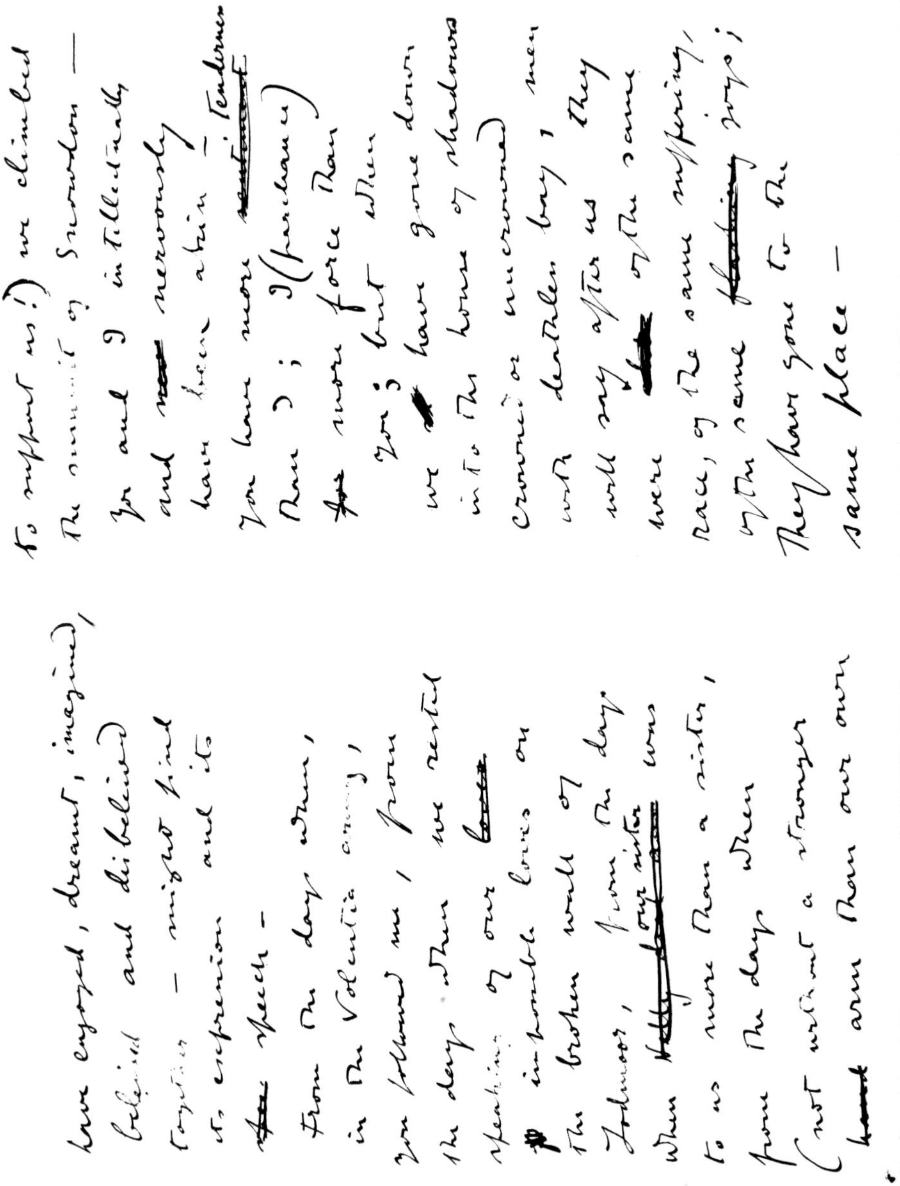

have enjoyed, dreamt, imagined,
believed and disbelieved
together – might find
its expression and its
speech –
From the days when,
in the Volentia army,
you followed me, from
the days when we rested
speaking of our ~~loves~~
impossible loves on
the broken wall of
Lodmoor, from the days
when our sister was
to us more than a sister,
from the days when
(not without a stronger
arm than our own

to support us!) we climbed
the summit of Snowdon –
you and I intellectually
and nervously
have been akin – Tenderness
you have more ~~sentiment~~
than I; I (perchance)
more force than
you; but when
we have gone down
into the house of shadows
crowned or uncrowned
with deathless bay, men
will say after us they
were of the same
race, of the same suffering,
of the same ~~fleeting~~ joys;
They have gone to the
same place –

From the letter to T. F. Powys, March 15th 1902.

PLATE (7) C

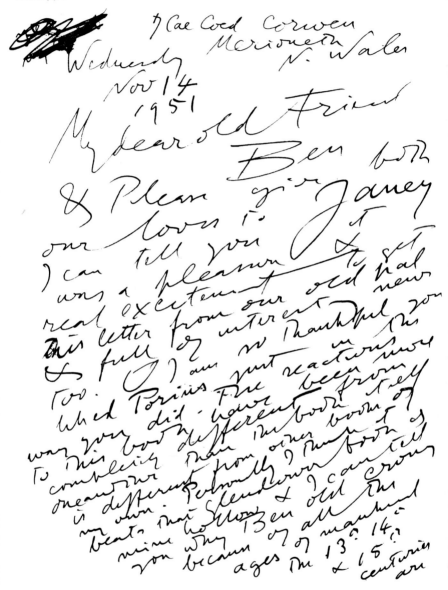

From the letter to C. Benson Roberts, November 14th 1951.

Appendix 1(b)

A CHRONICLE OF THE WRITING OF THE MIDDLE WORKS, EXTRACTED FROM LETTERS FROM AMERICA TO LITTLETON C. POWYS, 1927 TO 1934

October 21st 1927.

I think I shall decide to call my long novel about Sherborne "Ripeness is All" from a passage in King Lear. I bring in the Slopes where I behaved like that to you—so disgracefully. I am ashamed. But *not* that incident! and a lot about the Abbey. I am writing at top speed, but it won't be finished, heigh ho!, before I leave but I do enjoy writing it so *very* much.

January 1928.

I needn't say how I was shocked by this news of the death of Godfrey. Lulu heard of it simultaneously from old King. I can well imagine how you felt in that cemetery. By the way I was writing of that cemetery in the last chapter of my long book called "Ripeness is All" at the moment, or nearly so, when I got your letter. That cemetery plays a large part in my story for the father of its hero is buried there—an ex-schoolmaster who died a pauper in the Sherborne work-house! Soon the book will be done—and then I shall revise it.

May 9th 1928.

Well I have at last sent my huge book—I am, I think, going to call it *Wolf Solent* after the hero's name, tho' Lulu prefers the title "Crooked Smoke" which was one that was thought of —to my first choice of a Publisher—namely those Jews "Simon & Schuster" . . . But if he rejects it "Longmans Green" are very keen to see it—the old solid English firm who in 17— published *Robinson Crusoe*. . . . I'm giving them (S. & S.) an awfully short time to make up their minds—only a little over three weeks—& this book is twelve hundred typed pages—it'll have to be in two volumes of about six hundred pages of print each. . . . But they write very civilly about it & seem to understand my necessity of haste in the light of my having to leave New York for New Mexico by the second of June.

June 29th 1928.

No publisher could possibly have done less for a book than Doubleday did for *Ducdame*. Grant Richards did better for it—much better—in England—but went bankrupt before he paid *any* royalties! Every single one of my books is now out of print & un-obtainable—so its really necessary to get something out soon. I think I shall probably stick to "Wolf Solent" as the title . . .

July 30th 1928.

I think it looks as if Simon & Schuster will take my book but insist on my shortening it by something like 60,000 words. And I am inclined to think I must unwillingly agree to this. It will be in two volumes anyway.

Sept. 14th 1928.

Well the good news that now I've got to tell you is that Schuster *has* accepted my book and yesterday (no, the day before) (Sept. 12) the contract was signed in his office in red ink. Now you can believe how I am at work copying out cuts & corrections from the Carbon Copy to the Fair Copy. He thinks of publishing it in May—just before I start for England. But except for "Wolf Solent" which he thinks will not induce people to read the book—we *cannot* think of a good title. It is teasing how long I've tried, searching through Shakespeare, Milton—everything—& all in vain hitherto. I am to get ten per cent on every copy sold up to 10,000 copies & after that 12½ per cent. How annoying it is that Mr Keedick takes ten per cent of all I make by my writing.

[November] 1928.

I am now slowly composing, very slowly in these strange places, a book entitled *The Meaning of Culture* for an academic publisher called *Norton*, but this won't appear till next September; whereas my two-volume novel still called *Wolf Solent* for want of a better name will appear (D—V) in the spring— in *March* even maybe! That month when I remarked (in my first printed book) upon the unusual fragrance of the Lime-trees!

Good Friday [29th March] 1929.

The latest bulletin about Wolf Solent is very good namely a thrilling letter from the great Edward Garnett the most authoritative of all English critics and its acceptance by *Jonathan Cape* for England. The alterations suggested by Garnett were all "artistic" ones not "moral" ones. He says that "after the first shock" the book will be accepted. One little annoyance is that now it is too late to change it for the first edition—note my conceit in assuming more than one!—I find I have buried the wrong king in the Abbey . . . . .

[June] 1929.

P.S. I am thinking about my next long novel which I am inclined to make occur with *Glastonbury* as its background. So I hope to visit Glastonbury this time and perhaps *more than once* while I'm in the *West Country.*

January 22nd 1930.

I am reading everything I can lay hold of about the Arthurian legend. I came across a very good book called Snell's "The Arthurian Country" and I have found quite an extensive literature about the mythology of the Grail which goes back to old Druidic and Pagan days & has an irrefutable Celtic origin. I often think of that friend of yours who actually had a vision of the Grail. I would so like to have seen him. I shall think a lot of him when I really begin my Glastonbury book this summer. Meanwhile I am writing—when I get the chance: which hasn't been of late—a queer rambling fantastical poetical mystical book on my own philosophy, putting in many mystical & odd thoughts that were too wild for the Culture book . . . but which I do so very much desire to say aloud in print.

April 8th 1930.

Now when I'm out at Route 2 Hillsdale [J.C.P's home address in New York State from April 1930 until he left America in May 1934 to settle in England] I am going to settle down and

write my new long romance with Glastonbury as a background
—so any pamphlets you may pick up about Glastonbury or
Wells or those parts do'ee let me have them! I think I will not
use any *sham* names in this book; I mean about the places. I'll
use the real names.

May 2nd 1930.

Now on Sunday (Easter Day) I began my long Romance
that is to end up in Glastonbury *via* Stonehenge and is to start
at Northwold. I am going to make one of my heroes & one of
my heroines have a terrific conversation gazing at those big
fish in Harrod's Mill! And I hope to bring in Ely—from the
little book on it which I hurried to buy while you were getting
the car out of the garage. Do you recall in Ely how drastically
you aided me to escape from that very unpromising tea-shop
& how comfortable we were in that old Inn dining-room,
where you wouldn't let me smoke cigarettes! I have got an
Ordnance Map of Bridgewater & the Quantocks & one of
Wells & the Mendips; but Glastonbury is just at the edge
between these two so that it is rather hard to deal with them
together. I have nailed up the one that has Glastonbury on it
behind the Stove on the wall of this room.

July 27th 1930.

I begin my great Glastonbury Book (Mrs Hardy has sent
me the blessing of Max Gate upon it) with Northwold &
Alder Dyke & Dye's Hole. I make my hero and heroine make
love at Dye's Hole & I do not forget either Winnie Joy or
Mary Carter! In fact another character I call *Tom Barter*. I am
very interested in this book. It will take 2 years; it is *very* long;
it includes Stonehenge; due to your assistance for I had not
taken it in before at all. All the characters without exception
(except Grandfather William Cowper Johnson) are *purely
invented* & he is only brought in as a GHOST!

October 14th 1930.

I *hope* to be able to live thro' a year on my Royalties. I have 4 lectures during Nov.—weekly—at Columbia University (Extension) but only $30 (dollars) net to me each time; & Keedick is going to make me debate with Chesterton for about a Third of what Chesterton will get! . . . but never mind! The thing will be what Marian in her spirited way would call "a bit of sport" & it should be a very equal Duel of wits, and ever so much more lively and entertaining than the Russell one which was, in my opinion, a fiasco: & not really amusing. However with this damned ulcer to help me to "malinger" out of going "on the road" this year I ought to get on finely with my great Glastonbury book which I *am* enjoying so!

November 19th 1930.

My ulcer has been very trying of late owing to 4 weekly trips to New York (at Columbia University). I have 4 Extension Lectures—The Iliad The Inferno King Lear & Faust (in translation). I put "in translation" because I read the others holding the original & the crib side by side but German I know naught of . . . . . . I've now got to page *590* of my vast Glastonbury Book & as it is to be of 1500 pages that means that I've done a third. I must stay out here all next Spring & Summer *till it is done.*

January 5th 1931.

I have reached page *800* of my Glastonbury book in my Mss but it will be 2,000 pages ere it's done. I have two Ordnance Maps of Somerset. I hope there won't be any mistakes!

February 10th 1931.

I did so particularly like your account of that early "Mass" (as my son would say!) with King looking so Beauteous Frail & like the "Fisher King" in Malory, who guarded the Grail. I must surely keep in my mind with all reserves of deep-diffused

disguisements (& discreet transformings of person, place,
conditions etc. etc.) your tale of your friend Nash and the
Grail. That is just the sort of thing I desire to be in my book
on Glastonbury along with other things. What shall I call it?
Just alone "Glastonbury" Llewelyn says. "A Glastonbury
Romance" is what at present my publisher says. I also thought
of "Never or Always" as a title but Lulu *and* Schuster both
reject that . . . I have reached page *1070* of my Glastonbury
book—that is in my long-hand Mss. I hope to finish it this
Autumn however & then it ought to be published next year.
I expect this silence and hush & solitude is splendid for my
book. I have, what I've never had before, *real time* to write in,
hours and hours of time. I can *shuffle time*, like you shuffle
snow, in a great wooden spade. I can let time fall, freeze, and
thaw—So I can enlarge & ramble & digress at will & at my
pleasure—with all this *time*—but I can tell you its not wasted,
like these delicious red-cheeked Baldwin apples [referred to
earlier as rotting in millions on the ground within half a mile
of his house], for *it is used*—and my huge book *advances*—
slowly—a sort of mixture of Wilhelm Meister, Faust, the
Niblungenlied (about the Gods & the Giants) & I know not
what sort of crazy thoughts Sir John—Jack—Johnny!

April 25th 1931.

I've read nothing but the Loeb Classics with Greek on one
side of the page & English on the other all winter: but I've
read very little for I've been writing so much on my vast
Glastonbury Romance which has now reached page *1600* of
my long hand Mss!

May 21st 1931.

I try to keep my mind from getting worried over the publication problems of my vast Glastonbury book. I must be considerate to Mr Schuster in these matters for I depend on him
for my living entirely now I have given up lecturing and have
resolved to live by my pen. But it isn't only Mr S. I have to

deal with, but his energetic staff of publicity agents & editorial readers; & these gentlemen have invaded my retreat like an army—and this too while nearly a third—certainly a quarter of my book remains to be written. It seems likely that it will be published in two parts, the first this Autumn, and the second next Spring. I expect I'll have to allow a certain amount of cutting and shortening which as you can guess always goes against the grain but on the other hand its no good being a too truculent author if I've resolved to earn my living in this manner & chuck lecturing & travelling about! I wish I lived within a walk even a five mile walk of Quarry House—say at North Cadbury—or Marston Magna, then I would bring you over my huge Mss by relays for I am so afraid that there may be Linden flowers (as in that famous Poem!) coming out in March. What I find difficult as I talk of twilights so often is to remember *when* twilight *begins* in March—in April—in May etc etc etc. I am worse at that than even at the order of plants which is also a somewhat weak point! But they are rushing things on now so fast at the office—5 typists at work (for I was so unwilling that this huge Ms should be *sent out* to be typed) *in the office* itself . . . . . when you have read it in Print you must note bad mistakes of every sort in this Autumn *Part I* & then I can correct them or avoid them in the Spring Part II— a year from now. Meanwhile I ought to finish the whole thing by September *before* the Part I is out.

September 11th 1931.

I've now finished the last chapter of my book & the last but one & am working (for I am now going Backwards, which is as if God created the world, *beginning* at *Man*, & ending with the Ichthyosaurus!) on the last but last but one . . . but as this is will be 100 pages & there may be yet another the end is not yet. It is to come out Part I & Part II *together* in January . . . but I shall have to cut it nearly a third. O deary I!, indeed I shall very likely have soon to start cutting this Part II which I am now finishing.

November 20th 1931.

Do you know I have good hope now that my Publisher is going to be content with my cutting my Romance one fourth instead of one third . . . . . it will be a very very long book— as long or nearly as Tolstoy's *War & Peace.* I wonder if the present potentates whoever they are—Bankers, Manufacturers, Lawyers, Doctors, Clergymen, Tradesmen, Artizans, Gardeners, Mayor, Town-Clerk, Landowners, etc etc., not to speak of beggars, procuresses, waitresses, servants, saints, poets, miracle-mongers and so forth—will any of them make any protest about my description of them? I have written a brief Author's note to the effect that *everything is invented* which is indeed the truth most literally for my rule in this book has been to invent every character and take not a single one from real life. I've never done this before—& it has interested me a lot doing it. The only two persons with the remotest connection with reality are our Northwold Grandfather (& he only *in his coffin*) & no one would imagine it was the same, save for his white curly head, & his fondness (formerly) for reading Lycidas: and *Bertie* as a London Architect coming down to Glastonbury. But he only appears in his architectural work—not in person. All the rest are absolutely and entirely invented.

February 6th 1932.

My idea now is to write my next romance about Weymouth & Portland—so if you have any old tumbled to bits guide-books and books about those places more familiar to us both from childhood than *any others* you might despatch them to me. I wrote to Lulu about this—and he has already—the kind one that he is—sent me enough, bought at Weymouth, I expect, of guide books. But I am an ogre, *insatiable* over materials of this sort—for you never know! Twas in the most unlikely book on the Grail that I picked up the best clue to that Mystery which I used in Glastonbury—& I'm always ready for *More than Enough*!

March 19th 1932.

I have just sent off to Lucy and to Lulu the two advance copies of my book because I fancied you & my son were off on a fishing trip to Dartmoor but don't 'ee, either of ye, be cross over this! *Lucy* I dedicated it to; so she *had* to have the first copy that crossed the Atlantic anyway. Yours and my son's shall follow quick when I've got my next lot from the city. For its essential that you should have this American copy & have it quick too before the book comes out lest on one side or other of the water-way the Police suppress it & make it illegal to send it across. . . . . I fancy as a real fact no one will read it with more interest than you. I am *very* pleased with its general get-up & appearance & so far I have found very few mistakes except my own—for instance I seem to have called at least *three* of my leading characters—"this sturdy short broad-shouldered man". This must be in a desperate attempt not to have any characters resemble Wolf Solent! But I know you will find plenty of mistakes about nature and times and seasons. . . . . . O I can't wait to hear what you think of it old friend. You'd better vow not to write to me one other of those noble foolscap letters of yours, that are one of the chief delights of my declining years, until you've got this book in your hands! . . . . I daresay very few of my friends will have the gall not to patiently finish it but *some* will boldly & bravely say "I hate long *novels*" & let it go unread! But it'll be what you find mistaken & wrong over the Nature descriptions that will be the greatest help to me for I may be able to change it for future editions. This is, I think, *by far* my best work up to date! You must not be alarmed by what the English Publisher (*Gollancz* his name is) requires in expurgation; it is in order that the Circulating Libraries in England would buy the book. American readers having more extravagant ways buy the books more . . . . The book is not as a whole anything that *you* will dislike; nor indeed would anyone, I think really, unless *out* for being shocked, condemn it as an *immoral* book or with an immoral tendency. O it is so hard to make such things clear. It is very, *very* long however! 1170 *pages*! I believe its the

longest English novel—think of that! What future M.C.Ps. will
be reading it I wonder 100 years hence to what future C.F.Ps.?
It has a very good pause after the scene of the Glastonbury
Pageant so it *could* be divided into two parts if necessary.
Aye! but I do wonder what they will think of it in Glastonbury
itself. . . . . . I always call myself an *English* writer of course
just as Turgeniev who always lived in Paris, Turgeniev who was
just a pal of Flaubert etc., was a Russian writer because he
wrote in Russian. So I have compelled my American printers
to go through this book changing back the labors and rumors
and glamors etc. etc. . . . Heigh! Dreary I! I wonder what the
reviewers (who are critics I respect) & *real writers* will have to
say? *And poets* who are critics too—they are the ones I would
like to like this book but the books are so short & so "artistic"
& "poignant" & "airy" & "sophisticated" that are the fashion;
& this book—so slow & pondering and slowly advancing,
retarding, delaying, retreating, spiralling, debouching, off at
this, and off at that tangent—can it by itself, one book, revive
& stir up that old love of a lingering story—with a romantic
background—that every one *does* feel really & truly—if they
are not too perverted, too flippant too "mondaine", too
"metropolitaine"! . . . . . O I want 'ee to read it so carefully &
meticulously with all your wits clear and take note of mistakes
. . . . . . Would for instance anyone see a Clifton Blue at Glastonbury on June 25th, St. John's Day, Midsummer Day? . . . .
I want [Mabel's] attention too, for mistakes . . . actually in the
skeleton of the narrative itself where I've forgotten what I said.
I have at this very second writ a letter to the Publishers to
send me copies to send to you & to my only child . . He is 30
and I am 60 this year! Will he have the Classic Piety to read
clear to the very end his "Elder Pliny's" lucubrations? ' . .
Mr. King is the only person I have mentioned by name in my
Glastonbury Romance. In a passing little sentence I give him
(I don't care whether correctly or not) the whole and sole
credit for the Sherborne Pageant—"when the headmaster
played St. Aldhelm."

April 15th 1932.

Sure I'll add to my other revisions which I am collecting together for the 2nd edition the changes you mention, cutting out Mr. King's name as you say & substituting "bullied at School always bullied" for the other more definite phrase. I am so distressed that you should have been worried & upset over this . . . . . . Its a shame we cannot—& I fear *never* can—see these things quite in the same way, but *there it is*! I thought I gave a word on the other side when I spoke of the School coming so quickly to Glastonbury's rescue in the flood but you haven't got to *that* yet! But you know I cant regard that allusion to the psychological effect on a particular character of being bullied at school as an "attack", as you feel it to be, on *our* old School. In "Tom Brown" there's that detailed description of the proceedings of the Bully Flashman; but no one has ever regarded that as an "attack" on Rugby. All Public Schools have these incidents I fear and to mention them does not seem to me an attack but rather a recognition of a deplorable fact that must take its place as counterbalanced . . . by the good aspects of School life. I don't feel as if this passing allusion to bullying would offend the dear & sacred ghost of our old friend Carey; for many a time has he told me of how he himself suffered in this way & when I think of Deacon's bullying of Puckle & that even worse chap in Wilson's house in Bertie's time who so bullied him & his friend Room; & of Romer's still worse activities (which Carey always condemned to me in early days) it does seem that there is justification for my rendering of the effect of such things on poor Barter in my book. I feel as if our old School were as strong & proudly secure in its noble traditions (to be able to bear the truth of these more seamy sides of School life) as Rugby was to bear with the exposures of Flashman's bad conduct. I cannot agree with the policy of crying "hush" in the presence of abuses because they touch a well-loved institution. Its the same with Oxford & Cambridge and indeed with one's Country itself. I think only harm comes from the method of hushing up all bad aspects of the life of one's school or one's country—

... & it seems as if the true & better patriotism & true affection were in recognising these bad aspects & trying to reform them just as our heroic and noble Godfrey always tried to do. ... Of course you might argue that my Barter was too tough a bloke to be permanently hurt by bullying at School but I cannot agree with you there. I think for certain types of people deep harm is irrevocably done & I think an allusion to such unhappy possibilities, . . can only do good; by stirring up the nicer characters among people like the Duffers (who would be the only ones likely to read such a book) to do all they can to make sure that these secret persecutions do not go on any more. How far masters can do very much I'm sure I don't know. . . . . Well—as I say, old friend, I regret deeply that this sad spiritual difference in our emotions—both so strong & mounting up so quick (with upper-lip trembling & pit of stomach heaving) form our emotional inheritance on *both* sides! I fear in matters of this kind between Littleton & Johnny its like those old Chess Games and drawing ships *versus* "Volentia Army"—its the heart speaking & carrying the head away on its tide. You are an emotional Conservative. I am an emotional Radical. . And as it was when we rolled in that ditch between Cooksbridge & Court House (over the question of Ireland) so in a sense I fear it will be to the end of the story. On your grave could be writ "I defended Sherbourne for the good in it"—& on my grave could be writ—"I never forget the wickedness of Deacon"!

June 10th 1932.

No. No! My long delay in writing has been due to my having had a rather trying time in one way and another. The United States Supreme Court decided on May 28th that authors must pay *State*-Taxes out of their Royalties (which are Federal Royalties) and as the New York State Taxes have to, at this Bad Time, support some three hundred thousand unemployed in *New York City* alone these taxes are very high. I shall have to produce nearly a hundred dollars. Well! it is only right that those who *have* work in these days should keep from absolute starvation those who have none & there it is! Lucky am I to have "Royalties" at all! No, I had my publisher Mr. Simon out here . . . (there I have taken one of my "powders" & my ulcer grows quiescent again) and he was very pessimistic over the sale of all his books. The book-trade is in sore straits, the shops hardly selling anything . . . . In despair over the bad sale of my Glastonbury but all books are selling badly —even *best* sellers—my publishers have set me to write another short philosophical book entitled "A Philosophy of Solitude" of which I have now completed the 1st chapter—and I am going on with it side by side with my new book about Weymouth & Portland. I hope to finish it . . . by the Autumn so as to pick up my finances . . . The provincial reviews of Glastonbury from such towns as Richmond, Baltimore, St. Louis, Kansas City etc etc could not have been better—extravagantly worded & piling it up (perhaps a bit too thick) but the cynical and blasé New Yorkers found it heavy and long—Except "The Nation".

July 21st 1932.

I greatly fear that my Glastonbury will not, no! not yet for years!—be published in England . . . . . this is the Devil of a disappointment to me . . . . But there it is—Aequans memento— and really I am far too peaceful & happy in my mind from day to day in this lovely place, and in this lovely *cool* summer weather, to worry much. Evidently S. & S. feel that . . I owe it to them to write quickly a more saleable work & under the advice of my worthy ally & old friend Will Durant the Philosophy-Populariser they want me to write a little philosophy or semi-demi-philosophy-book to bring out I think in the Fall; & this I am now doing: having left my Weymouth work in a drawer for a month or two! When I return to it 'twill be (please God) with a new and fresh inspiration & I *may*—nay! I almost surely *will*—set myself to re-write it, from the start— so patient & thorough an ARTIST has your ancient Johnny become!

334

August 15th 1932.

I have nearly finished my book called "A Philosophy of Solitude" now it remains to get it typed. . . . . Do you know I had actually to pay *five hundred dollars* for having Glastonbury typed? Think of that! You can believe it cut badly into the not at all extensive Royalty I am expecting from this work . . . . I really *must* make my Weymouth book much, much shorter or I'll never be able to earn my living by writing books.

October 23rd 1932.

I have got off my little Philosophy book (safely revised and cut & improved with additions) to the publishers . . . . Mr. Schuster is now in England. I pray he'll manage to sell my Glastonbury to someone . . .

(*To Theodore* on *November 15th 1932* J.C.P. wrote:

I have now before me the hard task of re-writing from the very start my Weymouth Romance: for I'd made it too big too long, & since Glastonbury won't sell I *must* write shorter. So I've *got* to make the foundation smaller . . . for this foundation (begun when I was of proud look and high stomach thinking to myself that Glastonbury wd. win the Nobel Prize) was huge—the biggest foundation since Romulus & Remus jumped over the foundations of Rome; and I must get all the stones nearer the Centre now.)

January 1st 1933.

No more news of Glastonbury since John Lane was "considering" it . . . I am now back again in my Weymouth story and am re-writing it from the start so as to make it shorter.

February 9th 1933.

This morning my philosophical book comes out! and I shall hope when I get some more from the publisher—to get one off to you—in a few days—for from no one I long more to hear about opinion of it. Aye! but I pray it sells; for my income, and everything connected, depends on the selling of books! . . . . Thank the Lord Schuster says that John Lane has really formally & definitely taken my Glastonbury for English Publication; but *when* it will come out I do not yet know.

March 23rd 1933.

my Philosophy . . . was a "non-fiction" best-seller for one week anyway, in Chicago and in Washington!—but think how many copies will have to be sold to earn me my year's income when I only get 20 cents on each copy! . . . I must have written about a 3rd of my Weymouth & Portland book . . . I'd like to finish it in time for publication in the Autumn . . . I'm having this typed, chapter by chapter, by a good typist in that same factory where my unequalled gardener has his job as a weaver . . .

April 6th 1933.

I have now come to just about the middle of my Weymouth Romance. I want to finish it if I can by July 1st. . . . my present custom of going to bed from 12 to 4 when I write quietly in complete un-interruption helps me a lot to get ahead with it. I *was* so thrilled, old friend, with all you said about my Solitude book. I've just heard from the office that they are making a contract with an English publisher to bring this book out.

June 27th 1933.

Every Second is now occupied in racing *Against Time, Contra Temporum,* to get finished my Weymouth Book by *July* 15th which I must do if 'tis to be published in the Autumn as it *must* be for good Economic reasons . . . I have decided on the Title which is a great achievement to me for I find *Titles* the hardest part of a Book. *Weymouth Sands.*

August 4th 1933.

They tell me that the Mayor of Glastonbury has written an attack in a publication called Time & Tide in Bristol. Someone

is going to send me this work . . . *Weymouth Sands* is safe in
the publisher's hands. I am now thinking of writing a curious
sort of *Autobiography*. Don't 'ee be frightened! For I have
decided so to write it that no one's feelings whether living or
dead could possibly be hurt. I have decided to bring into it
not one single woman not even our mother—not even our
sisters. And of the men and boys . . . . I shall speak only *PRAISE*
. . . . *But* to compensate for this I shall exert my full imaginative
analysis upon my own bad qualities—except in so far where
I am too mad to do it—and I intend to make the book a
History of the development of Ideas, of the sense of Good and
Evil, of the artistic sense, of the moral sense, of the mystical
sense—I will NOT . . . . bring in DEACONS name or ROMER's
name and as for our friend Carey you yourself could not say
nicer things of him than I will say! In fact to all except *very
psychic* and *imaginative* persons this Book will be lacking in
the sort of sensation that the Vulgar Public love to welcome . . .
I *am soon after* a rest going to start upon this.

August 12th 1933.

I must soon really start my Autobiography which shall be
an Autobiography *without Scandal* . . . . . the main portion of
it will be the History of the Growth of and Development of a
solitary Human Consciousness & its reaction to Books and
Nature. So it will bring in all the sort of thing *you* like best in
my writings & little of what you *don't* like! In fact hardly
anything of what agitates you most. Though I *shall* bring in a
lot of my own badness but of an Impersonal kind! . . . My chief
worry at the moment is my doubt lest these Publishers of mine
should delay . . . so long over "Weymouth Sands" that they
don't get it out till [after] Nov. 1st . . .

September 3rd 1933.

I have now finished the first chapter of my Autobiography
all about Shirley. Now I must come on to Dorchester and the
regime of Miss Osborne in that stone house near the Great
Western and Victor Hussey and Georgie Frith and that little

boy whose mother lived at Old Fordington Rectory with a stone wall & grass field round it. Was not his name called "Joe"? . . . . . Twas so sweet of you to want to help me— "From one who *can* lick you" but no! I must deal with these matters myself in my own way . . . But I shall enjoy writing about our excursions to the Stinsford meadows. Was it you who fell in and was very nearly drowned? . . . . Sometimes I even *play* with the notion that I may eventually *settle in Wales* for the rest of my days & be buried in the land of my fathers! For I sometimes think I could write a book that I would enjoy writing more than anything I could possibly write and I see it as an extraordinary book—a book of wonderful possibilities—a book into which various qualities more naturally adapted to poetry than to prose might be thrown. But I cannot do this *in a hurry* . . . . . . I would *not* think of *buying* a cottage to end my days in only leasing it—but *where*? . . . Have you by any chance an old Baedekker of Wales that you could send out to me? . . . Do you recall our climb of Snowdon? And how I was so stingy with the money? And how you and Theodore (encouraged by me) fought in a field; and then old Theodore had some kind of a drink? or am I inventing & mixing things up?

September 29th 1933.

I have now in my Autobiography finished the 2nd Chapter & got you to 9 & myself to 10 & in Chapter III I'll describe our life at the Prep beginning with our room under the "good" steady reliable Williams . . . but I won't *name* him, or any of 'em! I went to New York and interviewed my Publisher . . & I *think* gave them the first jolt from me—their most submissive author they've ever had! . . . .

[October 31st 1933] Hallow-e'en

Dearest Littleton, O my friend I cannot tell you how the writing of my Autobiography so much about Johnny & Littleton—so much about Powys Ma & Powys Mi—does affect my hard heart & does bring back the Poet & bring all

338

those old days of our unequalled companionship back. I have only to call up one episode after another to feel every feeling I had mount up & surge up and brim over as I write. Certainly I think that Littleton Charles will be delineated in touches here & there all along the way that draw his lineaments, so extraordinarily dear to me, in such a way as make the future people —if this Book lasts, & I am trying hard to make it good enough for that!—know him as he was. Except a few confessions of wicked feelings of my own—I don't think you will take exception to anything—certainly not to anything where you yourself come in—& quite contrary to the attitude—do you recall?— of my old friend *Miss Heatly* (God preserve her—she must be 80 now!) I have said very little about cricket and football— *hardly anything*! *Indeed,* though you have come in so much— all the while—I have not *so far* even indicated that you were Captain of both the Eleven & the Fifteen. For that was the case, wasn't it? Of course this *Grand Cut* of mine—the leaving out of *all women* completely leaves me free to devote much more time to sensations and ideas and also to the men I have known . . . . . & in all these things I am as frank as can be— short of offence! I do trust, my dearest friend, that you approve of the way I make this *Same Cut*? I do think trust believe and know that this *is* better. What is the use of adding to the reader's burden of sympathetic indulgence that cannot help but be in certain cases, in *yours* for instance! against the grain? God! but I do know well that whatever confessions I made in my recollections in this Book, would not lead to the sort of outburst of moral and what shall I say—Detective Zeal!— *that I displayed*—Oh I blush to think of it! . . . . . & I have not dared—from *pure shame* to bring that little episode in—though I *ought* to—but not *fortunately* according to my Principle—no real "Winnies"—not even as little a one as Winnie Joy are allowed! With the exception of this *Grand Cut* dealing with all my relations with *all* women, in this Retrospective "Descriptive Letter" to you—for such all this first part of my Autobiography inevitably becomes, I don't think I keep much back, very, *very* little! I *did* bring in that wicked (even sadistic, God help me!) act, of running you down against the Slope Railings—

that is the sort of thing—just short of "I-am-cold-and-I-want-to-Bog!" that I *have* shamelessly introduced in a few places! I tell you what does present itself to me very strongly—and *that* is, how much more *all the worst of me you know*, than anyone else in the world—even than poor Margaret (not so very "Poor" all the same!) who, I suppose, would know the worst SECOND to you! But of course Llewelyn—I *must* endeavour to explain that in this Book when I come to him—has an *ideal image* of me lodged in his mind—& of course this leads him to be the more outraged when I fall below the Standard!—but to Littleton none of the most outrageous peculiarities of Johnny and the meannesses and basenesses & cowardices & priggishnesses of Johnny have *ever* been concealed. Good God!—it isn't a person's grand or large lapses that really damn him—these lapses are only condemnable to certain types, & certain moods in us all, & certain people—& situations! it is a person's *little* nasty mean priggish odious ways, and a person's subtle round-about *cruel* ways that damn him! And these, in me, you are the only person who knows—in and out & through & through—as I with you also! But in these mean little odious things—Good God!—my dear how much better off you appear than I! Not only do you not commit any grandiose "sins" but when I think of your long-lasting & most romantic & nobly passionate devotion to that boy-friend of yours who later actually saw the Holy Grail. That episode—don't ee be *scared*! This Book is *my* autobiography not *your* biography! —*yet*!—but that episode is really one (because of its romance) that you could never look back upon without feeling glad that you had such an experience. The "brown-coated" choir boy at Dorchester I did *just*, O so lightly, allude to in passing— (& though she, I suppose, *was* a woman), I *did* also refer to Georgie Frith's "Spanish Maiden"! But seriously my old friend you may be sure you are safe in my hands over this Book . . . . I shall certainly close my autobiography—cutting out American women just as resolutely as the rest!—with a eulogy upon Columbia Country—for it *is* beautiful here. Wonderful! Marian (May) gave me a Ward's (I think) Tourist's Guide for North Wales and Ernest Rhys' book on

South Wales. She is always so Daring that tho' she would miss
me if I really went very *grievous* she encouraged me in this
idea. But for many reasons (which make it seem difficult &
unwise) just now, I have let this Welsh idea *recede* in my mind.
I do *not* think, however, of living *here* till I die—or of laying
my bones here—but for the nonce—*pro-tem*—I rather believe
that I will leave matters in statu quo.

November 25th, 1933.

. . . . My hope now is that Weymouth Sands will
come out in the Spring, in the *early* Spring, the *very* early
Spring—& my Autobiography in October. Didn't I really
comment on your Court House letter & thank you for the
flowers? Well I was certainly thrilled by both letter & flowers
you can be sure and it made me think of that time you walked
with poor old Thora to get a decent meal in Lewes and Thora
pursued you into the grand dining-room there! And that
shameful day when I made you walk—or is this an invented
story?—*behind me* like a Tramp's wife on the road beyond
Offham so that I might the better meditate! "*I must think*"
was it? And of course our wrestling in the Ditch about Ireland.
God! I *must* bring that in! Heigh ho! I shall never be able to
bring in everything even if I do shorten matters by leaving
out—as if it were the Autobiography of St. Anthony!—every
living, or dead, possible—mother-of-men! But I have now just
come to *Mr. de Kantzow* & my time under Mr. Pollard's
Roof . . . . . I shall soon be coming on to Court House . . . .
but first I want to describe how you & I walked to *Rodwell*
near Lewes all the way from Brighton looking for a House.
How well I recall that splendid walk! I can now so clearly see
that house in the low flat marshes near the Sussex Ouse.

February 6th, 1934.

Dearest old Friend, I *did* so enjoy your letter . . about the new
Headmaster . . . & old Lutyens's Mediaeval view of Glastonbury
. . . & your garden & Willy's visit with you to Camelot &
Glastonbury. I have now got the *Advance copy* of Weymouth

Sands beautifully printed & bound—such big clear print & such a noble looking book . . . . they've done it well. But O dear! I find it so hard to deal with these Publishers. Not one penny yet have I had from Glastonbury. My affairs are pretty low . . . but we will see if Weymouth Sands over here does me any good; I learn that it has been advertised in England so may be it will soon appear there too. Aye! but I pray you will like it! We shall see . . . . . I was so interested, my dear, in your words about your own "Life". May it grow under your hands to your satisfaction even *if* slowly with all you have on hand in the garden etc. etc. . . . . . . It will eventually be such an interest to me to see all the things that you remember from our early days that I have forgotten. *My* Autobiography now has reached the point of the beginning of Lulu's illness & of our exciting but agitating time together on the Continent . . & of my own visit to Spain. The next chapter will be the first in which I introduce America for I am taking matters in sections rather in accordance with the subject than in exact chronological order! *Dates*, my dearest friend, were ever my weak point and I am simply letting them go to the devil!

Appendix 1(c)

EXTRACTS FROM LETTERS TO
C. BENSON ROBERTS

October 16th, 1944   *Corwen*

The great event in Phyllis's and my life of the last fortnight has been the Visit of my eldest sister *Gertrude*, THE PAINTER! And she has painted a Wonderful Portrait of me—second to a little one of our Father drinking a cup of tea at the end of his Many Days . . . and equal, I really think, to one she did of our old nurse, Emily Clare "Little Emily" now dead and buried! the Best of all her works! It is against a Background of my Bookshelf and it represents old Mr. John lying on his couch in profile writing away at the last pages of his Rabelais; one hand holding the paper and the other the pen. I've got—*that* and an *early* unknown or little known Walt Whitman when he was editor of the Brooklyn Eagle I think, long before the first Leaves of Grass—a picture card of Erasmus by Holbein in profile with sweet-disillusioned eyes drooping lids and the hands holding his pen—and Gertrude's picture is like this—really and truly it is!—only with this rich brown Bodley Library old Folio background.

December 28th, 1948   *Corwen*

I'm so glad you've got Love and Death as a Xmas present. Aye! I would that Llewelyn could learn of your words. Miss Gregory has given me a photo of a *death-mask* she had taken of him. I like it O far more than any other picture of him. I think because when you see a Person Fast Asleep you feel more affectionate of them than at any other time. *Why*? I think because there's always a LITTLE tho' may be only a *very* little Miching-Mallecho mischief and danger even in the most loving human eye—but when the eyes are closed in sleep—or is it . . . the Devil whispers . . . that you get an unfair advantage an almost cruel advantage? *You* possess a person you look at *when they're un-conscious* while *you* remain yourself *unpossessed!*

November 14th, 1951   *Corwen*

The reactions to this book [*Porius*] have been more completely different from one another than the book itself is

344

different from other books of my own. Personally I think it beats that Glendower book of mine hollow and I can tell you why Ben old crony because of all the ages of mankind the 13th 14th and 15th centuries are to me the most odious detestable and wholly unsympathetic—I even hate their costumes and weapons! and O I love the way the grand Italian Renaissance spread to France and England and helped by Erasmus destroyed that horrid epoch! But the *Dark Ages*—before that doubledyed old Father of all Royal Asses, with his song of Roland, *Charlemagne* put an end to them with the smoky candles of crusading Franks!—are my favourite of all ages. Because learning *did* exist (Greek and Latin of the best) if you *wanted it enough!*—and for the rest the Roman Empire was over and done with, and *anything might happen!!* but as I say (if you could make out that blurred sentence) the uttermost wisdom of life *was* available in *Papyrus MSS* for those who could hunt it up! it existed. *Plato existed*—Pythagorus who got his wisdom from both Greeks and Etruscans and whose Italian School in Italy started off the Druidic philosophy *was* to be found in fragments of MSS tho' hard to come by if you weren't a traveller!

October 15th, 1960   *Blaenau-Ffestiniog*

Her parents, my mother's I mean, lived in Norwich Norfolk and were Johnsons and Pattesons. These latter were *Brewers of Ale* and so were richer than the Johnsons. But individually they were very nice people and, I well remember how my mother's mother read to me as a child the whole of "The Children of the New Forest" by Captain Marryat. The first Book I ever read to myself was *Alice through the Looking Glass* by that wonderful inventor of the Jabberwok and of those queer words such as uffish and beamish and tulgy and burbling and of all those imaginary Persons like the White Queen and King and the Red Queen and King and all those exciting Figures from a *Game of Chess*. What an inventor he was this Lewis Carroll! He was a great help to *Liddell and Scott* the authors of that wonderful Dictionary of Greek and English. And I think myself that he must have been in love with little Alice.

Appendix 1(d)
THREE POEMS

John Cowper Powys

In a letter to Littleton C. Powys of August 2nd 1928 from "Bay View", Michigan, John Cowper Powys wrote: "I have just composed this poem which I now append."

SATURN

Dark moss thick lichen on his sleep
Leaf wrapt a thousand years
But in such place the dryads keep
Feeding him with their tears
And now tonight and who am I
So strange a thing to see?
He who fell from the liquid sky
To where the roots of the forests lie
Heaves up that greenery.

Who would have thought the sun could be
So heavy and so round;
And yet go down into the sea
Without a splash or sound?
Who would have thought the moon could fill
So small a space of air
Yet hold the boughs of a great hill
Tranced in its atmosphere?

How strangely coloured is this sky!
How phantom-like this deep!
One stoops, one rises wistfully,
And they kiss in their sleep.
How large that moon! I did not think
The sun could sink so red!
Earth stirs upon some unknown brink—
Mutters—but ere a star can wink
Falls back upon her bed.

What scent of mosses through the slim
Birch-boughs! How light they float!
The ripples gurgle round the rim
Of a deserted boat.
Ah! well I know what that small stream
In charméd forest air
Is whispering in some beech-trunk's dream—
Saturn, great Saturn is its theme;
"Saturn!" it whispers there.

But that white moon—ere she escape
Rise, tree! against her sway!
Become an isle, a reef, a cape—
Take any other curious shape
Ere she can glide away!
Out of what glade comes this strange air
To stir a tree so old?
Saturn, Saturn it has left there!
Leaves in his lap, leaves in his hair,
Leaves round his loins cold!

How slow the water-beetles spin!
How their heads the rushes hide!
And each small fish with silvery fin
What mystery it is folded in
And the moor-hen by its side!
How faint the stars! This is the hour
When every leafy sense
When every vein in every flower
And every grass-seed feels a power,
A touch, an influence!

In moss and lichen he slumbers dim
But tonight he heaves him up
And he knows his own and his own know him
And we drain the same strange cup
A fungus-cup of old brown rain;
For Saturn, Saturn, has come again!

TEIRESIAS

This wind has blown the sun out of his place!
I look towards the West and lo! a vast
Lost-battle-broken bastion covers up
The natural sky! To what rain-ramparted
Region of disaster do these hills
Toppling above each other, ridge on ridge
Of trees that in the night are heaped like moss,
Of trees that darken into tapestries,
Of vaporous moss, of roads that travelling
Thro' terraces of twilight lose themselves
In green-black tumuli of mystery
In piled up mounds of moss and mystery,
Lead my soul thro' the silence? Not a stone
But talks in muffled tongue to other stones!
It's a conspiracy to lead me on!
There's not a wild, wet-beaked, night flying bird
That does not scream upon this tossing wind
To other darker birds, its baleful sign,
Its madness-wrought Eumenidean sign
Of rumours and of runes of prophecy!
Of rain-whirled, storm-wrack rolls of prophecy!
And I Teiresias, riding on these hills,
And on this twilight, and on these heaped mounds
Of mystery, and on these wild birds wings,
Death-runes, death-rumours, ruins and rains of death,
Am now myself, this wind, this wind, this wind,
This wind that's blown the sun out of his place!

[*1928–1929*].

350

THE STONE   *October 12th 1933*

Stint and go! Stint and go!
Tarry not so long
Let that tree its burden strow
And the birds their song!

Cold the stone you sit upon
And the nights be chill
She has firelight where she's gone
Candles at her will!

Leave that tree and leave that stone
Let the wind and rain
Take to them what is their own!
She'll not come again—

"Bide I must and bide I will
"Where we used to sit.
"She will cry to see our hill
"And no man by it!"

Stint and go! Stint and go!
Night be on that stone.
"Nay! A stones a good pillow
"When you be alone!

"Bide I must till man and tree
"Rot into the clay!
"Stone will take her on its knee
"When she comes this way.

"Stone will watch when I be dead
"Stone my bones will keep.
"When she comes she will not cry
"She'll lie down and sleep!"

Appendix II

Additions to *John Cowper Powys:*
a record of achievement

Derek Langridge

My survey of Powys's work was published in the Autumn of 1966. Its fortunes are part of the story of Powys's reputation. There were few reviews, though these were mainly favourable, and in five years the book has sold only a little over 700 copies. For consolation I received many letters of appreciation from Powys admirers, friends and relations. Some of my correspondents kindly sent details of items not included in the book. These are listed below, together with items I have since discovered myself. Owing to pressure of other work I have not systematically collected this information and cannot claim that I am giving a comprehensive account of additions since 1966.

An incident attending publication of my book deserves recording. Having checked all proofs, including those for plates, I left for a year's stay in the United States shortly before publication date. When I finally received the long awaited copy it was only to discover the almost unbelievable error that had replaced a head of Powys as a young man with the well-known portrait of Erasmus! The original block had mysteriously disappeared from the printers and another had to be made. I still have a proof to show that the first block really did exist. A number of copies were sold with the Erasmus plate before the error was detected.

The incident was given point when I discovered later that for many years Powys kept a picture of Erasmus on his bookshelf. Miss Playter wrote to me "I think it would have pleased J.C.P. to have his (Erasmus's) eidolon slip past and take a place with his own as if by some unknown volition".

Shortly afterwards Bertram Rota's catalogue offered the following item for sale: Huizinga, J. *Erasmus of Rotterdam* . . . . Inscribed on the half-title page: "From John Cowper Powys For Frederick Charles Owlett to commemorate the feeling we have now discovered for certain celebrities and against certain celebrities. November 6th 1958."

354

ADDITIONS TO THE WORKS

Early 1930's. An Englishman up-state, pp. 5–15, Philobiblon Number 8, Winter 1966.

1936 Letter to A. R. Orage in Mairet, Philip. *A. R. Orage: a memoir*. Dent, pp. 101–103.

1957 The Recruit and Duality (poems) in Causley, Charles (ed). *Peninsula: an anthology of verse from the west country*. Macdonalds, pp. 83–84.

1961 Shillyshally (short story). Between Worlds: an international magazine of creativity Vol. 1, No. 2, Spring–Summer 1961, pp. 205–213.
Probably 1962. Foreword to Reid, Elspeth Douglas. *Verses*. National Antivivisection Society.

1964 Letters to Glyn Hughes. London Welshman, July–August.

1964 Letters to Clifford Tolchard. Meanjin Quarterly. No. 1, pp. 89–92.

1971 Jones, Bernard (ed). *Letters from John Cowper Powys to Glyn Hughes*. Stevenage, Herts.: Ore Publications. 23p.
Unknown Date. Anti-vivisection. British Union for the Abolition of Vivisection. 4p.
To be published November 1971. Letters to Nicholas Ross.

ADDITIONS TO THE REPUTATION

Reprints (including translations)

1937 The Art of Happiness (Swedish). *Lyckans Näsen*. Stockholm, Natur och Kultur.

1965 Introduction to Dorothy M. Richardson. *Toits pointus*. Paris, Mercure de France. (1st French edition of *Pointed roofs*.)

1966 Maiden Castle. Macdonalds.

1967 Autobiography. Macdonalds. (The only edition with an index.)

1967   Maiden Castle (French). *Camp Retranche*. Marie Canavaggia (trans.) Paris, Grasset.

date? Wolf Solent, translated by Suzanne Rétillard, Paris, Plon.

In preparation: French translations of Ducdame, Glastonbury Romance and Rodmoor.

Books, articles and reviews referring to J.C.P.

1928   "English novelist and lecturer who will speak here," Globe-Democrat (St. Louis), April 22.

Haldeman-Julius, E. *The first hundred million.* New York, Simon & Schuster, pp. 40, 41, 108, 109, 149, 181, 192–3, 194, 261.

Who's who among North American authors. Volume III, 1927–1928. Los Angeles, Golden Syndicate Publishing Company. Includes entry for J.C.P.

1930   Dobrée, Bonamy. Review of *Meaning of culture* in The Criterion, Vol. X, No. 38, October, pp. 178–9.

"Woman's Club hears Powys." Fort Worth Star-Telegram, February 7.

c. 1931. Morgan, Louise. *Dorothy M. Richardson.* William Jackson, 8 p. Quotes J.C.P. and T.L.S. review of his Dorothy M. Richardson.

1942   Frierson, William C. *The English novel in transition: 1885–1940.* University of Oklahoma Press, 1942. pp. 283, 296–9, 320, 321, 322.

Sawyer, Ruth. *The way of the Storyteller.* New York: Viking Press. p. 149 quotes from Enjoyment of Literature.

1943   Macdiarmid, Hugh. *Lucky poet.* Methuen. pp. 3, 82, 355, 397.

1948   Review of *Rabelais*. John o'London's, May 28.

1949   Clemo, Jack. *Confession of a rebel.* Chatto & Windus, p. 94.

1951 Horricks, Raymond. *These jazzmen of our time*. Gollancz, p. 210 quotes from Visions and Revisions.

1955 Miller, Henry. "When I reach for my revolver", pp. 78–102 in Puma, F. (ed). *7 arts, No.* 3. Indian Hills, Colorado: Falcon Wings Press.
Täckmark, Sven Erik. "Mit möte med enwalesisk filosof." Fornby-Kamnaten, No. 3, July.

1956 Reynolds, Reginald. *My life and crimes*. Jarrolds, pp. 50–51, 208, 209.

1957 Gardner, Martin. *Fads and fallacies in the name of science*. New York: Dover Publications, p. 43 refers to J.C.P. and Charles Fort.

1958 Clemo, Jack. *The invading gospel*. Geoffrey Bles, pp. 78–80.
Gregory, Alyse, "A famous family". London Magazine, No. 50.
Norman, Charles. *The magic maker: E. E. Cummings*. New York: Macmillan, pp. 166, 169, 195, 196, 324.

1962 Miller, Henry. *An interview with Henry Miller*. Folkways FL9724 (Gramophone record). Includes some discussion of J.C.P.
Wilson, Colin. *The strength to dream: Literature and the imagination*. Boston: Houghton, Mifflin, p. 68.

1964 Burrow, Trigant. *Preconscious foundations of human experience*. New York: Basic Books, pp. 67, 70–71 quotes from Confessions of two brothers.
Knight, G. Wilson. "Homage to Powys", pp. 80–84 in Young, K. (ed). *The second bed Post: a miscellany of the Yorkshire Post*. Macdonald.
Miller, Henry. *Nexus*. Weidenfeld and Nicholson, pp. 304, 306, 326.

1965 André, Robert. "La sensibilité de John Cowper Powys." La Nouvelle Revue Française, August. pp. 299–304.
Gresset, Michel. "Le rôle de l'humeur dans la création litteraire de John Cowper Powys". pp. 76–103 in

Actes du Congrès de Lille, 27–29 March 1965. Paris: Didier.

Hughes, Glyn. "Writer and wizard: a portrait of John Cowper Powys". Prediction, October.

Swanberg, W. A. *Dreiser*. New York: Scribner's. Many references to J.C.P.

Tjader, Marguerite. *Theodore Dreiser: a new dimension*. Norwalk, Connecticut: Silvermine Publishers, pp. 3–4, 7, 10, 20, 28, 69, 95, 108, 133, 148.

1966   Knight, G. Wilson. *Byron and Shakespeare*. Routledge and Kegan Paul. Many references to J.C.P.

Philobiblon (The Journal of Friends of the Colgate University Library). Number 8, Winter 1966.
A special issue devoted to John Cowper Powys, with contributions by Louis Wilkinson, Russell Speirs, Kenneth Hopkins, Malcolm Elwin, Thomas Davies. Essay by Powys listed above.

Priestley, J.B. Introduction to second edition of Tilden, Marjorie. *Star crossed*. Macdonalds.

1967   Anderson, Arthur J. "John Cowper Powys: a bibliography." Bulletin of Bibliography and Magazine Notes. Vol. 25, No. 4, September–December 1967, pp. 73–78, 94.
Lists a few items not seen by me.

Gale Research Company. *Children and books: the 1967 Gale literary datebook*. Includes J.C.P.

Glover, William. "The genial grouch". Sunday Star (Washington, D.C.) March 19. On Lou Jacobi, refers to J.C.P.

Hopkins, Kenneth. *The Powys Brothers: a biographical appreciation*. Phoenix House.

Joost, Nicholas. *Years of transition: the Dial 1912–1920*. Barre, Mass.: Barre Publishers, p. 248.

Knight, G. Wilson. *Shakespeare and religion*. Routledge and Kegan Paul, pp. vii, 17, 18, 19–20, 24, 188.

Täckmark, Sven Erik. "John Cowper Powys redevivus". Svenska Dagbladet, August 9, p. 4.

Wilson Angus. "Evil in the English novel." Kenyon
Review, March, pp. 188–9.

Reviews of Maiden Castle (French translation by
Marie Canavaggia).

Cixous, Helene. "Un univers fantastique. 'Camp
retranché' de J. C. Powys". Le Monde, March 29.

Faraggi, Claude. "Un compagnon de lévergondage".
Nouvel Observateur, March 8–15.

Galey, Matthieu. "Un devouement obstine". Arts,
March 14.

Kanters, Robert. "Une place forte du roman con-
temporain". Le Figaro Littéraire, April 6.

Mayoux, Jean-Jacques. "Un débutant de soixante
ans". La Quinzaine Littéraire, April 30.

1968   Mackenzie, Compton. *My life and times: octave seven,*
1931–1938. Chatto and Windus, pp. 142–3 refers to
Daily Mail reviews in 1933 and quotes from his review
of Glastonbury Romance.

Mayne, Ellen. "The new mythology of J. C. Powys".
13th New Atlantis Foundation Lecture, given at
Swedenborg Hall, Barter St. London, W.C.1 on
November 1, 1968—unpublished?

Tolchard, Clifford. "Getting to know Mr. Powys".
Sydney Morning Herald, January 27.

1969   Breckon, Richard. *John Cowper Powys: the solitary
giant.* Loughton: K. A. Ward, 8p. Limited edition of
150 copies.

Hanley, James. *John Cowper Powys: a man in the corner.*
Limited edition of 200 copies.

1970   Langridge, D. W. *Your jazz collection.* Bingley, p. 14.
quotes from Art of happiness.

Musgrave, Clifford. *Life in Brighton.* Faber. pp. 336–338.
quotes from Autobiography.

1971   Knight, G. Wilson. *Neglected powers: essays on nineteenth and twentieth century literature.* Routledge
and Kegan Paul. Includes five essays on J.C.P. and
many other references.

Macaulay, Rose. *Letters to a friend* and *More letters to a friend* contain references to J.C.P.

The following items appeared in recent years in Preuves, Critique and Le Monde: reviews of Wolf Solent and Maiden Castle by Diane Fernandez, review of Maiden Castle by Las Vergnas, L'extase et la sensualité by J.-J. Mayoux. A new French literary magazine, Granite, is planning a special J.C.P. number for May or June 1972.

Honours (dedications etc.)

1938   Ficke, Arthur Davison. *Selected poems.* Doubleday, Doran. pp. 175–6. "King of salamanders. To John Cowper Powys."

1956   Anderson, John Redwood. *Almanac.* Macdonalds. p. 117. "The choice. To John Cowper Powys.".

1962   Anderson, John Redwood. *While the fates allow.* Beckenham: Bee and Blackthorn Press.
p. 52. "Anniversary, August the 30th, 1957. To John Cowper Powys."

1966   London Borough of Camden. Exhibition of J.C.P. at Central Library, Swiss Cottage, November. Library issued pamphlet "John Cowper Powys 1872–1963: a selective bibliography."

1970   Young, Ian. *Year of the quiet sun* (poems). Totonto: House of Anansi. 'Dedicated, with admiration and affection, to the memory of the greatest of modern writers, John Cowper Powys (1872–1963)'.

John Cowper Powys's death mask is to be seen at the country address of booksellers Peter Eaton—Lilies, Weedon, near Aylesbury, Bucks.

Appendix III

Editions in English of the books by John Cowper Powys

compiled by Derek Langridge

Editions in English of the books by John Cowper Powys, compiled by Derek Langridge.

The following list includes distinct editions only. For full details including impressions and translations see *John Cowper Powys: a record of achievement*, by Derek Langridge (London, Library Association, 1966.)

1. *Poetry.*

   Odes and other poems. London, William Rider, 1896.

   Poems. London, William Rider, 1899.

   Wolf's-Bane. New York, Arnold Shaw, 1916.

   Mandragora. New York, Arnold Shaw, 1917.

   Samphire. New York, Thomas Seltzer, 1922.

   Lucifer. London, Macdonalds, 1956.

   John Cowper Powys: a Selection from his Poems. London, Macdonalds, 1964. (Selections from the above six volumes).

2. *Prose Literature.*

   Wood and Stone. New York, Arnold Shaw, 1915. London, Heinemann, 1917.

   Rodmoor. New York, Arnold Shaw, 1916.

   Ducdame. New York, Doubleday, Page, 1925.
   London, Grant Richards, 1925.

   Wolf Solent. New York, Simon & Schuster, 1929.
   London, Jonathan Cape, 1929.
   New York, Garden City Publishing Company, 1933.
   London, Macdonalds, 1961.
   Harmondsworth, Penguin, 1964.

   The owl, the duck and—Miss Rowe! Miss Rowe! Chicago, William Targ, 1930.

   A Glastonbury Romance. New York, Simon & Schuster, 1932. (Trade and limited editions).
   London, John Lane, 1933.
   London, Macdonalds, 1955.

Weymouth Sands. New York, Simon & Schuster, 1934.
London, Macdonalds, 1963.
as *Jobber Skald* (with changes of personal and place names
in text):—
London, John Lane, 1935.

Maiden Castle. New York, Simon & Schuster, 1936.
London, Cassells, 1937.
London, Macdonalds, 1966.

Morwyn. London, Cassells, 1937.

Owen Glendower. New York, Simon & Schuster, 1940.
London, John Lane, 1942.

Porius. London, Macdonalds, 1951 (Trade and limited
editions).
New York, Philosophical Library, 1952.

The Inmates. London, Macdonalds, 1952.
New York, Philosophical Library, 1952.

Atlantis. London, Macdonalds, 1954.

The Brazen Head. London, Macdonalds, 1956.

Up and Out. London, Macdonalds, 1957.

Homer and the Aether. London, Macdonalds, 1959.

All or nothing. London, Macdonalds, 1960.
Calcutta, Rupa, 1961.

3. *Biography.*
Confessions of two brothers (with Llewelyn Powys).
Rochester, N.Y., Manas Press, 1916.
Autobiography. New York, Simon & Schuster, 1934.
London, John Lane, 1934.
London, Macdonalds, 1967.
Letters of John Cowper Powys to Louis Wilkinson 1935–1956.
London, Macdonalds, 1958.

4. *Literary essays.*
Visions and Revisions. New York, Arnold Shaw, 1915.
London, Macdonalds, 1955.

One Hundred Best Books. New York, Arnold Shaw, 1916.
New York, American Library Service, 1922.
Girard (Kansas), Haldeman-Julius, 1923. (Little Blue Book 435).

Suspended Judgments. New York, Arnold Shaw, 1916.
New York, American Library Service, 1923.
Girard (Kansas), Haldeman-Julius, 1923.
(Little Blue Books 448, 450–453).

Dorothy M. Richardson. London, Joiner and Steele, 1931 (Trade and limited editions).

The Enjoyment of Literature. New York, Simon & Schuster, 1938.

as *The Pleasures of Literature* (with some differences).
London, Cassells, 1938.
Second edition, 1946.

Dostoievsky. London, John Lane, 1947.

Rabelais. London, John Lane, 1948.
New York, Philosophical Library, 1951.

5. *Philosophical and general essays.*
The War and Culture. New York, Arnold Shaw, 1914.
as *The Menace of German Culture:*
London, William Rider, 1915.
The Complex Vision. New York, Dodd, Mead, 1920.
The Art of Happiness. Girard, (Kansas), Haldeman-Julius, 1923. (Little Blue Book 414). (not same work as 1935 publication).
Psychoanalysis and Morality. San Francisco, Jessica Colbert, 1923.
The Religion of a Sceptic. New York, Dodd, Mead, 1925.

The Secret of Self-development. Girard (Kansas), Haldeman-Julius, 1926. (Little
Blue Book 112).

The Art of Forgetting the Unpleasant. Girard (Kansas),
Haldeman-Julius, 1928 (Little Blue Book 1264).

The Meaning of Culture. New York, W. W. Norton, 1929.
Tenth Anniversary edition, 1939.
London, Jonathan Cape, 1930.
Enlarged edition, 1940.
New York, Garden City Publish-
ing Company, 1941.
Toronto, Blue Ribbon Books,
1941.
Calcutta, Rupa, 1960.

as *Culture and Nature,* and *Culture and Life:* Tokyo,
Hokuseido Press, 1958. (selected and annotated
edition).

Debate! Is modern marriage a failure? (with Bertrand
Russell). New York, Discussion Guild, 1930.
Powys's part is included in *John Cowper Powys: a
record of achievement,* by Derek Langridge.

In Defence of Sensuality. New York, Simon & Schuster,
1930.
London, Gollancz, 1930.

A Philosophy of Solitude. New York, Simon & Schuster,
1933.
London, Jonathan Cape, 1933.
Tokyo, Kinseido, 1954.

The Art of Happiness. New York, Simon & Schuster, 1935.
London, John Lane, 1935. Second
edition, 1940.
Bombay, Jaico Publishing Company,
1960.
(not same work as 1923 publication.)

Mortal Strife. London, Jonathan Cape, 1942.

The Art of Growing Old. London, Jonathan Cape, 1944.

Obstinate Cymric. Carmarthen, Druid Press, 1947.
In Spite Of. London, Macdonalds, 1953.
        New York, Philosophical Library. 1953.

NOTES ON CONTRIBUTORS

FRANCIS BERRY is Professor of English in the University of London at Royal Holloway College. His publications include poetry, *The Galloping Centaur, Morant Bay, Ghosts of Greenland,* and criticism, *Poets' Grammar, Poetry and the Physical Voice, The Shakespeare Inset.*

JOHN A. BREBNER of the University of New Brunswick, Canada, has published on J. C. Powys in *The Anglo-Welsh Review.* As a Canada Council Fellow he spent two years in Wales for research on J. C. Powys and has recently completed a study of Powys's novels as a Ph.D. thesis for the University of New Brunswick.

GLEN CAVALIERO, formerly a Research Fellow of St. Catherine's College, Cambridge, is the author of articles on J. C. Powys in *Theology,* no. 495, and in *The Penguin Companion to Literature.* He recently completed a full-length study of Powys's novels which is awaiting publication.

H. P. COLLINS, author of *John Cowper Powys: Old Earth Man* (1966), published a pioneer work of New Criticism, *Modern Poetry,* in 1925, was the literary editor of *Adelphi,* 1926–28, has edited several periodicals and contributes to many on an astonishing variety of subjects.

FREDERICK DAVIES, Head of the English Department, Pensby School, Cheshire, Fellow Commoner, Churchill College, Cambridge, is the translator of Goldoni and Labiche (Heinemann and Penguin Classics) and has published two novels for children.

MALCOLM ELWIN, professional writer, since his early biographies of Charles Reade (1931) and Thackeray (1932) has written mainly on the Romantics period, including the biographies of De Quincey and Landor, his most recent books being *Lord Byron's Wife* (1962) and *The Noels and the Milbankes* (1967). He has published essays on J. C. Powys and is the author of *The Life of Llewelyn Powys.*

368

DIANE FERNANDEZ of the Sorbonne is the author of articles on numerous 19th and 20th century English writers in *Les Lettres Nouvelles, Preuves* and *La Quinzaine Litteraire.* She is completing a doctorate thesis on J. C. Powys and is translating *Ducdame* (Editions du Seuil).

RAYMOND GARLICK, Director of Welsh Studies at Trinity College, Carmarthen, edited *The Anglo-Welsh Review* from 1949 to 1960, being responsible for the J. C. Powys number, 1956. His Collected Poems, *A Sense of Europe* were published in 1968, his *Introduction to Anglo-Welsh Literature* in 1970.

MICHAEL GREENWALD, Assistant Professor of English, Wilkes College, Pennsylvania, was formerly a teaching fellow at Harvard where he obtained his Ph.D., 1972, for a thesis on J. C. Powys.

JEREMY HOOKER, Lecturer in English Literature, University College of Wales, Aberystwyth, has published many essays on Anglo-Welsh writers, some early poems in *Poetry Introduction I,* Faber 1969, and is preparing a study of J. C. Powys for the *Writers of Wales* series.

BELINDA HUMFREY is a Lecturer in English Literature, St. David's University College, Lampeter.

TIMOTHY HYMAN, artist, emerged from the Slade School of Fine Art in 1967, lectures at The Working Men's College, and has read two papers to The Powys Society.

BERNARD JONES, Lecturer in English, Darlington College of Education, is the author of numerous articles on 19th and 20th century writers, also of poems, *The Chanceful Season*, and editor of *The Poems of William Barnes.*

JONAH JONES's sculptural works include walls at Coleg Harlech and the Flintshire Law Courts at Mold, and "Y Tywysogion", a commemorative group in the village of

Aberffraw in Anglesey, last seat of the native Welsh Princes, also portraits of Bertrand Russell, Clough Williams-Ellis, Gwynfor Evans, and Lord Morris of Borth y Gest.

G. WILSON KNIGHT, Emeritus Professor of English Literature, University of Leeds, is well-known for his method of critical interpretations of works through their patterns of imagery, and for his many books on Shakespeare and the Romantic poets. His published writings on J. C. Powys include *The Saturnian Quest* (1964) and a valuable chapter on Powys's poetry in *Neglected Powers* (1971).

DEREK LANGRIDGE is the Principal Lecturer, School of Librarianship, Polytechnic of North London.

ROLAND MATHIAS is Editor of *The Anglo-Welsh Review*. His publications include a work of historical research, *Whitsun Riot* (1963), his latest volume of poetry, *Absalom in the Tree* (1971), an article and many reviews on J. C. Powys.

GWYNETH F. MILES is writing a Ph.D. thesis on J. C. Powys at the University of British Columbia, and has visited Britain for research as a Canada Council Fellow.

ROBERT NYE, professional writer and literary critic, has published three books of poems, *Juvenalia 1* (1961), *Juvenalia 2* and *Darker Ends* (1963), a novel, *Doubtfire* (1968), a volume of short stories, and some books for children.

C. BENSON ROBERTS corresponded with J. C. Powys from 1939 when he arranged some lectures for Powys in Bridgend on The Mabinogion and Shakespeare's Tragedies. He is the Chairman of The Powys Society.

INDEX